URBAN ALCHEMY

Restoring Joy in America's Sorted-Out Cities

W9-DDP-321

URBAN ALCHEMY

Restoring Joy in America's Sorted-Out Cities

Mindy Thompson Fullilove, MD

Published in the United States by
    New Village Press
    @ Centre for Social Innovation
    601 West 26th Street, Suite 325-11
    New York, NY 10001
    bookorders@newvillagepress.net
    www.newvillagepress.net

New Village Press is a public-benefit, not-for-profit publishing venture of Architects/Designers/Planners for Social Responsibility.

In support of the Greenpress Initiative, New Village Press is committed to the preservation of endangered forests globally and advancing best practices within the book and paper industries. The printing papers used in this book are 100% recycled fiber, acid-free (Process Chlorine Free), and have been certified with the Forest Stewardship Council (FSC).

Original paperback ISBN 978-1-61332-010-5
eBook ISBN 978-1-61332-012-9

Publication Date: June 2013
First Edition

Library of Congress Cataloging-in-Publication Data

Fullilove, Mindy Thompson.
    Urban alchemy : restoring joy in America's sorted-out cities / Mindy Thompson Fullilove, MD. -- First edition.
        pages cm
    Includes bibliographical references and index.
    ISBN 978-1-61332-010-5 (pbk. : alk. paper)
    1. Community development--United States. 2. Urban ecology (Sociology)--United States. 3. City planning--United States. 4. Urban policy--United States. I. Title.
    HN90.C6F844 2013
    307.1'416--dc23
                                2013011796

Front cover design by Pam Shaw
Illustration "Musicians" by William Henry Johnson
Interior design and composition by Larry B. Van Dyke

To Bob
for everything

For a long time, I have been trying to mobilize our leaders so that the cities, where our money and brainpower are concentrated, innovate for better functioning. What is the problem that we must solve? It is the fracture that exists between the wealthy neighborhoods and the others. Each day, this chasm grows. I am convinced that there is a close connection between the signs of exclusion and the shape of the city, whether it is poor neighborhoods or whole cities that have been shut out. We find neighborhoods far from everything, without means of transport, where many are unemployed, and where there are numerous young people. We find the names of those neighborhoods in the newspapers. We also know that those neighborhoods are the neighborhoods with high rates of illness.

But, paradoxically, if we want to improve life in those neighborhoods, *we can't just treat the neighborhoods*. We have to remove the chasm that is dividing the poor neighborhoods from the other parts of the city. Doctors know that if you want to treat a boil on the skin, you have to treat the whole body. It's the same for the city. If we want to solve the problems of the poor neighborhoods, we must treat the whole city. We must eliminate the fracture.

—Michel Cantal-Dupart
Colloque Triville, 1993

Table of Contents

Illustrations

Foreword

Jean Nouvel

In this book, Dr. Mindy Fullilove leads us on a magical journey.

The childhood of Michel Cantal-Dupart did not predispose him to become the expert specialist on questions of urbanism that he is today. He was born in the southwest of France in what is known as Gascony in that immense forest of maritime pine trees planted in the middle of the nineteenth century on unstable, shifting sands. This is a forest that in modern times is almost metaphysical in its stature, where the same tree is infinitely repeated along a straight, rectilinear beach two hundred kilometers in length, a beach shaped by the tireless waves of the Atlantic. Gascony endowed Cantal with his great stature, built upon stilt-like legs that have served him almost as well in his profession as his head has. His size enables him to survey every urban and semiurban space it has been his passion to confront. It gives him the capacity to physically explore that which his colleagues are unable to do with anywhere near the same facility, enthusiasm, or appetite. This appetite, which I understand well since, like Cantal, I too am from Gascony, is sparked by a complex peculiar to us country bumpkins who dream both of discovering the secrets of the Big City and of losing ourselves somewhere within it. As students of the city, we hurried first to see Toulouse, the terracotta-rose city of the southwest of France, then to Bordeaux, a classic among French cities, and then to Paris, which for us exists as a distant mirage. These cities inspired in us a fascination for things urban and spawned in Cantal the desire to become an expert on urban forms, an urbanist.

He will not be disappointed in his life journey. He—the concrete but also earthy man, lover of physical realities, landscapes, marketplaces, urban streets, and, most assuredly, with all things living there—he discovered the tools of urbanism, the "potatoes,"[1] the "crosshatching,"[2] the zones, the coefficients, the norms, as well as the profession's blind spots. Far from being discouraged, he would forever be in pursuit of his art, as befits a native of Gascony and a spiritual heir of Cyrano de Bergerac.

I met Cantal in those conspiratorial days after the revolution of 1968 in Paris. We were a handful of optimistic architects who wanted to believe that the rules and regulations of urban planning imposed on all French cities, which had created segregated urban spaces as well as "new cities" that were neither urban nor new, could be stopped. In the 1970s, with a couple of the leftist-leaning architects with whom Cantal was particularly close, we created the March 1976 Movement, a group that was decidedly against the urban planning trends of the era. Subsequently, with the creation of the Association for Democracy in Urbanism and Architecture (ADUA), we created something called the Union of Architects—the first antiestablishment group of its type in our profession—in order to defend the purity of architecture and to set ourselves apart from the mandarins of architecture of that era. It was an era of meetings, an era of new ideologies, of involvement and participation. It was an era of engagement with the members of tenants's associations. It was an era noted for surveying the terrain. One can easily understand how the verve and dynamism of the Gascon Cantal-Dupart expressed itself with such magnificence under such historic conditions. Cantal constructed his own style of urbanism and created a network of associates that included mayors and activists.

His power to propose solutions to urban problems comes first and foremost from his never-ending desire to understand the nature of things, from his love of other people and other places, and from the sheer pleasure that comes from the discovery of new neighborhoods and of new cities. And from all of that arises an immense desire for urban solutions that emerge from long hours of self-reflection and from countless hours spent in offices or at the bargaining table with elected residents, officials, and politicians. Thus, these solutions and the power to deduce them are at the core of his diagnostic arts. But in order for his diagnosis to produce effective solutions, he will throw himself into an effort to persuade others, by speaking with the enthusiasm, the lucidity, and the tenacity that is so characteristically his. From the Medina of Tunis at the beginning of the 1970s to the city of Nantes where he pursued his studies, he developed an understanding of the need to preserve the ancient streets of historic sites and he came to appreciate the joy that comes from developing waterfronts, rivers, and canals. And thirty years later in America, in the city of Pittsburgh, he reconnected the African American inhabitants of that city's famous Hill District with the rivers that gave birth to the steel industry where so many of their forefathers worked. And, of course, in the metropolitan regions of Paris where he spent the 1980s in the company of another of his famous cronies, Roland Castro, the two managed to convince French president François Mitterrand to develop "Banlieues 89" (Suburbs 1989) that changed forever the perceptions that Parisians would have of Paris.

And it's very logical that I found Cantal in 2008 to be part of the international initiative known as the Grand Paris. This was an initiative that brought together ten international, interdisciplinary teams to create a series of proposals that would guide the evolution of Paris. In the spirit of complementarity, our team was guided by a trio of experts: an urbanist with a vast understanding of the places, the spaces, the residents, and their elected representatives (Michel Cantal-Dupart, obviously); an architect and engineer from École Polytechnique with expertise in the area of transportation (Jean-Marie Duthilleul); and a jack-of-all-trades in the area of urban forms and design (i.e., yours truly, the author of this foreword). And at the core of this wonderful team was a group of consultants—including the author of *Urban Alchemy*, whose book sits in your hands—who worked for almost a year surveying the territory, developing the ability to diagnose complex problems, and struggling with the details, through joyous charrettes to dinner discussions in which we reshaped the contours of the world.

And then there was Cantal, who was everywhere, speaking to everyone, who pumped up our spirits, and who provoked lively discussions.

And, if the evolution of streets, riverbanks, and neighborhoods is in each moment to be reinvented and reevaluated; and if the reasons must each time be debated democratically to arrive at creating the real, the profound urban truths, this is all to say, quite simply, that the good Doctor Cantal, with his urban potions, has not wasted his time!

Notes

1. *Patates*—potatoes—is an expression Cantal developed to denounce the use of black circles around poor neighborhoods by city planners. See Chapter Three.

2. *Hachures*—crosshatching—was used by artists of the Beaux-Arts school to make their work beautiful. When used by architects, the word implies a denunciation of academicism.

Introduction

Dear Mr. Potter,

We are pleased to inform you that you have been accepted at Hogwarts School of Witchcraft and Wizardry. Please find enclosed a list of all necessary books and equipment. Term begins on September 1. We await your owl...

Questions exploded inside Harry's head like fireworks and he couldn't decide which to ask first. After a few minutes he stammered, "What does it mean, they await my owl?"

—J. K. Rowling, *Harry Potter and the Sorcerer's Stone*

This book represents a psychiatrist's views on how to fix the American city. When I tell people I am a psychiatrist and I study cities, they look at me intently. "Psychiatry" and "cities" don't fit neatly into one box.

I agree. This was not my plan. As a black woman, to some extent it was inevitable that I would be outside the box of American psychiatry. But when I started to do research, I wanted only to fit in. I thought I had found an excellent niche in the study of AIDS, an epidemic that has disproportionately affected people of color and that is spread by behaviors dear to the hearts of psychiatrists: sex and drug abuse.

But things happen, and two of those things happened to me. An ecologist, Rodrick Wallace, explained how the AIDS epidemic was linked to neighborhoods. Then an urbanist, Michel Cantal-Dupart, explained that, if I wanted to help neighborhoods, I had to treat the whole city.

"What does it mean, 'treat the whole city'?" I asked him.

Shortly thereafter, I left behind studies of individual behavior (and my little niche) and started to study the ways in which American cities were the source of jeopardy for AIDS and a long list of other ills. Happily, my master's degree in nutrition had used a systems approach and my training in psychiatry had included a good deal of family and systems therapy. Those became my starting points.

The thesis of systems therapy is that what are labeled "problems" are often better understood as "symptoms" of disorder in the mechanism of a larger whole. For example, when a toddler is having constant temper tantrums, the parents will bring him to the therapist saying, "We are so worried about his problem." The family therapist will seek to understand the child, but will also start to examine how the whole family works. In no time at all, a deeper problem, like poor communication in the marriage, will likely surface, and that is what the family therapist will treat. Once that problem is treated, the toddler will stop being a problem and become a normal "terrible two."

Cantal was applying the same systems logic to neighborhoods and cities. He contended that neighborhoods were seen as the problem, but what we really needed to examine was the organization of the whole city. It was there that we would find the issues that needed to be resolved. The search for the problem in the city was part of the work that I undertook. The other part was finding the interventions that would set the city on a better path. Just as I had ideas for ways to fix communication among couples, I wanted to have ideas for fixing the dysfunction in cities.

My ideas are anchored in many conversations with ecologist Rodrick Wallace. A fundamental lesson, which he has stressed on innumerable occasions, is that ecosystems are resilient. Ecological resilience, however, is *not* the happy we-bounce-back-from-disaster quality that people tend to think it is. Ecosystem resilience means that, after being disturbed, a system becomes stabilized again, but that stabilization can be achieved at a much worse point than before. Things do not go back to what they were before: they lurch forward from the point of disturbance. Evolution is a one-way street.

For example, a pond, polluted by fertilizer-rich runoff, may become turbid, and the life that was there may die out. This is called *eutrophication*. Once the pollution is stopped, the pond will remain in that state of eutrophication unless interventions are made to restore it to a more life-supporting form.

This is hard to accomplish. "Hysteresis," Rod said when I called to complain to him one day. "It's a principle of physics that teaches us that the past conditions the future. It is hard work to overcome the past destruction of communities. This applies to human communities, like neighborhoods, in the same manner that it applies to ponds. It is a process that requires that you both stop the source of injury, for example, the run-off of pollution to the pond, and reanimate the life of the community. The upward spiral of recovery is shaped by the downward spiral of destruction."

In this book, I argue that, for neighborhoods, the equivalent of the run-off of pollution is the sorting-out of the American city by policies that have divided us by race, class, age, sexual orientation, religion, and many other factors. The solution I propose is the restoration of the urban ecosystem's wholeness. This requires the hard work of both stopping the source of injury and restoring the upward spiral of function, a transformation dragged down by the weight of past injuries.

I have identified nine elements of urban restoration that I believe are the critical tools for repairing our cities and returning our nation to health. These elements are:

1. Keep the whole city in mind
2. Find what you're FOR
3. Make a mark
4. Unpuzzle the fractured space
5. Unslum all neighborhoods
6. Create meaningful places
7. Strengthen the region
8. Show solidarity with all life
9. Celebrate your accomplishments

These elements of urban restoration are drawn from urban restoration projects I've been following for years, some carried out by my research team, the Community Research Group, and some that I've learned about from the people who lead them. In order to create this book, I asked Michel Cantal-Dupart and nine other leaders—Terri Baltimore, Ken Doyno, Lourdes Hernández-Cordero, Molly Rose Kaufman, Bonnie

Young Laing, Michael Malbrough, Patrick Morrissy, Carl Redwood, and Dan Rothschild—to be co-storytellers, talking through what had happened and working on drafts of the manuscript with me. This co-storytelling resembles oral history, except that the medium for collaboration was not the transcript of an interview, but the actual chapters for this book. Happily, e-mail and telephone calls could augment face-to-face meetings with my ten collaborators.

My confidence that we can have great cities comes from France. I number among the legions of African Americans who have taken to heart their time in France and used it as a lens for considering how life at home might be improved. To me, sitting in a café in Paris, dipping my fingers in a fountain in Aix-en-Provence, or walking alongside the ocean in Capbreton have been moments of civility, beauty, and humanity that proved that cities could be quite different from the traumatized and underfunded urban centers in which I function in the United States. But it is watching the city of Perpignan grapple with sorting that has really convinced me that urban restoration is possible.

Drawing lessons from events that unfolded in many different places and in many different times requires attention to rhythm and a keen eye for movement. I have tried to supply these, but I am depending on you, dear reader, to complete the task. Indeed, this is a book that requires you to complete it. It is a working book—a book about making the city a better place. I hope you will let it sit on your desk and become worn with time and consultation. I hope you will return to these stories, as I have, and draw ideas and comfort for your own work.

I also hope that you come to see how these nine elements of urban restoration work together. I was going over them with Cantal while working out how to best translate them into his lexicon of urbanism, when suddenly his face lit up.

"You need to get a photograph of the Pittsburgh Steelers football team!" he exclaimed. "They understand the nine elements of urban restoration! Think about it. They have the city in mind—they understand that all the parts of their team have to work together, they understand their fans and their opponents, and they think about the whole city around them and how they will reach it as they play their games. They get it. They think about having a program—they *know* what they're *for*—they're going to win the Super Bowl. They are focused and they achieve their end!

"And what do they do at the end?" He looked me deep in the eyes and nodded knowingly. "They have a party! A million people in the streets of Pittsburgh celebrating the Steelers."

He pulled out his tablet and began to search for the ideal image to convey the Pittsburgh Steelers as the epitome of the nine elements of urban restoration. He finally found a dense action shot in which a black player had jumped into the air to catch a ball while his teammates pushed the opposition out of the way so he could run to the goal.

"There it is! That's the nine elements of urban restoration, right there!" he pointed jubilantly.

I was even more surprised when Zoë Levitt, a young urbanist in Oakland, California, told me that I should visit a community garden in Brooklyn. "Community gardens," she said in an email, "are the ultimate antidote to the sorted-out city, and there we see all the nine elements of urban restoration.

"In New York, where I first spent time in urban community gardens, I felt how transformative these places were. I saw how many of these gardens were the beautiful result of grassroots investment and rebuilding in the face of systemic disinvestment and despair. People had joined together with their neighbors, poured their sweat and love and labor into the earth and reclaimed what was rightfully theirs—true public space that was welcoming, healing, regenerating, and alive. Even as community gardens transcend the concrete jungle of the city, they allow you to have the whole city in mind. They almost make it more possible to understand the whole city because the second you step into a garden, you are met by an undeniable sense of nakedness about what the city means for all of us. In the garden, we confront the humbling reality that we are all living on this same earth with the same need for nourishment and respite and connection despite the false divides that have been imposed around and between us through the construction and demolition of our own relentless yet invigorating skyline.

"Community gardens represent a program of action—it takes a community of people to create and recreate a vacant lot into something positive, beautiful, and green—and they often go hand in hand with other efforts to reclaim and rebuild urban neighborhoods. They make a mark on an otherwise vacant and deserted space. Gardens literally bring color, music, and life to desolate city blocks. They create a meaningful sense of place—a destination, an oasis, and a community gathering space—where before there was a non-place, or a negative place to avoid because of danger, desolation, or ugliness.

"Community gardens connect and draw people in from different parts of the street and block. I have met neighbors in community gardens whom I would not have otherwise met, as well as people from different blocks or neighborhoods. They literally create new life in cities by facilitating cultural, social, biological, and economic/commercial growth and interaction.

"Working together in the garden, you develop a sense of solidarity with each other and with other parts of the city. Gardens are where I first felt a sense of loyalty to the city of New York, as well as a commitment to work for a more just city. Not to mention, they are amazing sites for parties! Some of the most magical parties I have been to took place in gardens."

I told Molly Rose Kaufman, my urbanist daughter, about the remarks Cantal and Zoë had made. Molly shook her head to agree. "It's Ironworks, our own neighborhood settlement house, where you can easily see all the nine elements of urban restoration. We restored the building by listening to youth. We work together with all the people in the neighborhood to make it a meaningful place. We influence the region by inviting youth from all over our area and hosting them in our space. We show solidarity by having an urban farm next door. And at our parties, we build community and have fun."

Cantal's book, *Merci La Ville!* (1994), opens with the sentence, "*J'ai vu un pré devenir Auchan.*" I'd translate this as, "I saw a field become a big box store." It sums up, for me, the dreadful feeling of things done wrong.

I got the idea that it would be lovely to know what the opposite was—how things might be done right and how urban alchemy might be captured in a sentence. Cantal, in one of our conversations, reminded me of some arrows he'd drawn on a plan that had great resonance in Pittsburgh (see Figure 10.2). "Those arrows became gold," he said, "the transmutation of the base element to the precious one. Those arrows helped strengthen a collapsing neighborhood."

J'ai vu une flèche animer une friche.

I saw an arrow give life to a collapsing neighborhood.

What have you seen?

What will you see?

What will you do?

PART I

The Madness of the Sorted-Out City

CHAPTER ONE

From Illusion to Solution

Mr. Darcy's letter she was in a fair way of soon knowing by heart. She studied every sentence; and her feelings towards its writer were at times widely different. When she remembered the style of his address, she was still full of indignation; but when she considered how unjustly she had condemned and upbraided him, her anger was turned against herself; and his disappointed feelings became the object of compassion. His attachment excited gratitude, his general character respect; but she could not approve him; nor could she for a moment repent her refusal, or feel the slightest inclination ever to see him again.

—Jane Austen, *Pride and Prejudice*

In 1954, the US Supreme Court, in the decision of *Brown vs. Topeka Board of Education*, ruled that racially segregated schools were inherently unequal and therefore violated the nation's Constitution. Of course, it was not just schools that were segregated and not just schools that were inherently unequal. Transportation, employment, housing—you name it—we had it segregated. Undoing the law and custom of segregation has been the work of decades. This book addresses the paradox that while we've been desegregating our society, we've also been aggressively partitioning it by race, class, age, religion, lifestyle, and sexual orientation through the use of a sorting process that has amplified rather than eliminated separate and inherently unequal conditions of living, working, worshipping, playing, and attending school.

This situation is both morally repugnant and pragmatically dangerous. The sorted-out city, which is the focus of concern in this book, is a dysfunctional city, plagued by illness and paralyzed in the face of problems. These ills are not just the sorry fate of those at the bottom of the pyramid, but a trap for our whole society. Inherent inequality gives birth to universal problems. This is a surprise for most of us, as we tend to think that our "group" offers a protection from the problems of other "groups."

Even the most oppressed groups are allowed to revel in the trump cards they believe they hold: African Americans can jump and dance; Jews are smart; gays are charming and well dressed; women are nurturing; and atheists are brave. And certainly, those who actually have power and wealth believe that they are outside of the problems. But scholars have attacked these concepts as false ideas putting us all at risk (Gilman 1996). They have explained that the system of inherent inequality creates problems for all. As shocking as it may seem, it turns out that even the most privileged people suffer in unequal societies (Wilkinson and Pickett 2010). For example, Sir Michael Marmot and his colleagues compared white, middle-aged American men to their counterparts in England. They found that English men with minimal education had better health than Americans with the most education (Banks et al. 2006).

It is bad that we have sorted our cities by race and class. It is even worse to know that we are continuing to do so, aggravating the inequalities rather than resolving them. Given the threat this poses to our well-being, what are we to do?

This is the question that has preoccupied me for more than two decades and taken me to cities around the world, searching for tools to fight sorting. But I didn't start as an opponent of the sorted-out city. I started out demanding the right to remain segregated. I was seven. Here is the story of how I changed my mind.

Inherent inequality is *not* my problem

In 1957, I was a student in Oakwood Avenue School in Orange, New Jersey. I lived in a sea of learning. I learned to read, sing, play hopscotch, like boys, do arithmetic, love my teachers, and make art. I loved walking to school, playing in the playground, trying hard, and being great. I loved it when my mother invited the whole class to our house for a picnic and we

SCHOOL DAYS 1955-56
OAKWOOD

Figure 1.1: Oakwood school days.
Mindy Thompson as a kindergartner
at Oakwood Avenue School.

all walked there together, but afterwards I didn't have to go back to school because I was home! I loved the thank-you notes everyone wrote to "Dear Mrs. Thompson." I hopped to school, skipped home, and reveled in my own magnificence.

At that time, the city schools were segregated by a line that wiggled through the south of the city in a weird design that collected up white kids for the "white" school and black kids for the "black" school. Though logically I lived in the district of the white school, as I was black, I walked across busy Central Avenue to Oakwood, the "black" school. Because my mom, Maggie, was white, she was able to get a copy of the map that showed this gerrymander. She handed it to my dad, Ernie, a great community organizer, and said, "Fix it."

In the spring of 1958, my parents told me that they had won and I was going to go to a new school. I staged my version of a sit-in. I wept so bitterly at the thought of leaving my dear school that I caused myself to have migraine headaches. I hated being desegregated with all my heart and soul and I hated my parents for making this happen to me.

Later that year, when I was in third grade at Heywood Avenue School, the "white" school, my teacher, Ms. Hilda Portuguese, created an apartment house out of oaktag in which she had cut little windows, one for each person in the class. The oaktag was cut so it opened like shutters. Our photos were inserted in the windows. Every day, we were asked a series of questions about our comportment, things like going to bed by 8 p.m., eating citrus fruit, and brushing our teeth. If we had done all of these things, our shutters stayed open. We could see ourselves all day long. But, if not, our shutters were closed.

I took this lightly at first, but after a time or two of looking at my closed window, I realized it was no joke. My family was poor and having oranges every day was a stretch for the budget. I ate a lemon on one occasion. One time, my mother had taken me with her to solicit donations for the Mother's March of Dimes. I realized we were going to get home after eight. I threw a tantrum and she finally hailed one of the police cars patrolling the streets to protect the canvassers. We whizzed home and I shot up to bed.

Maybe it *is* my problem

In 1970, when I was nineteen, and my dad's health was failing, he asked if I would help him finish the book he'd been working on for as long as I could remember (Thompson and Thompson 1976). I started to write down his stories, using my own words and imagination. I read him what I'd written. "That's awful," he said. "That's not what happened or what it was like."

I was furious. Here I'd worked so hard and he was just trashing my artistic endeavor. But, unable to escape the project, I said (some hours later), "Well, then you better explain."

He did. In bits and pieces, he showed me what it had been like growing up in the segregated South at the height of Jim Crow. The black farmers were powerless, which meant that whites could abuse them. To protest might mean death, so they handled the insults in a propitiating manner. Away from the eyes of the white population, life was eked out, short on food and other comforts. My father described the profound kindness of his mother and the harsh punishments of his father, the church that was filled with poetry and praise, and the school that was built on his grandfather's land. I slowly realized that, whatever I had had to suffer because of the change in schools, to have accepted segregation would have been worse.

Mad plagues

"Remember how God visited ten plagues on the Egyptians so that Pharaoh would let the Jews go? If a group of elephants is a parade and a group of lions is a pride, what's a group of plagues?" I asked my daughter Molly one day.

"Mad plagues," she said immediately. "That's mad plagues." She had learned the word "mad" in junior high school. The expression became very popular in Washington Heights during the summer of 2005 while Molly was leading our Family-to-Family teen filmmaking program. That was the year that the documentary "Mad Hot Ballroom" came out. It featured young people from the neighborhood who were in a ballroom dancing competition. "Mad" was synonymous with "a lot."

My experience with mad plagues started in 1986. I was working as a psychiatrist in community mental health in San Francisco. The infamous real estate tax-cap, Proposition 13, had just been passed, and one of the effects was that it decimated mental health services. I decided to do research instead of clinical work, and I happened to get a job studying the AIDS epidemic in black and Hispanic communities. But just at that time, the crack cocaine epidemic was taking off. Soon, the neighborhoods where I was studying AIDS were convulsed by a wave of addiction that swept through the black neighborhoods. At the same time, the fight over the markets for selling crack triggered an explosion of violence. The violence, in turn, tripped an avalanche of mental illness related to violence. Just as I was beginning to understand all of those epidemics, an epidemic of multidrug-resistant tuberculosis broke out.

I followed the epidemics as they appeared. I talked to the people who were suffering from the illnesses piling up in their bodies. I visited the clinics where doctors were passing out pills with all the aplomb they could muster, but sore in their hearts over the great gap between what they knew and the kinds of new diseases and comorbidities that were arriving so fast at the clinic doors. I gained a bit of fame due to the dubious distinction of being the first public health professional to report a series of "the next bad thing" (see Selected Publications by Rodrick Wallace and the Community Research Group for more information on mad plagues).

In Harlem, I encountered patterns of despair I had never seen before or heard described. The environment was a wreck. A third of the buildings had been destroyed. Almost all of the blocks had lost one or more buildings. Some had lost nearly all. The empty lots were filled with rubble and garbage. There were strong smells and large rats. Nothing new was being built, and little was being fixed. The houses that were standing were ragged and sagging.

The people were thoroughly stressed. In focus groups and interviews, I encountered levels of discomfort that exceeded anything I'd previously encountered. On one occasion, I went to a drug treatment center where seven women joined me for a conversation. I was trying to understand the connection between crack use and the risk for HIV infection. Even before we got to the most sensitive part—trading sex for drugs—the women were agitated. When we started to talk about sex trading, one woman said she hadn't done that; she just had sex with friends who gave her drugs. The other six started screaming at her that that was the same thing. She refused to consider this, and the screaming became even more frenetic, if you can imagine what that must have sounded like. I had never heard anything like it. The noise was so loud, it aroused the concern of the whole treatment center and a dozen people collected outside the door, wondering if they should come in and rescue us.

Looking at the broken environment and talking to the distressed people, I felt the same sense of confusion I'd had as a new psychiatric resident, unable to decipher the language of madness. It was my mentor and friend, Rodrick Wallace, who helped me get a handle on the geyser of pathology. Rod is thin and disheveled, with brilliant blue eyes that are intensified by his bright white hair. He loves his own jokes and insists on truth telling, however inopportune the moment. Rod has a love of words that I count on. He passes along great science fiction, gives thoughtful presents for big birthdays, and, as someone nine years ahead of me, has kind advice on aging. His research has focused on the ecology of disease in American cities.

When I first met him, he had just published a very major paper called, "The Synergism of Plagues: 'Planned Shrinkage,' Contagious Housing Destruction, and AIDS in the Bronx" (Wallace 1988). Rod showed in that paper that a New York City policy called "planned shrinkage" had triggered the mad plagues of the 1970s. It was a policy so evil that it seemed like something a science fiction villain like Dr. Strangelove would invent.

At its heart was a decision to close fire stations and let the poor minority neighborhoods, including the South Bronx and Harlem, burn down. This would displace people, clear land, and allow the city to "shrink" its services. When I try to explain to students that this really happened in the United States of America, they look at me in total disbelief.

Rod demonstrated that the buildings destroyed by the fires set off a domino effect called "contagious housing destruction." This is a process of ecological catastrophe in which each lost building undermines the integrity of the buildings next to it or near it. One fire could eventually cause the loss of acres of housing. Indeed, in the South Bronx, some sections of the neighborhood lost 80 percent of their housing.

He estimated that the implementation of planned shrinkage caused a hundred thousand deaths or more—there's never been an official reckoning. It triggered the epidemics of AIDS, crack addiction, violence, mental illness related to violence, and asthma. The plagues were not contained in the neighborhoods burned by planned shrinkage, but rather they were spread throughout the city, the region, and the world. These are what I call mad plagues.

I wanted to understand the mental links between the broken environment and profound agony. "Read about mazeway disintegration," Rod said. "Go get the paper by Anthony F. C. Wallace (1957) that's in *Human Organization*."

The journal was housed on the lower level of the library at the Columbia University Medical Center. I pulled the dusty volume off the shelf and carefully photocopied the short article. It took only a few minutes to read the pungent description of the mazeway, the set of codes and social habits we develop for living in a place at a given time. When the mazeway falls apart, Wallace argued, we are at a loss. Deprived of the plan we had, we literally don't know what to do next. A paralysis follows. It is difficult to rebuild, and fanaticism, whether religious or political, can take hold.

When I was working with my father on his book, he often spoke of Harlem. His work as a union leader and civil rights activist had often taken him there in the 1930s and 1940s, and he always described it as an exciting place. David Swerdlick (1990) spent the summer taking photos of Harlem as it was in 1990 and comparing them to photos that he found in the archive of the Schomburg Collection. Those older photos—of fine buildings, stately parades, young women in their Sunday finery, gents out for the evening, night club stars, and more—were glimpses of a lively neighborhood capable of nurturing children, fighting injustice, and producing and enjoying music, art, and literature.

That was the mazeway, the way of life that made sense, which had been destroyed by fires and mad plagues. The screaming that became more frenetic in that drug treatment center was the language of loss, not simply of one person's home, but of many people's collective way of life. It was a language of the agony of upheaval, an agony that was made sharper by the heavy toll of death from the mad plagues.

Alexander Leighton (1959), a key theorist of social psychiatry, had said that communities that are working together might be called "integrated," while those that had lost that social glue might be called "disintegrated." I postulated that planned shrinkage and other antiurban policies had led to a step-wise collapse from integration to disintegration (Fullilove 1993). In my "Stage-State Model of Community Disintegration," I proposed that at each turn of the screw, the matrix within which people were functioning became distinctly different. The people shifted with the changing times, adapting to increasingly harsher social realities by changing the whole behavioral language that they were using.

These adaptations included the adoption of what people in public health labeled "AIDS risk behaviors," but what Rod pointed out were behaviors essential to the survival of one's dignity and worth under excruciating circumstances (Wallace, Fullilove, and Flisher 1996). It was evident to me that people were profoundly shaped by their environments. If we wanted to have healthy people, we had to have healthy neighborhoods.

I looked around at the acres of empty lots and wondered, "What is to be done?"

Fix the city!

In 1993, I went to Paris for a conference on AIDS, homelessness, and substance abuse with that question on my mind. As a serious student of the mad plagues, I'd been to many meetings on those topics. At none of them was there any talk about the devastation of the neighborhoods. But no sooner had the conference started than a Frenchman strode to the podium and said, "There is a very strong interaction between the questions that preoccupy doctors and the form of the city." I sat up straight and elbowed my husband, Bob—I was a doctor and I was wondering about the form of the city!

"For a long time," the speaker, Michel Cantal-Dupart, said, "I have been trying to mobilize our leaders so that the cities, where our money and brainpower are concentrated, innovate for better functioning. What is the problem that we must solve? It is the fracture that exists between the wealthy neighborhoods and the others. Each day, this chasm grows. I am convinced that there is a close connection between the signs of exclusion and the shape of the city, whether it is poor neighborhoods or whole cities that have been shut out. We find neighborhoods far from everything, without means of transport, where many are unemployed and where there are numerous young people. We find the names of those neighborhoods in the newspapers. We also know that those neighborhoods are the neighborhoods with high rates of illness.

"But, paradoxically," he continued, "if we want to improve life in those neighborhoods, *we can't just treat the neighborhoods*. We have to remove the chasm that is dividing the poor neighborhoods from the other parts of the city. Doctors know that if you want to treat a boil on the skin, you have to treat the whole body. It's the same for the city. If we want to solve the problems of the poor neighborhoods, we must treat the whole city. We must eliminate the fracture."[1]

We can't just treat the neighborhoods—that made sense to me. In the medical model of disease, we know that symptoms arise from disorder in an organ, like the heart. The symptoms alert us to trouble, but what we treat is the problem in the organ. Arguing by analogy, the neighborhoods had the symptoms of disorder, but the city was the organ with the defect of fracture.

In Figure 1.2, we follow this process. The African Americans who moved to Harlem during the Great Migration established an orderly way of life, as seen in the 1930s photo of a Harlem street, one of the historic photos selected by David Swerdlick (1990) for his slideshow, *Mazeway Disintegration*. The fires of planned shrinkage contributed to the loss of 30 percent of the buildings in Harlem and disrupted the functioning of the community. In the 1990 photo, we see abandonment at its nadir. The downward spiral is my model of community disintegration, in which each

The fire next time

Sense of order.

Figure 1.2: These photographs depict how the Harlem community burned down and fell apart socially. This collapse is modeled by a downward spiral, which raises the question: What next?

Photo credits:

Above: Sid Grossman/WPA. Harlem Tenement in Summer, where Harlem residents gathered and sat around the entrance to the residential building, 1939. Some tenants are peering through the windows. From the Photographs and Prints Division, Schomburg Center for Research in Black Culture, the New York Public Library, Astor, Lenox and Tilden Foundations.

Top: Harlem Fire, Rodrick Wallace, used with permission.

Top right: Stage-State Model of Community Collapse by Mindy Fullilove.

Bottom right: Street Play, David Swerdlick, from the Community Reasearch Group (CRG) Collection.

Question: How do we restore the neighborhood?

Fire acts as a destabilizing event.

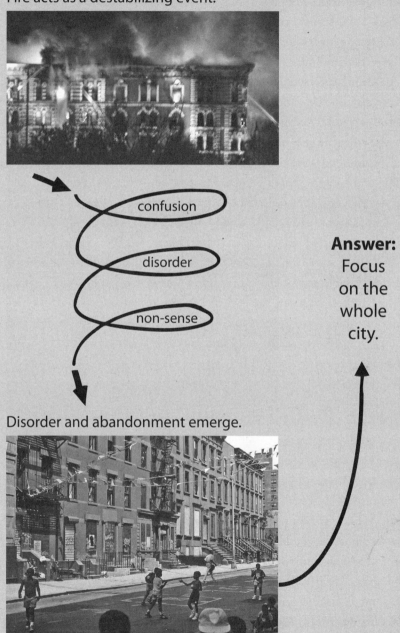

confusion

disorder

non-sense

Answer:
Focus
on the
whole
city.

Disorder and abandonment emerge.

insult that hit the community caused further disintegration, as the community shifted from the well-organized state of the 1930s to the "non-sense" of the 1990s (Fullilove 1993). We can see this shift when we compare the orderly street scene from the 1930s, where street play is overseen by adults sitting on the stoops, to David's photograph of a street scene in 1990, where street play cannot be watched by people on stoops as the buildings are largely abandoned.

According to Cantal, the solution rested not in simply fixing Harlem, but in fixing the city. Indeed, the policies of segregation, redlining, urban renewal, and planned shrinkage, which had caused the problems, were policies set by the city, not the neighborhood.

"Would you please teach me how to fix cities?" I asked Cantal in my halting and badly accented French. He nodded, with great sympathy. The next day, he gave me an artsy book he'd written, *Les Ponts de Paris* (The Bridges of Paris) (Pattou and Cantal-Dupart 1991). What bridges in Paris had to with saving Harlem was anybody's guess, but I was game to learn.

In 1996, Cantal came to New York and we walked Harlem together. I pointed to the legion of empty lots. He pointed to a red balloon. "Someone had a birthday party," he told me. It was my introduction to the elements of urban restoration. He continued, "If you want to understand the city, you need to study in a Latin country. When you're ready, come to France."

What is a city?

Cantal is tall and embodies that Alexander ideal of fluid, upright posture. He is dapper, charismatic, and French, not simply as a national origin, but as a sense of style. He *never* drops food or drink on his clothes, and always knows how he is supposed to act in any given situation. He is marked by the imperiousness of French white men of his generation, those born during World War II, but he imbibed decolonization by spending seven years in Tunisia at the beginning of his career. This opened doors for him that few others could access. His time in Tunisia created the territory he and I share. He is very serious about his work. He can also be very silly. One time, Bob and I got sick while visiting at Cantal's country home. He arrived in our room, ready to leave for a costume party and dressed as a World War I aviator. He tucked us in very tenderly, kissed us goodnight, and strode off down the hall, singing at the top of his lungs. He is an artist of the city, a lover of a *bon gueuleton*, and a loyal friend.

In the summer of 2000, Bob and I packed our bags to stay for two months in France. My goal was to learn about urban renewal for my 2001 book *Root Shock*, Bob's was to immerse himself in the food, wine, and language of the country. Cantal had arranged for us to be housed in the sixth *arrondissement*, a neighborhood just off the Seine, cut by urban renewal in the nineteenth century and never made whole again. Despite that ancient wound, it was the busiest, most interesting urban place I had ever lived. It was a street people had been walking for a thousand years. I loved listening to the drunken tourists singing loudly at four in the morning. "You don't know," I thought, "that you're following in a flow that is ever so old."

Cantal taught me that for many millennia, people had been gathering in urban centers, and this is where they had amassed the social and cultural treasures of humanity. People then used that wisdom, inspiration, and ingenuity from urban centers to build pyramids and space ships, to solve riddles and quadratic equations, to remember the great and honor the living, to make, in sum, civilizations and culture. We send the products of the mines and mills, fields and factories to the city so that it may take on this special function as a convening place of the society. The city is a location for generating culture and an economy, for inventing language, for deciphering mysteries. A city is a node in the net of the nation, essential to its supply lines and communication systems.

One day, when he thought I'd got the basics of what a city was, Cantal took us on a "healing the city tour." He showed us what fracture looked like and some of the ways in which he was fixing it. The first place we visited was a small village called Sore. We drove into a parking area in the center of the village. We walked a couple of steps forward and he stopped. A quaint church had come into view. "That's the first problem," Cantal said. "They need to reveal their assets." People driving by couldn't see the church and weren't drawn to stop. "These roadside towns need to invite people to stop—that's how they survive."

We walked around the side of the church and he pointed out the walled-up *cagot*, or leper's door, an ancient form of sorting the city by excluding those with a dreaded illness. We walked a little ways away from the church and stopped by a stone wall. "This wall was the edge of the village. The lepers had to live on the other side, denied access to the church and God. But," and he winked, "they had the science of numbers and they could do carpentry. This village has a great story to tell in this historic church and its relationship to the lepers and their struggles. But they are not doing anything about it."

We walked a little further back behind the houses that fronted on the main street to a sandy, disorganized lot. A few houses were scattered around, in no particular order. "I tried to get them to develop this section, as it would strengthen the Main Street. They weren't willing to do it." We walked up to the main street and Cantal pointed silently to several stores that had "Going Out of Business" signs. He shook his head at each one.

Our next stop was Mont de Marsan, where we saw a second version of "hidden assets." Cantal drove through the interior of a housing project and pointed out the ways in which people had nestled in, planting gardens and making areas to barbecue. It was a very attractive lively place, and I have a vivid memory of the lovely flowers everywhere.

Then we went back to the street and he stopped the car to show the fence around a basketball court that interrupted the view of the buildings from the street, cheapening and isolating them. "The city wants to tear down these housing projects—it's a policy that's popular in France right now. I told them not to tear the buildings down—there's a lot of evidence that the buildings are sound and house a contented community—I told them to tear down the fence and create an elegant entrance so that the housing project is connected to the larger city. That wasn't what they wanted to hear, but it's what is right."

When I got out of the car in St. Sever, our third stop, I saw a poster that said that Cantal was the urbanist for a project that was going on. "It is an unusual village," he explained, "because it is built around the monastery. In most places, the monastery was outside of town."

The monastery was right on the central plaza, which was clogged with parked cars. The parking had overrun the center—there was no place for people to gather. This lack of a center is a very common problem of cities. Without such a heart, the city's "blood" will stop flowing. This is as deadly for cities as it is for people.

He explained what he was doing while we lunched at a restaurant on the plaza. "My plan is to make this area a real plaza for city life. But the cars can't be too far from this area, so we are creating a parking space just behind. It will strengthen the back area—what I proposed for Sore—while opening up this center for public use. In my view, the key to city life is making the public space beautiful and attractive—in the sense of pulling people in. Once they're pulled in and using the space together, the action of the city will start to work. The city has its own logic—my job is to create the effective kinds of space in which the city can work."

"By pulling all the parts together, are you creating a more democratic city?" I asked.

"Exactly!" he exclaimed and beamed at me. He paid our bill and said, "Let's go see Rion des Landes!"

This was, Cantal recounted, a progressive city with a dedicated mayor, a leader who had understood and identified with Cantal's democratizing intent. We started our tour in the center. From there, we worked our way around the panoply of interventions that had given a once forlorn city a deep hum of beauty. We sat on benches by the Rights of Man Fountain, and Cantal, blissed out by his own work, chortled, "This is how you make a place!"

In the background were low-income apartments as beautiful as the rest of the center. Across the street, the church had been freed of distracting fencing and given a splendid pavement for wedding photos. "Very important," Cantal explained, "because people keep those photographs, and when they come to the city, they will look for the church, and it will give them a connection with their history, with the very spot where their ancestors stood on a happy day many years before."

We paused before the World War I monument in which Patria, in flowing garments, embraced a young soldier, his eyes uplifted in a pose of grace. "I moved it from the side of the road to this place. People will gather to pay tribute and they will have more fun if they have some room, and they're away from the traffic."

A bit further down the gravel path was a château, abandoned for some years, but then made into city hall. "City hall was down the road in a shabby building, but they wanted to move it here. I made a park to provide a glorious setting for town events."

The list went on: the church fence had been moved beside the creek; the schoolchildren had been given a bicycle path; the bullfighting arena, a traditional part of village equipment in that part of France, had been refurbished with a splendid courtyard; and public housing was being built nearby to flank the bullfighting ring, providing a wing for the public plaza as well as housing for people.

Form follows perspective

BEFORE Sandy and unstructured (looking west).

AFTER Lines of perspective to church and tree (looking east).

Cantal had tackled the same problems we had seen in the other cities: the lack of a center, a weak area surrounding that center, and hidden assets that were disconnected from one another. He had made a center, strengthened the back, connected the parts, and revealed hidden treasures. He had

Figure 1.3: Rion des Landes, like many villages in the Southwest of France, has a bull-fighting arena. It was located in an unstructured plaza. Cantal used the visual lines of perspective to the church spire and the village's Tree of Liberty to give meaningful structure to the plaza and create new allure for the arena.

Photo credits and plan of intervention [site plan]: Courtesy of Michel Cantal-Dupart inserted social housing without denigrating it. He used a principal tool of French landscape design, the creation of perspective, to give the space order and connection. Thus, the plaza by the bullfighting ring, shown in Figure 1.3, is not simply attractive because it has pavers. The pavers define the space and create visual links from the front of the arena to other key parts of the city, including the church spire in the distance.

"You know that game that kids play where there are numbered dots and you connect the dots to make a duck?" he asked.

I nodded.

"That's what I do. I'm Mr. Fix-it, *Bricoleur-des-Villes*—I connect the dots to reveal the city. Then I unveil, modify, strengthen, harmonize— whatever's needed to make it work."

I visited forty-three cities in the fifty-six days I spent in France that summer. I learned to see the city, which caused a revolution in my thinking. One day in Bordeaux, sitting by the perfectly turquoise pool of a local architect, I shared how tiring my trip was. "I know," he said sympathetically. "You are studying space, and space is all around you, everywhere you go. How are you to rest?"

The city's injury

In 2005, I was invited to Charlotte, North Carolina, to celebrate World AIDS Day. I proposed to the organizers that we have a tour of the city as part of the festivities, a program they called, "Stop AIDS: Keep the Promise. The Importance of Neighborhoods in the Fight Against AIDS." They asked Tom Hanchett, historian at the Levine Museum of the New South, to lead it. He and I met beforehand, and he gave me a copy of his 1998 book, *Sorting Out the New South City: Race, Class and Urban Development in Charlotte, 1875-1975*. "Look," he emphasized, showing me a map from 1875, "the surprising fact in this book is that we weren't always segregated."

Hanchett dissected how Charlotte in 1875 was a city in which people of both races and all income levels were intermingled. By 1975, it was heavily segregated. We can see in the map from 1980 that well-to-do white people are concentrated in the southeast, African Americans reside in the northwest, and lower-income whites occupy the northern perimeter.

The sorting process is not a once-and-for-all process, but rather a repetitive process that continually relocates people, making finer and finer distinctions among them. As Hanchett (1998, 259) noted about Charlotte,

Once in place, segregation begat segregation. People increasingly out of contact with their diverse urban neighbors came to take separation for granted as a natural law in human affairs. This tendency was accelerated after 1930 by actions of the federal government. Washington—acting on assumptions shared by many urbanites—underwrote suburban housing development, shopping centers, urban renewal, and other programs designed to promote "homogeneous" and "appropriate" land use. Thanks to federal aid, local leaders could carry sorting-out to its logical extreme. The result was the creation of the late twentieth century's pronounced sector pattern of separation by color and income.

Each of these policies pushed people into increasingly homogeneous spaces. Each of these policies was, for the people affected, a turn of the screw as I showed in Figure 1.2, a time of upheaval and disorder. When the American nation wrote inequality into the US Constitution and then intensified that division with a time series of segregation, urban renewal, highway construction, planned shrinkage, and other practices that fractured our cities, it both warped the mind of the polity and shattered its body.

Rod Wallace has done a lot of research examining the functioning of shredded networks. He called me up one day to talk about his new idea.

"There is a theory that says the brain works by the cooperation of its parts to create a 'Global Workspace.' The cognitive activity takes place in this combined space. I have been considering the ways in which work teams cooperate to get work done. I think they create something analogous to the Global Workspace. When teams are cooperating, we run into many opportunities and some problems. They have to share information and that takes time. They might not be able to see some issues, and that's a kind of blindness. They might ignore issues because of ideology and policy.

"But the worst problem is that the fractured networks intensify all of these problems of cooperation and might keep people from even attempting to cooperate. That's a really terrible situation that leads to many kinds

The sorting of Charlotte

1875. People of all races and incomes are intermingled.

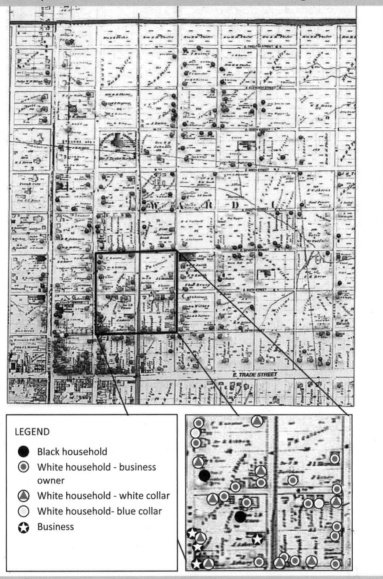

LEGEND

● Black household

◉ White household - business owner

⬤ White household - white collar

○ White household- blue collar

★ Business

Figure 1.4: In 1875, people of both races and all income groups lived mixed together in Charlotte, North Carolina. By 1980, people had been sorted out by race and class into pie-shaped wedges. See also the graph of sorting in Figure 4.3, Charlotte neighborhoods as viewed through PRIZM.

1980. People are sorted by race, class, and lifestyle.

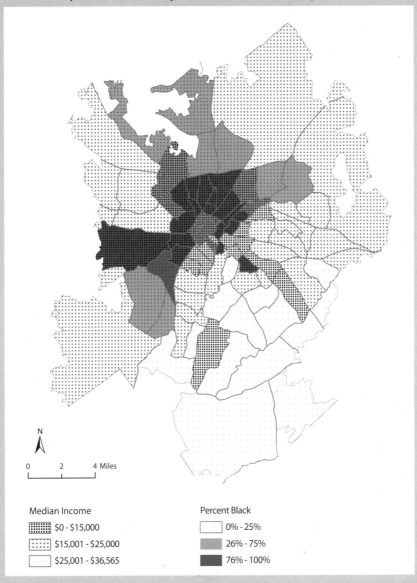

Median Income
- $0 - $15,000
- $15,001 - $25,000
- $25,001 - $36,565

Percent Black
- 0% - 25%
- 26% - 75%
- 76% - 100%

1875 map courtesy of Thomas Hanchett; call-out by Sarah Schell.
1980 map made by Sarah Schell.

of problems. I was wondering if you'd like to write about this for the book I'm working on, *Collective Consciousness and Its Discontents* (Wallace and Fullilove 2008)?"

He prompted me to think in a new way about a group of studies my research team had done on the AIDS epidemic. One study had looked at the slow and erratic way in which health care organizations had gotten involved in AIDS (Garcia-Soto et al. 1998). Another study had looked at the religious and social problems that kept the black clergy from responding to the epidemic (Wallace and Fullilove 2008). The third study had looked at how the funding provided by the Ryan White Care Act was working to help minority women living with AIDS (Madoff 2002). In all three studies, the fractures between groups defined by race, class, sexual orientation, addiction, and any other difference we could think of—religious sect, education, and on and on—were interfering with the creation of the intergroup global workspace.

Without that common platform for collective thinking, the groups could not solve the problems with which they were confronted. They were caught in a profound paralysis, unable to recognize and respond to patterns of threat and opportunity. In that context, the AIDS virus made its merry way from person to person, unhampered by the multitude of impediments an aroused public might have thrown in its path. American society dickered for nearly two decades about whether or not it was OK to save the lives of gay men and intravenous drug users. The mammoth worldwide AIDS epidemic is directly proportional to those years of debate, and those years of debate are directly proportional to the degree of collapse of the intergroup workspace in America's sorted-out cities.

Rod and I were talking about this one day, and he said, "You know, it's the inverse."

"What's the inverse of what?" I asked.

"Well, the powers that rule America have always used divide and conquer to maintain their power. That's the purpose of the sorting process—to divide the mass of people so that the powers that be can control everything. But divide and conquer is what's making us flounder. What we're proposing is the opposite, to unite people, to share what we have."

Mesh and prosper

For twenty years, my search to understand the South Bronx, Harlem, and the mad plagues has been shaped by Rod's encouragement to study social disorganization and Cantal's encouragement to study the form of the city. During that time, I worked with a remarkable team of researchers that included Lesley Rennis, Caroline Parsons Moore, Véronique Héon-Klin, Jennifer Stevens Dickson, Lourdes Hernández-Cordero, Beverly Xaviera Watkins, Moriah McSharry McGrath, Molly Rose Kaufman, Evelyn Joseph, Howard Joseph, Arelis De La O, Mark Boutros, and many others.

We called ourselves the Community Research Group. We studied AIDS, violence, mental illness related to violence, tuberculosis, the psychology of place, the rebuilding of Harlem, the Berlin Wall, spiritual awakening, mass incarceration, urban renewal, and social cohesion. We reacted to the events of our times, from fatal school shootings to the 9/11 terrorist attacks on the World Trade Center. (See Selected Publications by Rodrick Wallace and the Community Research Group for more information.)

From this body of work, I became convinced that our cities were mired in a profound contradiction. Human beings create cities so that they will have a site for social and cultural interaction and development. Cities fulfill this function because people connect with each other and exchange goods and ideas. The sorted-out American city cannot do what it is meant to do, as division is antithetical to connection, conquering to exchange. It is this deep contradiction that rumbles in the guts of our cities: we feel the unease, suffer from the dysfunction, and act out the madness.

Cantal likened the dysfunction of the sorted-out city to a mill whose grinding surfaces were not aligned and could not function. The solution for our cities, he argued, was to ensure that the parts met meticulously to unleash the power of the machine. This is the meeting point of my work, Rod's work, and Cantal's work: the broken city speaks a language of madness, which is embodied by its citizens as violence, despair, family fracture, and mad plagues. Whether broken by class or race oppression, religious hatred, or patriarchy, cities that are broken must be realigned if we are to be free of disease and have a hopeful future.

Architect Dan Rothschild, whose work has inspired much of this book, reflected on this analogy of the mill. "The wheels of the mill," he pointed out, "actually intersect. This is a much more robust relationship than simply connecting, which might mean two entities merely touch. For the mill to work, we must *mesh* the parts to create a fit where one side supports the other."

Living in the solution

At the Community Research Group, we loved the oft-told tale of a man standing by the side of a stream and pulling drowning people out, one by one. Suddenly, he left the stream and started to run. "Where are you going?" asked one of the people he'd rescued. "There are more drowning people coming down the stream."

"I'm going upstream," the man replied, "to stop the person who's throwing all these people in the water!"

To go upstream—to stop the sorting and repair the city—I propose we use the science and mystery of urban alchemy.

Alchemy, which dates back to ancient Egypt, was a study of life processes. The alchemists were interested in creating life and making it last forever. They used philosophical, mystical, and experimental approaches. This rich combination gave birth to modern chemistry, made major contributions to medicine, and inspired artists and philosophers.

Urban alchemy starts with a version of the alchemist's question: How can we make the sorted-out city whole again? Urban alchemy takes a broad array of methods—experimental, spiritual, and philosophical—and arrives at hitherto unimagined answers and powerful results. Like alchemy, urban alchemy is a search for rules. This search for rules is a place of invention and exploration necessary to power through transformation. In furthering this quest, I am proposing nine elements of urban restoration and the key rules for how they are to be considered.

I've taken plenty of chemistry courses and the periodic table of the elements was the principal decoration in many of my classrooms. Its mysteries of discovery and organization were my first introduction to the idea of building blocks. Everything in the world arises from combinations of those basic atoms. I thoroughly enjoyed learning the facts of those elements—their names, symbols, weights, type, and actions in the world. And good thing I did, as much of the medicine I've practiced has been about giving people chemicals to change their pathophysiology.

Strunk and White's (2007) *The Elements of Style* was my second introduction to this concept. They, too, used "the" in the title, announcing the fact that the "little book" is a definitive guide. On page 1, they tell us, "Form the possessive singular of nouns by adding 's. Follow this rule whatever the final consonant. Thus write, Charles's" (Strunk and White 2007, 1).

They are not, you will note, suggesting that you consider the idea—it might be helpful *if*. They state the rule and you are supposed to do it—period, end of discussion. I don't know a serious writer who doesn't have a copy of *The Elements of Style* near her desk. And if in this book there's a possessive singular noun without an apostrophe and an s, it's not my copyeditor's fault!

But the proximal source of the idea for the elements of urban restoration is Joe Eck's (2005) monumental work, *Elements of Garden Design*. Wayne Winterrowd, Eck's husband and co-gardener, recounted how the idea for the book was born in an English pub. The editor of *Horticulture* had asked Eck what he thought was missing from the magazine. "Gardening philosophy… Theory… Argument… Garden design," he replied. From that conversation came the agreement to write a series of essays for the magazine (Eck 2005, xxi). Those essays were eventually collected into the book.

Eck, like Strunk and White, was proposing a series of rules, but he hoped that his rules would be challenged. He welcomed critique and exploration. "All of these imagined responses, even the first one, will further the fundamental aim of this book, which is, quite simply, to encourage a dialogue on how gardens are made" (Eck 2005, xx).

Eck's book offers us a rich language for thinking about the gardens in front of us. On the concept of the scale, for example, he emphasizes, "Many gardens in America fail because they are too meager" (Eck 2005, 41).

How many foundation plantings flash into my mind when I read this! Suddenly, my dissatisfaction has been articulated and the search for the solution offered. I even understand my own problem. In my front yard are two magnificent Japanese maples. They offer dense, welcome shade in the summer and let the sun in in the winter. They are perfect trees, but they easily overwhelm the house and the postage-stamp lawn. The exuberant trees and meager lawn are out of scale with each other, which I had not

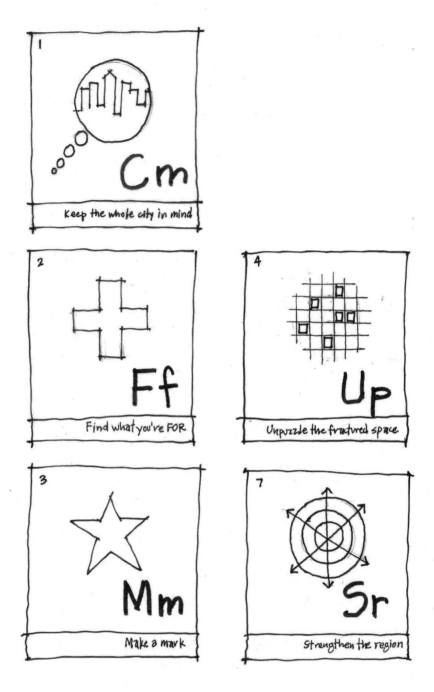

Figure 1.5: The order of elements refects the three parts—align, create, connect.

The periodic table of the elements of urban restoration

Design: Sarah Schell and Dan Rothschild.
Illustration: Dan Rothschild.

understood before I read Eck's comments. It is this richness of thought that has made his book so dear to me. From that deep pleasure, I took the idea that there must be similarly helpful elements people are using to make cities better.

It is a bold proposition to identify the basic rules of any discipline. I like Eck's positionality. Therefore, these are not *the* elements of urban restoration, the way the elements of the periodic table are *the* building blocks of life on earth or the rules of grammar propounded by Strunk and White are *the* rules to write by. But I do think these are important elements, fundamental to the restoration of the sorted-out city. The periodic table of the elements of urban restoration is shown in Figure 1.5.

The first element for restoring the sorted-out city is that we learn to **keep the whole city in mind**. This poses a profound challenge to much of our current practice of "community" and "neighborhood" development. It locates our community and neighborhoods in the city and asks us to fix the larger system so that its smaller units can prosper.

The second is that we **find what we are FOR** and use that to develop a clear program of action. Many social movements are initiated in order to *stop* something—nuclear testing or the use of animals in experiments. A programmatic approach, by contrast, asks us to articulate a vision of the world we want to see. It is the idea proposed by Stephen Covey as the second habit of highly effective people, that we start with the end in mind (Covey 2012).

The third is that we **make a mark**. The mark changes the world by reordering the streams of people and events. By understanding our marks, and by placing them in powerful locations, we can begin to realize our programmatic goals.

These first three elements help us *align* our ideas with one another.

The fourth is that we **unpuzzle the fractured space**. The sorting-out of the city has twisted our urban space and created barriers to free movement that leave us confused about how to live together. Unpuzzling opens the space and frees us to get to know each other.

The fifth is that we **unslum all neighborhoods**. Jane Jacobs (1991), the great American urbanist, was the first to define a slum as a place where people didn't want to stay. She observed that when people decided to stay and invest in a place, improvement began. Our work, she argued, is to understand this natural process and to support its unfolding.

The sixth is that we **create meaningful places**. Place provides comfort, security, and well-being to the extent that it gives us a sense of belonging. This requires that the place have meaning in the social system of those who live, work, and play there. Urban restoration is, in no small part, the effort to show to advantage the symbols that have been tarnished by neglect and disrespect.

This group of three elements helps us *create* the city we want to see.

The seventh is that we **strengthen the region**. The sorting-out process that partitions cities also operates in the same manner at the level of the region. The strength of the restored city can be used to repair the tears in the fabric of the larger region.

The eighth is that we **show solidarity with all life**. Ecosystems are vulnerable to the intense exploitation we have imposed on them in the course of industrialization. In this process, we are creating threats to all species and perhaps, most importantly, to our own. To ensure survival, we must find ways to moderate our pressures on the earth and bring harmony into our ways of living with others.

The ninth is that we **celebrate our accomplishments**. In the sorted-out city, people are demoralized and disempowered. We will not become powerful overnight, but we can lift our morale by recognizing and celebrating every step we take toward living in the solution.

These last three elements help us *connect* to one another.

Mending our destiny

The downward spiral of community disintegration is a powerful force undermining our nation's cities and, therefore, our nation. Urban restoration can stop this process and can transform the sorted-out city, characterized by *divide and conquer*, into the welcoming city, characterized by *mesh and prosper*.

In its simplest form, what I am proposing is that the downward spiral of community disintegration can be halted by stopping all the processes that sort us by race, class, and other differences. Patrick Devine-Wright (2009) has called such actions "place-protective behaviors."

Then, using the nine elements of urban restoration, we can reintegrate the city, restoring our ability to recognize and solve problems. Following the logic of Devine-Wright, we can call these "place-restorative behaviors" (Fullilove, forthcoming). Through their use, we are able to return our society to sanity.

The Reverend Martin Luther King, Jr., (1963) in his famous *Letter from a Birmingham Jail*, wrote, "Injustice anywhere is a threat to justice everywhere. We are caught in an inescapable network of mutuality, tied in a single garment of destiny. Whatever affects one directly, affects all indirectly."

In sorting our cities, we have torn that garment of destiny, which poses a fundamental threat to our health and well-being as a society. We are rushing towards the terrible consequences of rupture. By protecting and restoring our places, we can mend our destiny and create new hope for a bright collective future.

CHAPTER TWO

Our Hearts Inspired

Athena, her eyes flashing bright, exulted.
"Father, son of Cronus, our high and mighty king!
If now it really pleases the blissful gods
that wise Odysseus shall return—home at last—
let us dispatch the guide and giant-killer Hermes
down to Ogygia Island, down to announce at once
to the nymph with lovely braids our fixed decree:
Odysseus journeys home—the exile must return!
While I myself go down to Ithaca, rouse his son
to a braver pitch, inspire his heart with courage."

    —Homer, *The Odyssey*, translated by Robert Fagles

In 2007, I went to see August Wilson's *Radio Golf* at the Cort Theater on Broadway. The play opened with developer Harmond Wilks exulting in his plan to raze an old building and get rich from a new development, the Bedford Hills Redevelopment Project. The creaky door of the old office opened and Elder Joseph Barlow walked in. "You know where I can find any Christian people?" he asked, despair ringing in his voice.

I was startled by the juxtaposition of the ecstatic celebration and the pained question. Where was this going? "I'm looking for some Christian people," Elder Barlow continued.

It emerged that there was a plan to tear down Aunt Ester's house, and Elder Barlow wanted to stop the process. In fact, it was Wilks himself who was about to destroy the house, and the confrontation quickly became quite personal. Slowly, I got that this was a play about Ms. Della and Ms. Edna and all the leaders who rose up to oppose the HOPE VI program's demolition of the housing projects in Pittsburgh's Hill District. My excitement grew. I turned to my cousin Linnie Golightly. "I was there!" I told her, with great excitement. "I saw this happen!"

I was not surprised to learn that, indeed, *Radio Golf* was set in 1997. We can imagine that August Wilson, sitting up in Eddie's Restaurant on Wylie Avenue, had heard about the protesting of HOPE VI over in Allequippa Terrace and Bedford Dwellings and the coming threat to the projects. He remembered the agony of urban renewal and he transformed that need for salvation from the bulldozers into a simple question: "You know where I can find any Christian people?"

What have you loved about this place?

In 1997, Della Wimbs, Edna Council, Tamanika Howze, Terri Baltimore, and other African American leaders in Pittsburgh's Hill District knew that HOPE VI plans were being adopted for their city. HOPE VI was a federal initiative that was designed to alleviate the problems of distressed housing communities, that is, federal housing projects that were deemed to be dysfunctional. Public housing had gotten such a bad reputation among the general public that most people viewed the destruction of the towering apartment buildings as a welcome intervention. "Mothers can't watch their children play from the eighteenth floor. Tall buildings don't work for the poor," was what I often heard asserted as a justification for the program, even when the housing projects in question were two-stories high. HOPE VI would give money to cities to demolish the housing projects and rebuild mixed-income communities. Glowing images of New Urbanist townhouses replacing ugly housing projects swept the United States.

But the leaders of the Hill District had lived through urban renewal—the 1950s federal program that had promised to clear blighted slums and create beautiful new urban terrain. The truth was that people lost their homes, businesses, churches, friends, and neighbors as a result. The neighborhood was devastated and had been on a downhill course since then. The Hill leaders recognized in HOPE VI an eerily familiar program of displacement and feared the worst.

At about that time, Don Mattison, dean of the University of Pittsburgh Graduate School of Public Health, read my paper, "The Psychiatric Implications of Displacement: Contributions from the Psychology of Place" (Fullilove 1996). In that paper, I reviewed studies of upheaval and argued that displacement posed serious problems for individuals and groups. "The major proposition presented here is that the sense of belonging, which is necessary for psychological well-being, depends on strong, well-developed relationships with nurturing places. A major corollary of this proposition is that disturbance in these essential place relationships leads to psychological disorder" (Fullilove 1996, 1517).

An astute internist, he saw the seriousness of this statement. "You're raising issues we need to consider in Pittsburgh. Please come and give a talk at our school," he said to me.

On February 17, 1997, I spoke to an auditorium full of people at the Graduate School of Public Health. "People love their homes," I told the audience, "and this love is not trivial, it is not superficial. Four-hundred years ago, physicians recognized a life-threatening illness they named 'nostalgia,' meaning the pain caused by loss of home, which threatened people who had moved, sometimes even to what we would think of as very short distances. I have interviewed people who lost their homes due to urban renewal, and they are still grieving the homes and communities lost forty years ago. We cannot overestimate the extent to which we love and need our homes and neighborhoods.

"It is crucial to protect people's neighborhoods," I concluded, "because they are the source of their well-being and they are not easily replaced."

The women from the Hill caucused immediately after my talk and said to each other, "Why isn't she giving this talk in the Hill? People need to hear this."

A dozen organizations pooled their money and other resources to support a visit. Rich Brown, a graphic designer with a deep sensitivity to community issues, created a bold leaflet that asked, "Do you know you're moving?" This leaflet sent shock waves through the housing projects and brought many out to hear what I had to say.

The group had sent me HOPE VI documents in preparation for the visit. I was shocked to read that a distressed community was defined as one with rent arrears and other problems that were patently linked to poor management and not in any way measures of the people in the community. This was a blatant case of "blaming the victim." I knew that people attacked in this way might become paralyzed, as is the case with all victims of abuse.

Dr. Steve Goldstein, one of my teachers in 1981 when I was a psychiatric resident at Morrisania Neighborhood Family Care Center in the Bronx, was stern on this point: "The victims' chances are a lot better if they are angry and fight back. And you have a better chance of helping if you show that you're really mad. Shout, be loud—show people that you think it's really serious. Many things can change if people stand up for their rights."

This wasn't just a theoretical point. I was working with a family in a therapy session, and Steve was watching through a one-way mirror. He called me on the phone. "Please come out," he told me. I went to the adjoining room. "We want you to be even louder." I went back and remonstrated with the parents in the biggest, boldest way I could. "Yeah," Steve said, "That's what I wanted to see."

I know he was looking over my shoulder that day. At each of the housing projects I visited, I said with all the force I could muster, "They are blaming you for their inefficiencies. They are saying you are a bad community, but you are *not*. Before you leave here, you must tell the *true* story of this place and all that it has meant to be neighbors here. You must stand up for all the good that has been part of your history in this place. Don't let them put you down!"

I remembered, too, Steve's admonition that people needed to change in the therapy session if they were going to be able to be different at home. Therefore, I asked the people to gather in small groups and answer four questions: What have you loved about this place? What are you proud of? What do you hope for the future? And how will you take your memories with you? People worked hard in the small groups and began to articulate a reality opposite to the community-in-need-of-reinvention-through-destruction rhetoric of HOPE VI.

We ended the day with a commitment to continue, though we did not know what we would do or how.

From safety to unexpectancy

My new friends, these leaders of the Hill, knew its story in their bones and hearts. African Americans were among the first settlers of Pittsburgh's Hill District, but they were a distinct minority until World War I, when the Great Migration brought thousands from the South to work in the steel mills. These new migrants crowded into the Hill, which had been welcoming newcomers for more than a hundred years. African Americans joined a vibrant multicultural community that had established churches and synagogues, settlement houses, youth programs, and many businesses. African Americans, facing discrimination· in many facets of Pittsburgh life, organized themselves politically and socially. Through the 1930s and 1940s, black organizations flourished, bringing together, among others, deer hunters, numbers runners, beauty contestants, and young artists.

Figure 2.1: Wylie Avenue with Crawford Grill No. 1 and Crampton Drugs on left, Hill District, c. 1947-1952. This photograph, taken by the great African American photographer Charles "Teenie" Harris, captures the complexity and density of the Hill District in the 1930s and 1940s. Like Harlem, it was a place where African American migrants had built a functional community.

Photo credit: Charles "Teenie" Harris, American, 1908-1998, black and white, Kodak Safety Film, H: 4 in. x W: 5. in. (10.20 x 12.70 cm.). Carnegie Museum of Art, Pittsburgh. Heinz Family Fund. 2001-35.2495.

Doctors and lawyers lived next door to shop owners and millworkers. African Americans began to add to the complex mix of enterprises that filled the Hill. In spite of oppression, people were able to have a rich life that included hard work complemented by public celebration and refreshment. The area grew in political strength and began to have sufficient political power to challenge the white-only political rule in the city and county. The African American neighborhood of the Hill began to have national influence through the *Pittsburgh Courier*, which was distributed by the Pullman porters throughout the nation. The Crawford Grill jazz club and all the stores on Wiley Avenue, the main street of the Hill, were part of this exciting and functional urban space (Figure 2.1).

The sorting-out process, which had its roots in the segregation of the city, was intensified in the late 1930s by the institution of "redlining," the assignment of risk scores to neighborhoods based on the age of the buildings and presence, or threatened "infiltration," of nonwhites and foreign-born people. This was a program carried out by a federal agency, the Home Owners Loan Corporation (HOLC). In 2012, three students—Sarah Schell, Samantha Hillson, and Amy Yang—and I made a visit to the National Archives at College Park to get a copy of Pittsburgh's redlining

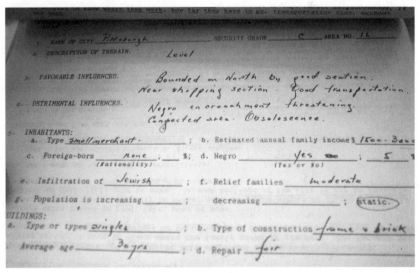

Figure 2.2: Residential Security Survey Form. The Home Owners Loan Corporation created this form to rate neighborhoods with an eye toward the identification of "undesirable" elements, like minorities, the foreign-born, and the poor.

Photo credit: Sarah Schell.

map. While there, we looked at the maps of many other cities and examined the rating forms that were the basis of the risk assessment. In the example shown in Figure 2.2, you can see that, in the comment area at the top, there is a note that says, "Negro encroachment threatening." In answer to the specific question about "infiltration," the surveyor noted "Jewish," and in answer to question about the presence of "Negroes" among the inhabitants, the surveyor wrote "Yes" and "5 percent."

The rating forms were used to color the neighborhoods, indicating how desirable they were for loans or insurance. Neighborhoods rated "A" were colored green, and those rated "D" were colored red, giving rise to the term "redlining." The maps were made as the world lurched toward World War II and genocide. They firmly linked the era's racial discrimination to national banking policy, and they steered money away from the Hill and other neighborhoods that were home to people of color. This set in motion decades of economic malnutrition and made massive physical decline inevitable. A black-and-white version of the map that determined the fate of Pittsburgh is shown in Figure 2.3.

Urban renewal played a direct role in the history of the Hill. In the 1950s, the Lower Hill, the commercial heart of the neighborhood, was demolished to clear land for the Civic Arena, which was built, and a cultural plaza that never materialized. Eight thousand people were dispersed from the area. The white people who were displaced were able to move to many parts of the city. African Americans were forced to stay in segregated neighborhoods, and class divisions were intensified. Those with the most money moved to Homewood or East Liberty, while the poor moved to housing projects in the Hill and many other parts of the city.

The next major development in the sorting-out process was the precipitous loss of the city's industrial infrastructure, largely in the 1980s (Haller 2005). Vast steel mills, once employing thousands or tens of thousands of people, vanished like thieves in the night. Eventually, Pittsburgh lost half of its population, bleeding people from every neighborhood. As the city regained its economic footing—*Forbes Magazine* declared in 2012 that it was a "comeback city"—the renewal came from industries that employed people with a good deal of education (Bruner 2012). For the most part, the people left in the Hill were not included in the transformation of labor that enabled some workers to move into those new sectors. Deep and

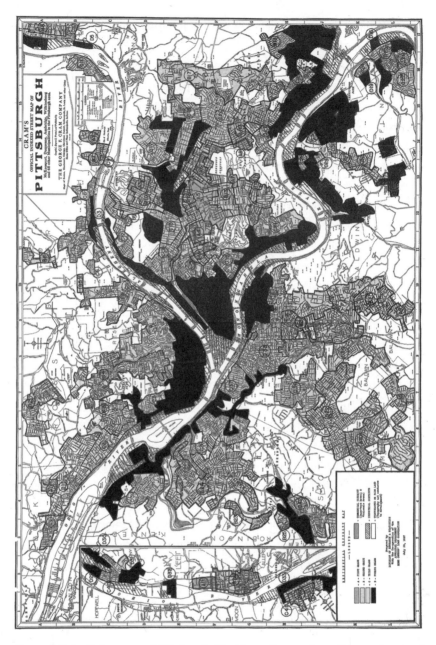

Figure 2.3: Redlining map of Pittsburgh. The Home Owners Loan Corporation used the information gathered on the rating sheets to create what came to be known as "redlining" maps. These full-color maps were part of major shifts that firmly linked banking practice to segregation. The color version of the map and the rating sheets can be found at www.universityoforange.org/redlining.

Scan of the original document, housed in the National Archives at College Park, Maryland.

persistent unemployment of the unskilled became the order of the day. In that vacuum, the drug trade became a dangerous but definite way to make money in an otherwise bleak situation.

The economic straightjacket sapped the last strength from the old houses in the Hill District, many deprived of investment since the 1930s. The buildings began to collapse, burn, disintegrate, and disappear, following the well-known pattern of contagious housing destruction that Rod had helped me see in Harlem and the South Bronx. The once dense and crowded landscape evaporated, leaving voids to be filled with weeds and litter that worked to shoo people inside the homes and buildings that remained. Only those who were up to no good remained outside, ruling the streets with violence and addiction. Under the combined pressures of the collapse of industry and the collapse of housing stock, the population of the Hill declined dramatically, falling from 38,100 in 1950 to 9,830 in 1990 (Acker 2009, 81).

My research on Harlem in the 1990s had taught me that the way of life changes as neighborhoods collapse, and the sorting process moves forward (see Figure 1.2). I have found Eva-Maria Simms's (2008) paper on childhood in the Hill to be one of the clearest expositions of the effect of neighborhood collapse on social organization. When Simms looked at her data on childhood play in the Hill, she was surprised to discover that there were remarkable shifts in the context and content of childhood between 1930 and 2004. She was able to identify three distinct eras: 1930 to 1960, 1960 to 1980, and 1980 to 2004. I call these three eras, respectively, Simms I, Simms II, and Simms III.

Simms I, dated from 1930 to 1960, was characterized by a strong net of relationships that anchored the young. "You thought it was just your little world," one of her respondents said. Simms noted,

> Their "little block" became the anchor for venturing into and understanding the larger world. "We knew each other, the neighbors knew us, they'd look out for us, it's much different than it is now... we weren't afraid of anything" (Willa). (Simms 2008, 78)

Charles "Teenie" Harris, a prolific photographer for the *Pittsburgh Courier*, documented the complex and interesting life of the Hill during this era. In thousands of photographs, he documented the safety that existed in the Hill during the 1930s and 1940s. His photograph of a youthful crossing guard protecting the schoolchildren (Figure 2.4) is an excellent example of an integrated social system working for the good of all.

The Carnegie Museum of Art, which houses the Teenie Harris collection, has asked residents of the Hill to provide information about the eighty thousand photographs in the collection. Because of the enduring nature of such a tight-knit community, the children in the photo supplied ample detail, which became the full title of the photo: "Boy school crossing guard holding back children, including Donald Christmas, Joann Collins, Elaine Robinson, Kenneth Holiday, Curtis Andrews, Beverly Myers, and Marlene Brown, on corner of Kirkpatrick and Reed Streets with A. Leo Weil School on left in background, Hill District, 1947."

Figure 2.4: Safe passage to school. This photograph captures the sense of safety and engagement that pervaded the Hill in Simms I, the era from 1930 to 1960.

Photo credit: Boy school crossing guard holding back children, including Donald Christmas, Joann Collins, Elaine Robinson, Kenneth Holiday, Curtis Andrews, Beverly Myers, and Marlene Brown, on corner of Kirkpatrick and Reed Streets with A. Leo Weil School on left in background, Hill District, 1947. Charles "Teenie" Harris, American, 1908-1998, black and white, Kodak Safety Film, H: 4 in. x W: 5. in. (10.20 x 12.70 cm.). Carnegie Museum of Art, Pittsburgh. Heinz Family Fund. 2001-35.3137.

Figure 2.5: Demolition.

Photo credit: Intersection of Wylie Avenue and Fullerton Street looking southwest toward demolition, Hill District, c. 1956-1959. Charles "Teenie" Harris, American, 1908-1998, black and white, Kodak Safety Film, H: 4 in. x W: 5. in. (10.20 x 12.70 cm.). Carnegie Museum of Art, Pittsburgh. Heinz Family Fund. 2001-35.3254.

The "little world," so well-endowed with a rich and energizing life, ended when it was declared "blighted" by the city fathers. Urban renewal cut the Hill District off from the rest of city by eliminating roads and public transit and installing a major highway between the neighborhood and downtown. Figure 2.5, a photo also by Teenie Harris, captures the demolition in midstream at the intersection where the Crawford Grill, shown in Figure 2.1, had been located.

Simms II, dated from 1960 to 1980, begins with demolition of the Lower Hill, which dispersed residents and disrupted the whole neighborhood. The disorganization of the community was intensified by deindustrialization, and chronic unemployment became a permanent feature of life. In the absence of legitimate opportunity, drugs and violence flourished (Acker 2009). Mass criminalization followed, adding another form of displacement and social rupture to the growing list.

Eva-Maria Simms found that memories of childhood related by people growing up in that period differed from those in Simms I, before urban renewal. The structure of the community had altered. Dense, interconnected neighborhood-wide networks that shared responsibility for rearing children had been replaced by a more patchwork system of extended families and some neighbors sharing responsibilities for their own children. One respondent told her,

> You mean, was it a community? Yeah. But it was changing.... On the one hand, certain people could correct me. But on the other hand, the people on the second floor had no say-so at all. Because we didn't know them all that well. People were moving in and out, so it was hard to really get to know people well. So it was only the older people in the community that was really the correctors. (Simms 2008, 80)

If people said there was "no clear path" during Simms II, they had even more dire conclusions about the state of neighborhood life in the decades that followed.

The character of Simms III, dated from 1980 and 2004, is captured in the quote, "It's crazy now in this world." The "village" of earlier decades was now limited to extended families, and many families had contracted so that only the single mother was responsible for raising the children. Uncertainty had given way to a sense of danger. Simms (2008, 80) reported,

> Darien [an interviewee] created a powerful neologism to characterize the mood that permeated his teenage years: *unexpectancy*. He said, "In general, you never know what might happen, you know, in the hood, just you coming out that door, just to see what's outside, could be a 'surprise' every day. Unexpectancy... You know, you never knows what lies around what corner, but you just gotta be able to be prepared and just hope, you know, you know as they say look both ways before you cross the street, so. That's basically how it is here. Just look both ways."

I arrived in the Hill District in the middle of Simms III. On a tour, that first day in the Hill, my hosts took me to a drug treatment center and the Dot Talley Center, a newly opened housing center for abused women in recovery and their children. These essential resources occupied spaces that had previously been used for the social and residential life of the neighborhood. It seemed a particularly poignant confirmation of collapse that

Figure 2.6: Don't ever give up! In 1998, in the middle of Simms III, this mural on a rickety building was testimony to the devastation the community was experiencing as well as its determination to hold on.

Photo credit: Mindy Fullilove.

people were getting drug treatment in the space where an earlier generation had learned to roller skate.

Yet, it also spoke to the determination to hang on, a sentiment that was captured on a mural I often passed (Figure 2.6). The central image, of a frog choking a bird that is trying to eat it with the words "Never give up!", was a popular one at the time, often seen on the walls of cubicles of people who had to deal with the public. But the artist had added scenes of despair across the top of the mural to link the frog's struggle to the intense problems that threatened the life of the neighborhood. The artist's signature, painted backwards, was an intriguing part of his adaptation of the common design.

I was also struck by Crawford Square. Situated at the edge of the neighborhood nearest downtown, this New Urbanist housing development stood in sharp contrast to the motley style of the Old Hill. It represented one of the largest economic infusions in the Hill in many decades and was a signal that change was coming. It represented the fruits of a decades-long struggle to place affordable housing at that site. Lois Cain, one of the leaders of the Hill, had moved back there, but shared with me that she found

Been in the storm so long:

Sorting leads to economic, social, and physical depletion of communities.

Centre Ave between Kirkpatrick and Divilliers, Pittsburgh, PA

1952

Figure 2.7: These aerial photographs, from 1952, 1969, and 2005, show the economic, social, and physical depletion of communities that follows the sorting-out process.

Photo credits: U.S. Department of the Interior, U.S. Geological Survey, earthexplorer. usgs.gov. Retrieved at National Environmental Title Research Online www.historicaerials.com. Quotes from Simms, 2008.

Simms, Period I, 1930–1960

"The closeness of the houses created a strong sense of community and shared public life, and the inhabitants of a particular block knew each other well and watched out for each other's children. 'We knew each other, the neighbors knew us, they'd look out for us, it's much different than it is now... we weren't afraid of anything.'"

the rents steep. In essence, Crawford Square, in its difference, represented the leading edge of gentrification, a bit of downtown that had leapt the Civic Arena and settled next to the Hill. If the Hill followed the patterns of gentrification I'd seen elsewhere in the US, then it was poised to become the New Hill, a place that would be renamed as it was reclaimed for a new cadre of laborers, workers in the new industries of Pittsburgh, industries for which the African Americans of the Hill were not needed.

Cantal has argued that people are deeply affected by where they live. People who are living in a mediocre neighborhood will wear mediocre clothes and delinquency will go up. Like me, Eva-Maria Simms had found that the deterioration of a neighborhood slowly alters how people live. To see what happened to the urban ecosystem, I have compared three aerial photographs of Centre Avenue between Devilliers and Kirkpatrick (Figure 2.7). The first, taken in 1952, shows the ecosystem in Simms I. The

1969   2005

Simms, Period II, 1960–1980

"Neighbors were no longer people you shared your life with because you knew their families, their churches, their work, and if they treated their neighbors well over time; neighbors now were often strangers next door who were tied to the 'little block,' and [had] no attachment to its inhabitants."

Simms, Period III, 1980–2004

"When [Shanika] was a child, 'everybody cared about everybody back then. Now everybody's for their self. Now it's just —I'm scared for my boys now. Because it's horrible now...You don't see kids outside anymore just to play...' "

second, from 1969, depicts the state in Simms II. The third, from 2005, reveals the massive changes following the accumulation of insults to the neighborhood.

Gut check

In 1997, I knew very little about rebuilding communities, but I had read a set of books that inspired my imagination. The first was a book I found on sale in the New York University Press catalog. Called *Seasons of Captivity* by Amia Lieblich (1995), it was an oral history of ten Israeli soldiers who were captured by Egypt during the 1967 war and held in captivity for several years while prisoner exchange negotiations went on. Each of the ten men was tortured and held in isolation before joining the group in a common cell, six meters by ten meters, with an adjoining courtyard. Together in their captivity, the ten men were able to create a society with rules, rituals, and a balance of group and individual needs. The existence of the group buffered the members from the worst horrors of captivity and helped them work through some of the traumas of the experience. In addition, they were able to accomplish many tasks: they turned their cell into a "jewel," carried out the official Hebrew translation of *The Hobbit*, built the Eiffel Tower from matchsticks, read books, and studied for pleasure and university credit.

The process of making an open-ended stay in enemy territory into a positive experience was a hard one, and every man contributed to the evolution of the group life. One argued for decorating the room, another for physical activity. Each idea was debated intensely; the collective decisions moved the process forward. When the time came to leave, one prisoner, Avi, remembered, "I said in my heart, how can I leave now? There are so many things I'm in the middle of doing: I had plans for two weeks more. It shows how we rooted ourselves in that place [laughing]" (Lieblich 1995, 133–34).

I lingered over every word of their stories, heartened by what they had accomplished. While still taking notes on that book in December 1994, I found myself at a book table at a conference in Chicago. One of the books on display was *The Golden Thirteen* by Paul Stillwell (1993), a history of the first African American naval officers. I was excited to read their story and pored over the book all the way home on the plane.

I was amazed when I read that the sixteen African American men had found themselves in a single room at the US Navy's Great Lakes training camp during World War II. They were not sure why they had been called together, but they were sure that the fate of the black race depended on their success. Like the Israeli soldiers in a single room in Egypt, they took stock of their surroundings, assessed their options, and created a group. The group buffered the rigors and terrors of their assignment: if they could pass the course, they would be the Navy's first black officers and break the color barrier. The stories in *The Golden Thirteen* were so similar to those in *Seasons of Captivity* that I actually made a table of those nearly identical quotes. Like their Israeli counterparts, the African American sailors found that, together, they could do what none could have done alone.

From those books and others, I proposed the idea of "empowered collaboration" in my paper, "Psychiatric Implications of Displacement."

At the heart of the experience of displacement is the sense that one is without a place to be. The reconstitution of order depends on the reestablishment of a health-promoting habitat and affirmation of each person's sense of belonging to that place. Success in accomplishing these tasks can be measured by the following criteria:

1. People live in a "good enough" place.
2. People feel settled in home, neighborhood, and region.
3. People contribute to caretaking of the personal and shared portions of the environment.
4. People know their neighbors and interact with them to solve problems.

To achieve these goals, a series of steps are required, a strategy called "empowered collaboration." At the outset, people must conduct a detailed assessment of the environment. On the basis of that assessment, they can create a list of priorities to guide the assignment of resources. Where displaced people lack sufficient resources of their own, negotiations with unaffected communities should be initiated. The next step is for people to start working together on rebuilding activities of all kinds. While the rebuilding is going forward, people must also attend to emotional needs to mourn the lost place and to bond to the new place. Rituals from the old place, as well as rituals from the new place, are essential to this process. (Fullilove 1996, 1521)

What made the next steps happen was the organic grant making of Phil Hallen, president of the Maurice Falk Medical Fund. Phil had been at my talk at the University of Pittsburgh Graduate School of Public Health in 1997, had followed what happened during the visit to the housing projects that July, and thought that bringing Bob and me to Pittsburgh routinely was a golden opportunity. He funded an eighteen-month fellowship with the University's Center for Minority Health that allowed us to visit Pittsburgh once a month from 1998 to 1999.

When the leaders in the Hill asked me, "What do you think we should do next?" I said, "What the Israeli soldiers and the Golden Thirteen did—empowered collaboration. It starts with an assessment of the situation."

I told them about a tool the Community Research Group had developed for mapping neighborhoods, the "Community Burn Index," which measured the extent to which a neighborhood had been destroyed by the many policies of serial displacement. "I got the idea after the tragic death of Dr. Betty Shabazz, wife of Malcolm X, who had been set on fire by her grandson and died of her wounds. Burn centers use a 'burn index' to rate the severity of the injury a burn victim has sustained. Burns can be first, second, or third degree, depending on how many layers of the skin have been destroyed. The third degree burns are the really life-threatening ones because that means that all the layers of the skin are gone. Dr. Shabazz had suffered third degree burns on over 70 percent of her body. Her chances of survival were slim: the body just can't contain fluids and fend off infection without the skin. It struck me at that time that communities might be assessed for third degree burns, and so we created a community burn index."

Tamanika Howze stopped me at that point. "You mean to tell me my community is dead?" she asked accusingly. I was terrified by the look in her eyes. If I did mean that, I wanted to take it back.

But Della, the spiritual center of the group, held up her hand. "It's upsetting when you get what Mindy's saying, but then you move on, you deal with it. We have to face the reality."

With that girding of our loins, we called a first teach-in on the Hill's Community Burn Index to be held in April 1998. Today, it has become popular for communities to carry out "asset mapping," looking not at their deficits but at their resources. Leaders want to be sure that demoralized communities are not rendered more powerless, which is an important goal. My guess, however, and here I speak as a psychiatrist, is that accepting the devastation is required. Denial is common and problematic. When Della said that we could look, she authorized unveiling the eight-hundred-pound gorilla in the room: the massive destruction the neighborhood had endured. It was like sounding the depth of the water so the ship could sail safely in dangerous areas. As a collective, we needed to know the reality.

But what is to be done with such a reality?

I invited Cantal to come as my consultant, supported by the Falk Fellowship. He hesitated when I asked him because he doesn't speak English. I said, "I think we need your eyes, not your ears," but he protested that his head couldn't be separated in that way. He finally agreed, but had low expectations for what he would be able to do. In preparation, he read about Pittsburgh and studied maps. When he got there, he toured the Hill, the city, and the surrounding region.

On the day of the teach-in, Cantal helped with creating the Community Burn Index for the Hill (Figure 2.10). As the day went on, he realized he had understood the problem despite the language barrier and asked if he might speak. "The people of the Hill were working people and they worked in the mills along the rivers. I want to know," he said, "how did the people who lived here get to work?"

Figure 2.8: Workmen coming from work on the 17th Street incline late in the afternoon, April 1951.

Photo credit: Richard Saunders, Pittsburgh Photographic Project; Pittsburgh Photographic Library, Carnegie Library of Pittsburgh.

The elders in the room brightened up. They eagerly offered answers, explaining the incline, the stairs, the many streets, the trolleys, and the buses that took people to work. Cantal nodded. "Yet many of these paths to the rivers have been lost since those days."

People nodded. If the burn index had been a heart-stopping reality, this was the opposite. This got hearts going again. A photograph by Richard Saunders captures an image from the Hill's incline, an image that was on the minds of many in that room (Figure 2.8).

"I urge you," Cantal continued, "to find the paths to the rivers and to re-create those paths as parks or trails or signs, to celebrate your ancestors and the way they lived."

There was a moment of general silence in the room. "Find the rivers" stuck in people's minds. Cantal later reinforced that advice and, in a memo and in a map, used arrows to indicate the connection to the rivers. It was the teach-in's two accomplishments—facing loss and looking toward the rivers—that made the resulting empowered collaboration work.[1]

Truth and reconciliation

Our mapping was picked up by the *Pittsburgh Post-Gazette*, and a sympathetic editorial accompanied the story. Terri Baltimore called me a few days after the event to say that the developers for Bedford Dwellings, one of the HOPE VI sites, wanted to meet. In July, she called to describe that meeting. The activists, she reported, were no longer gripped by anger, but rather engaged in a long and thoughtful investigation of the implications of the plan. Their informed questions were penetrating, and they raised issues the development team had not considered. The developers, in turn, agreed to think through the issues raised. Ultimately, that conversation led to a remarkable reorganization of the HOPE VI plan for Bedford Dwellings, a plan that took the community's deep experience into account.

The community leaders and I organized five teach-ins held in the Hill District and a conference held at the Carnegie Museum of Art. At the end of the eighteen-month fellowship, we created a scrapbook called "Hillscapes: Envisioning a Healthy Urban Habitat" (Robins et al. 1999). We liked the term "Hillscapes" so much that it became the nickname for the whole project.

I became committed to understanding the story before the story: the horrors of urban renewal that had conditioned the response to HOPE VI. My 2004 book, *Root Shock: How Tearing Up City Neighborhoods Hurts America and What We Can Do About It*, drew heavily on the story of the Hill. To a very major extent, the powers that be in Pittsburgh accepted the truth of the story that I passed on from the many people I'd interviewed, the story of the destruction of a brilliant neighborhood to erect the ironically named Civic Arena.

Meanwhile, Cantal, in asking us to find the paths to the rivers, had shifted our gaze to reconnecting the parts of the sorted-out city. Terri Baltimore, Denys Candy, and their many partners tackled Cantal's admonition, forming an organization called "Find the Rivers!" At first, they sought the paths, and, when they'd found them, they sought the funds to make them work. As they went down the slopes and out onto the water, they made new friends and broke the isolation that was the deep cause of the slow death of the Hill. Every time I visited Pittsburgh—which I did as often as I possibly could—Terri would tell me about new connections she had made.

Perhaps the most dramatic story was about a 2004 poetry reading and concert that had been planned at Hill House, the settlement house in the Hill. It featured artists from other parts of the city. On the night of the event, Hurricane Ivan brought torrential rains that Terri thought would keep everyone away. She was shocked as the audience kept coming and coming until sixty people from many different neighborhoods had shaken out their umbrellas and coats and had settled in for some good music. From such experiences of cultural and social exchange, new ideas began to travel from neighborhood to neighborhood, generating an enthusiasm for taking stock and making plans.

The neighborhoods, though in competition with each other, also began to recognize common cause. Institutions, like Leadership Pittsburgh, which convened leaders from every sector, built important bridges. Efforts, like Pittsburgh's Riverlife Task Force, which developed a vision of the three rivers of Pittsburgh as a gathering and connecting place for the entire region, began to connect the many neighborhoods to each other and the city as a whole.

Restoring the mind politic

But it wasn't simply people in the Hill District making overtures to others, but also other people arriving independently at the same conclusions and reaching out to the Hill. Two of many were Dan Rothschild and Ken Doyno, partners in the Rothschild Doyno Collaborative (RDCollab), a firm engaged in architecture rooted in commitment to community well-being and meaningful storytelling. In 1997, they began to do community planning, working with the Federal Hill community on the north side of the city to address issues of reconnection across a broad boulevard just north of another notorious urban renewal project called "Allegheny Center." Like Cantal, they believed that connected and interdependent neighborhoods were required for the city to function optimally. Their focus—whether working at the building, neighborhood, city, or regional level—was geared toward the restoration of the whole and the elevation of the social component of their projects. While one design challenge was to reconnect the physical parts of the larger body politic in concert with the communities they were aiding, they also discovered the need to get the mind politic working again.

At the heart of their strategy for restoring collective thinking was Dan Rothschild's invention, the "Design Sketchbook."[2] Designers, Dan noticed, typically made many drafts as they went through the design process, but these were usually consigned to the trash while finished solutions were conventionally presented. He decided to organize and save his own drafts as a record of the evolution of a project. He found that putting them together in an annotated book told the story and created an invaluable record of the design process, including the sharing and testing of goals, alternatives, and interventions.

The Design Sketchbook is conceptually simple—each page has a clear purpose, a title, graphics, written descriptions, and a date. Dan and Ken have trained their staff in the process and have found that this tool makes the design process accessible and transparent. It helps each person who contributes to the process feel a sense of ownership for the outcomes. Design Sketchbooks became stories of discovery and a means for people to connect desires and hopes with the design for physical change in their communities.

In my work in family therapy, I had encountered a process that shared many of these virtues. Called "generative graphics," the process was used to track conversations in family therapy (Karno, Brunon, and Waldron 1977). The team that invented the technique found that groups that could see their conversation were likely to move toward resolution, avoiding misunderstandings, and divisive debates. The use of images and symbols to track the metaphors used in a conversation was also an aid. It gave people something concrete to kick around.

It was easy to see how the Design Sketchbook could accomplish many of the same goals. I happened to be taking my capstone course in landscape design at the New York Botanical Garden just as Dan told me the story of his invention. My desk was literally covered with tracing paper sketches just as his had been. I carefully preserved them and, at the end, made a Design Sketchbook from them. It is, as Dan and Ken promised, a record of the process that reminds me of the many steps I took in getting to the end and allows me to share that journey with others. It deepened both my understanding and my ownership of what I'd done. I was quite proud to give a copy to my professor, David Dew Bruner.

"I have a card for you!" I said, when I encountered him at his shop in Hudson, New York.

"That's not a card, that's a book!" he exclaimed.

I liked the Design Sketchbook process so much that I assigned it to students in my public health course, Urban Space and Health. "Designing," artist Pam Shaw explained to me, "is the process of presenting something clearly."

In that view, the students accomplished much more than any previous group of students had. They learned to tell their stories and explain their ideas, not just regurgitate what was said in books. I observed that addressing social, geographic, and historical issues on Design Sketchbook pages led to a holistic view of the class materials and an appreciation for urban ecology that was deeper and more nuanced than that which students in previous years had experienced. And the final presentations demonstrated a confidence in working with visual material that no other class had shown.

The first of the RDCollab Design Sketchbooks that Dan and Ken showed me was about the design of "The Legacy," a massive project consuming an entire block of new construction on Centre Avenue, in the heart of the Hill District. As Rod has put it, "To get the social, cultural, and economic capital needed for effective collective thinking, we must restore the urban ecosystem."

Dan and Ken saw the future building as crucial to the restoration of the urban ecosystem. With that goal in mind, they envisioned the building as restoring memory and re-creating the main street as a place of activity and excitement. An earlier effort, by another design firm, to define the design standards for this corridor had envisioned a New Urbanist historic building. While attractive, this plan had lacked sufficient force to meet the great needs posed by urban restoration in the sorted-out city.

Urban restoration requires a very specific approach to the creation of new buildings or the restoration of the old. For RDCollab, this process began with a detailed study of what they term "site forces," where they recognize the many layers of the urban ecosystem, including its rich history. They identified that the building site sat between the Crawford Grill and the New Granada Theatre, two key locations in the flourishing Jazz Age of the 1920s, during which the Hill was known as the "Crossroads of

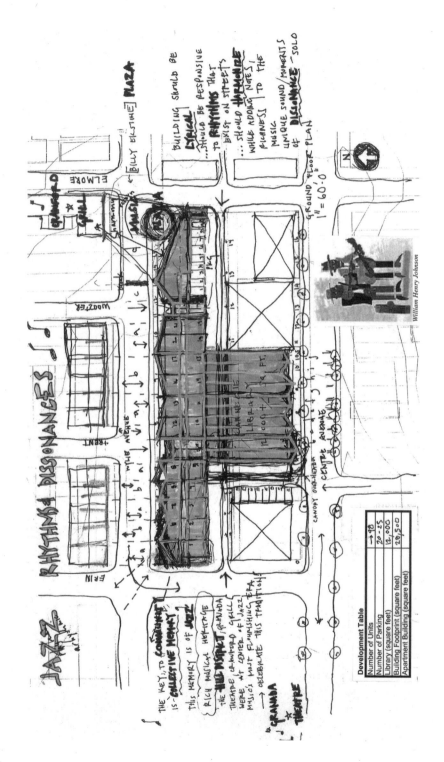

William Henry Johnson

Development Table

Number of Units	98
Number of Parking	20-25
Building Footprint (square feet)	12,000
Apartment Building (square feet)	28,500

the World of Jazz." The concept of "jazz-as-a-construct" emerged, which translated into a syncopated, rhythmic building that expressed the proud history of jazz in the neighborhood.

This concept evolved over several weeks and on many Design Sketchbook pages. On the page entitled, "Jazz Rhythms and Dissonances," we find at the base, two street musicians painted by William Henry Johnson, widely considered a leading African American painter of the twentieth century (Figure 2.9). There were many street musicians in the Hill during Simms I, 1930 to 1960, so the use of that trope has important resonance with the local history. But it also evokes the music played outside on the streets, as opposed to the music inside the great music halls. The Legacy, RDCollab believed, had to connect to the streets to serve in the area's restoration.

Part of RDCollab's design included a series of limestone panels carved with the names of local jazz greats selected through a vote by people in the neighborhood. Dan remembered, "I went to the construction site every week to meet with the builders. There was a lot of tension around the site—you could feel it. We were infilling an entire block at the center of the neighborhood. People were leery about the intent of this building—was it gentrification taking more of the neighborhood? But the day the first jazz panel went up, I was approached by neighbors who asked, 'What is that?' As I explained, they were thrilled to see names they knew. It broke the tension. This was a meaningful demonstration of respect. On the day the building opened, one of those honored—Roger Humphries—was playing. He told me he never expected to be so honored in his lifetime—to have his name on a building and to be playing at the opening party—and he teared up."

Terri remembered, "During the Hillscapes process, Della said she'd realized that the knot she had in her gut was grief—she'd finally named it. It was a great relief."

Figure 2.9 (opposite page): Designing The Legacy: Jazz Rhythms and Dissonances. Each Design Sketchbook page, according to its inventor, Dan Rothschild, includes a title, an illustration of some kind, and appropriate labels or captions. It is always dated. The great utility of the Design Sketchbook is that it supports shared understanding of the complex process of urban restoration. The page depicted here shows the search to understand the nature of the space in which The Legacy will be erected. See also Figure 8.8, Designing The Legacy: Jazz Fusion.

Credit: Design Sketchbook Page courtesy of Rothschild Doyno Collaborative.

How the Hill changed:

Community Burn Index, 1998 and 2011.

1998

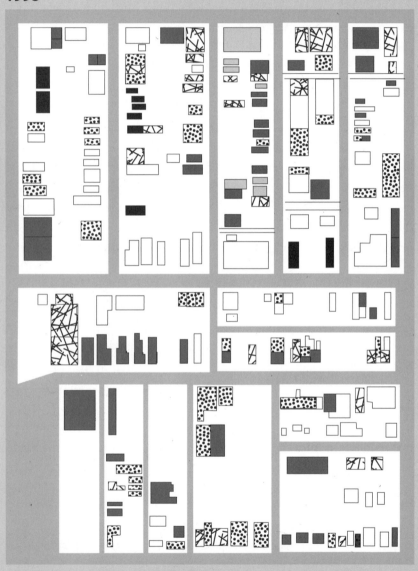

Figure 2.10: In 1998, as part of the Hillscapes Project, a community mapping was undertaken. It confirms the devastation shown in the aerial photos in Figure 2.7.

new

oldie but goodie

wearing out

severely deteriorated

demolished

2011

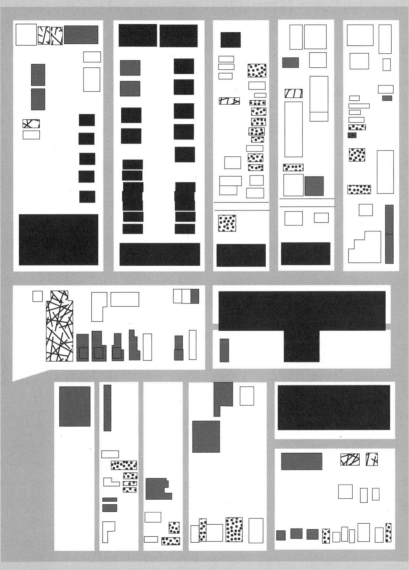

The community mapping was repeated in 2011. By then, rebuilding, which started with The Legacy, had begun. We can see the new buildings that are going up.

Diagrams created by Rich Brown, adapted by Sarah Schell.

When Roger Humphries shed a tear, he was crying from the joy of recognition and the grief of living without it for so long. Unnamed grief, the absence of recognition—every single person in a collapsing community carries these weights. In listening between the lines to what people are longing to tell, and in bringing those heartfelt messages into the design of The Legacy, Dan and Ken eased the weight of oppression. Such a force is bigger than one building, but each building that contributes to the work makes the oppression less and the freedom more.

We'll have fun

Shortly after Hillscapes started, the new awareness of place resulted in a victory for Bedford Dwellings. Within two years, the new construction on Bedford Avenue went up and people started to move to new homes while Bedford Dwellings was still standing. People were not being thrown out this time, but were moving on up. Gains and losses continued to reshape the neighborhood, but at every turn, the Hill community pushed for its right to be included in the future. The number of people willing to battle for the future of the Hill grew and grew. In 2007, a dispute over the placement of a casino erupted into a fight for a community benefits agreement, which I describe in more detail in Chapter Four. That successful fight represented the reconsolidation of the fractured community. It brought attention, respect, and resources.

In 2011, Terri suggested that it would be interesting to remap the twelve blocks we had first examined in 1998 (Figure 2.10). Lois, Terri, and I had been there for the first mapping, but others who had joined us were doing this for the first time. I found it remarkable to revisit the area building by building. Investment that was imprinted with the community was everywhere. The New Granada Theater had been stabilized so that it would survive while plans developed for its future. The Legacy had been built and a new YMCA—part of a community benefits agreement—was going up just across the street. The change hadn't been quick—it was fifteen years since we started Hillscapes—and it hadn't always been evident. Poet Marge Piercy (1971) wrote, "Connections are made slowly, sometimes they grow underground."

The Piercy Principle alerts us to the fact that the state of community affairs is not entirely evident from what we see on the streets. On the surface, it might have looked like Simms III, but something else was happening, something that Terri and I thought might well be called Welcoming I. When the change has surfaced, as it did during the fight for a community benefits agreement, it is possible that a community has reached Welcoming II. This is not yet the dense networks and vibrant community that existed in Simms I, but it is on the path to re-creating it, however it will look or whatever it will be called in the twenty-first century. The people living it, of course, will simply call their neighborhood "fun."

A toast to that future

In the winter of 2012, Ken invited me to join him for a planning meeting in Homewood, a Pittsburgh neighborhood that had suffered as much as the Hill. It also turned out to be a perfect time to go to the Charles "Teenie" Harris photography exhibit at the Carnegie Museum. "I was thinking it would be fun to have a dinner party," I said, thinking he'd invite a couple of people to his house.

Ken was facilitating the Homewood meeting that Friday, February 17th, exactly fifteen years after my talk on displacement at the University of Pittsburgh Graduate School of Public Health. We were meeting with a group of local leaders who had asked him to assist them in developing a comprehensive community plan. Ken said, by way of opening the discussion, "Who should lead and be engaged in the plan and what should it accomplish?"

One of the leaders pointed out that the neighborhood used to have fifty thousand residents and now had only six thousand. Sarah Campbell, one of the distinguished elders in the room, said sharply, "We've always had a plan."

She pulled out a 1953 plan for Homewood. The pointed implication was that sixty years of planning had not stopped the collapse. And the corollary for Ken was: what do you know that will make a difference?

I felt as I had when Tamanika asked, "Are you telling me my community is dead?"

I looked at Ken to see how he was taking all this. Firmly rooted in the work he and his firm had done in the Hill, East Liberty, Hazelwood, North Side, and other Pittsburgh neighborhoods, he could see the synergies that would make a difference and that had never existed before. The energy of that possibility was apparent in his eyes and voice. It was Sarah who was the spirit of Della in that room. She looked at Ken calmly and smiled her approval. The meeting moved on. Ken said, "How shall we proceed?"

Reverend Sam Ware responded, "We're all committed—that's why we're here."

Embedded in that answer was the response to the "how": let's work together to get things done and make this community better.

The next day was the dinner party. To my surprise, it had been organized as a dinner in my honor, hosted by the Design Center of Pittsburgh. Ken, as president of their board, spoke to the sixty guests, representing many neighborhoods, community associations, and the city of Pittsburgh. He has a runner's spare frame and a gentle manner. He'd told me he had a booming voice, which comes from his days of singing and playing improvisational music in his rock band. Still, I was not prepared for how much power he had, enough to fill Steve Glassman's vast East Liberty loft. "In 1997, a zeitgeist called us to action—Terri and others in the Hill, Dan and me in Federal Hill, others around the city. Slowly, we have emerged from the isolation of our neighborhoods to see the wholeness of our city. Together we have a chance to make Pittsburgh a 'welcoming city,' home to all who are here and any who want to join us.

"Mindy has gotten a contract for her new book, *Urban Alchemy: Restoring Joy in America's Sorted-Out Cities*. It will tell the story of our efforts here in Pittsburgh. Let us drink a toast to our future as a Welcoming City!"

And so we did.

PART II

Align

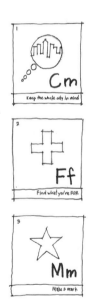

CHAPTER THREE

Element 1:
Keep the Whole City in Mind

Dick was beaten at home by the cross cook. She used him so cruelly... the poor boy decided to run away.... He walked as far as Halloway and sat on a stone to rest. While he was sitting there wondering which way to go, the Bells of Bow began to ring. Dong! Dong!

They seemed to say to him,

"Turn again, Whittington,
Lord Mayor of London."

"Lord Mayor of London!" said Dick to himself. "What wouldn't I give to be Lord Mayor of London!"

—Marcia Brown, *Dick Whittington and His Cat*

I first heard Cantal fume about potatoes in 2009. He had come to consult with us in Orange, New Jersey, as we were developing a plan for the center of the city. He had discovered a map of Marseilles with certain poor minority neighborhoods outlined with heavy black lines (Figure 3.1). He wrote on his PowerPoint slide, "The manager who identified these areas in this way, was he looking to imprison people on islands?"

Cantal railed to us, referring to the areas indicated by the dark circles, "You see these potatoes? Those are *not* potatoes—those are places where people live. The person who made this map wanted to tear apart the city. But let me tell you—the city is *not* a sack of potatoes to be divided with careless

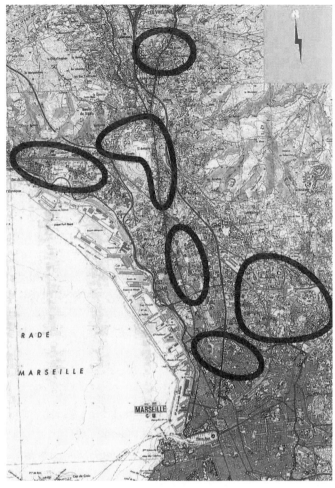

Figure 3.1: The city is NOT a sack of potatoes. Cantal argues against the use of maps annotated to pinpoint the areas in difficulty, as if they were potatoes, when, in fact, they are people's homes.

Map courtesy of Michel Cantal-Dupart.

thrusts of the pen. This is the way we destroy the city. What we're looking for is the way to save it."

The first element of urban restoration is that we must keep the whole city in mind. This involves:

- Understanding that the separation caused by sorting is blinding; and
- Facing the complexity of the whole city so that we can restore it.

Separation is blinding

Véronique Héon-Klin was one of twenty students in my Qualitative Research Methods course in 1996. I asked my students to help our research team understand the complex violence epidemic that was shaping the Washington Heights neighborhood where the Columbia University Mailman School of Public Health was located. Véronique was gripped by this project and became a major contributor to the report and the scientific publication we wrote (Fullilove et al. 1998). When she was preparing to return home to Germany, she decided to continue doing qualitative research. We kicked around ideas for a study. As she was going to be working in Berlin, the story of the Berlin Wall occurred to us. With the help of Erika Sieber, an East Berliner who had lived through the whole experience of the Wall, and Julia Huebner, an American in medical school in Berlin, Véronique was able to examine the story of putting up a wall to divide a city and then demolishing it not quite thirty years later. At the heart of the study were interviews with twelve people—six men and six women, six from East Berlin and six from West Berlin—who had been there from beginning to end (Héon-Klin et al. 2001).

Germany was divided into eastern and western portions at the end of the World War II. In 1949, the western section became the Federal Republic of Germany, with a new capital in Bonn. The eastern sector, which became the German Democratic Republic, had its capital in Berlin. Berlin, located in the east, was divided in half, with one portion given to the West and the other given to the East. The partition of the nation created divergence in culture, economics, and social organization from the start, but people in Berlin were able to move back and forth across the dividing line. They used this openness to take advantage of higher wages in the West and lower costs in the East, which put a strain on East Germany. Furthermore, the new East German nation was at a disadvantage in combating the propaganda of the Cold War.

In an effort to take control of the situation in Berlin, East Germany erected the Berlin Wall. A barrier along the East–West border went up suddenly in 1961, and the Wall was constructed within the same year. People who were used to moving back and forth were suddenly trapped on one side or the other. A woman in East Berlin said, "I drove aimlessly through Berlin, looking at checkpoints. For the first time, I had the feeling of being locked in forever. I suddenly had this feeling: I can never get out of here" (Héon-Klin et al. 2001, 371).

Families were torn apart by partition. A man told our research team,

The Wall was for me the concrete symbol of the separation from my parents. They were on the other side of the Wall, the symbol of hatred, and therefore I was very lonely in Berlin in the years following the building of the Wall. The support and caring of my parents was suddenly gone. I developed sleep disturbances and heartache as a result, as the doctor could not find any organic cause for these symptoms. (Héon-Klin et al. 2001, 372)

People on both sides learned how to live with the Wall, and in so doing, the two societies—the capitalist West and the socialist East—evolved along different lines, slowly becoming *Ossis* and *Wessis*. The sudden demolition of the Wall in 1989—just twenty-eight years after it first went up—ended the physical separation and introduced the *Ossis* and *Wessis* to each other. This was not a meeting of equals, as the West had "won" the Cold War and the East was a defeated nation with subjugated people. The Easterners lost institutions and an identity they treasured. One Eastern woman's relative from the West told her, "You Easterners have to learn how to work." Another Easterner regretted the sense of belonging that had arisen from shared hardship. And another commented on the loss of support for working people, including job security and childcare.

Seeing the West was a shock for East Berliners. One woman related,

What mostly impressed me was that in my whole life, I never had seen so many beautiful flowers in the winter. I thought I was dreaming, since something like that does not exist here. Here, we might have three roses and you had to fight to get them, or we had some green plants but no flowers, and I was also shocked by the fruit vendors with grapes and all that. Over here, we only have something like that around Christmas, some oranges. Otherwise, all year you get apples and seasonal vegetables and cabbage. Well, we did not have more. So when I saw the fruit vendors, I could not handle it. (Héon-Klin et al. 2001, 372)

Westerners were curious about the East, but did not find its massive buildings and lack of shops attractive. They did not continue to visit. Indeed, at the time of our study—1997 and 1998—people had settled into their "side" and life continued. In small and large ways, the East was being erased—their classic stop and go signals were replaced by the Western type and the streets were renamed, erasing the old socialist heroes of the East, like Ho Chi Minh. But this erasing was actually creating an enduring separation. We argued,

> There is no space for Easterners to remember the strengths of the old system, to mourn its loss, or to find a new identity that has meaning and pride. Easterners are expected to take on a new identity, while Westerners are not confronted with the need to realign their sense of self. As long as the adaptation remains unidirectional, healthy integration will not occur. (Héon-Klin et al. 2001, 274)

There was an interesting physical aspect of this ongoing separation. The Berlin Wall, we learned during the course of our study, was not a simple wall, but a massive complex of obstacles, 500 meters (1,640 feet, nearly a third of a mile) at its widest point. When the Wall was demolished, a huge area in the center of Berlin—capital of the reunified Germany—was opened for redevelopment. A massive construction zone erupted, sending sleek skyscrapers into the air that sharply contrasted with the low-rise buildings of nineteenth-century Berlin that stood on either side. Thus, the Wall became a forest of skyscrapers.

Véronique saw a cartoon in an exhibition in Berlin (Figure 3.2). The guide is saying, "Once a terrible wall separated the people here!" The people are still organized with a vast space between them, even though the wall is gone. There may or may not be solidarity within the groups on either side, but there is likely no solidarity across the great divide. Véronique found a great deal of evidence that *Ossi* and *Wessi* were antagonists, with the *Wessis* looking down on the *Ossis*. "The Wall will never be gone," Cantal opined.

Cantal knew that this kind of separation between people on different sides of a border was not limited to *Ossis* and *Wessis*, but affected all people who had functioned for a period of time with a line between them. That

Rebuilding without reintegration ≠ repair

Figure. 3.2: The guide is saying, "Once a terrible wall separated the people here!"
Cartoon by Barbara Henniger, used with permission.

included me. Cantal's challenge, in teaching me about the city, was to liberate my mind from the bonds of this system.

Truncated movement is fundamental to our sense of the sorted-out city. All place is embodied by our movements through space. The city that has been divided is internalized through the constant negotiation of borders, real and perceived, that mark the edges of that which is our space from that which is not. The edges turn us back, into ourselves. In that context, we do not see the city. We see what is ours, and we see what is not ours. We each belong to a set of fragments within the whole, and we generally stay on the tracks that link them. This is true of all of us who function under the parameters of apartheid—not just *Ossis* and *Wessis*. Violations of the rule to stay in your zone are plot devices that novelists love, as Tom Wolfe (1987) did in *Bonfire of the Vanities*, a book that centers on the madness that occurs after a rich white man gets off the highway in the poor minority neighborhood of the South Bronx.

At the heart of Cantal's instruction to me was the simple command, "Follow me." I did. I followed him into mayors offices and hippies' gardens, into housing projects and châteaux, on rivers and under bridges. Time and again, my body would be befuddled by the conflict between Cantal's "follow me" and my own command of "stop." I would nearly stumble on those occasions as my feet stopped, but my head kept going. He taught me to enter boldly, speak kindly, peek behind curtains, admire all efforts at placemaking, and laugh loudly. I loved moving as Cantal did, and it infiltrated my habits when I was by myself. I'd get to a city and start to walk and pretty soon I'd find myself saying, "But what is behind that?" And I would go see. One of the great opportunities I had to see the whole city was presented by my work on recovery in the aftermath of the 2001 terrorist attacks on New York City.

Seeing is restoring

New York has the power to heal us all

On September 11, 2001, a wave of shock and horror reverberated throughout the Greater New York Region, where I lived and worked, when terrorists attacked and destroyed the Twin Towers of the World Trade Center. While the tragedy came to be identified with the people who died in the attacks and those who tried to save them, the categories of victim and hero were too small to encompass the vast pain that consumed us. The Twin Towers were not small, insignificant buildings, but massive lighthouses, orienting us from as far away as Bear Mountain to the north and Sandy Hook to the south. The iconic rectangles were painted in every pizza parlor and on every panel truck in our area. The smoke of their destruction rose up and hovered over us.

I started—really for the first time—to use Cantal's lessons in thinking like a city, with its myriad organizations linking all of its citizens. I started to notice all the organizations that were around us, from the Hispanic Muslims of the South Bronx to the Hatzolah Volunteer Ambulance in Brooklyn.

"There are so many of them, I can't even imagine what they all are and I can't imagine what they need to recover," I said to my coworkers, Jen Stevens Dickson and Lourdes Hernández-Cordero. "But if every organization took on a piece of our recovery, we'd be able to help everyone. Organizations know their constituents so they could design interventions that would be culturally sensitive and specific. And it wouldn't cost much money because organizations gather people in the natural course of affairs. Think about holiday parties. If every holiday party had a small bit of recovery included, we'd have treated the whole population by New Year's. And, because we all go to so many parties, most people would have had the equivalent of a course of brief therapy at no additional cost to anyone!"

Jen and Lourdes liked this "thinking like a city," and together we launched NYC RECOVERS, a collaboration of organizations concerned with the social and emotional recovery of the New York City region. Our first event was a "Rally for Recovery" at which the newly formed NYC RECOVERS Choir performed a song called "New York Has the Power." It had the refrain, "New York has the power to heal us all," which was echoed by different voices, ending in an ecstatic, "New York has the power!" Although we don't always think of deep mourning as a time for assembly, it is essential to the human spirit to affirm our capacity to be together in the face of the splintering of death. That our wounded city might heal us was a startling and wonderful revelation of that day.

Because we were thinking like a city, we turned our gaze everywhere. And because it was an exceptional moment, a great many doors opened and we could go nearly anywhere we wanted. In the fifteen months of our "Year of Recovery," I went to meetings in the poorest neighborhoods and in the richest. I gave advice to one of the most prestigious recovery efforts—the Municipal Art Society's Imagine New York—and to some of the most humble. It was a time of exploring, meeting, learning, and linking in a city that is normally reified in a rigid hierarchy of class and race.

At the end of the Year of Recovery, our partners gathered for a celebration of our work. I thought it would be fun to sign a banner with our logo on it. But what happened instead taught me everything about what a city is. Our partners, so confident about making the city, began to draw and illustrate everything we had learned and dreamed. They reconnected the buildings to the ground, restored the empty space where the towers had

Rebuilding + reintegration = JOY

September 2001

December 2002

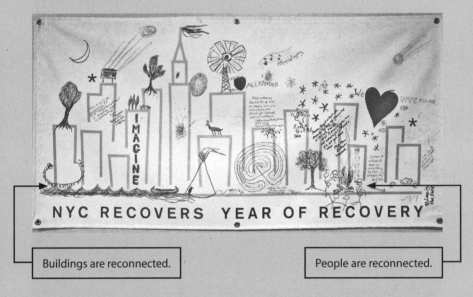

Buildings are reconnected.

People are reconnected.

Figure 3.3: In the original logo of NYC RECOVERS, the shadowy buildings, which are disconnected from the ground, spoke to our sense of disorientation. The banner of the Year of Recovery Project was decorated at the NYCR December 5th party in 2002. Our partners reconnected the buildings and added some new features to the city, like rooftop gardens and a campfire. This is an image of rebuilding *with* reintegration and it is obvious that the NYCR partners thought this would produce joy.

Photographs courtesy of the CRG Collection.

stood, and put canoes in the water and trees on the rooftops. The shadowy gray logo with which we'd started the Year of Recovery sprang into living color (Figure 3.3).

What's big enough to make the city?

When I thought about New York City as everywhere the Twin Towers had been visible—from Bear Mountain to Cape May in New Jersey—I was thinking on the scale that Cantal was urging. One day, as Cantal and I were standing in the street in Créteil, a city outside of Paris, he pointed out, "The street is too small a constraint to give structure to the city. So what is large enough to give the city its form?" He looked at me, pausing a beat for emphasis. "Water. Water gives the city its form." He then led me one block over to a man-made lake whose contours gave the city its edges. "Water shapes the city."

The world's first cities started where there was water for drinking, bathing, cooking, and transport. Situated on the banks of rivers or beside lakes or oceans, cities took their form from the water, as Paris takes its form from the Seine. I've never lived there, but I've visited the city over twenty times and twice stayed for two months. I've had to figure out the metro, the parks, and life in a Paris apartment. When I took my granddaughter Lily for her first visit to the city, I thought she should see the Eiffel Tower, the Louvre, the Musée d'Orsay, and Notre Dame. I know that these places are all disconnected from each other: making the circuit requires a lot of transfers on the metro, followed by reasonably long hikes.

In 2000, Cantal bought a houseboat on the Seine and, after extensive renovations, settled there. This had got me in the habit of going down by the water. His home is quite close to the Musée d'Orsay stop of the Batobus, *bateau* (pronounced bat-OH) being French for boat. Cantal, whose musings about the city lead him to think of everything, had had the idea for the Batobus. It is a great way to see the historic heart of Paris. When seen from the river, it becomes quite clear that Paris was built from the banks of the Seine and that the city's great structures hug the water, not the metro. You get off the Batobus at the door of the Louvre, and the same is true for the Eiffel Tower, Notre Dame, and the Musée d'Orsay.

The Seine threads the heart of the city, shapes the Right and Left Banks, and links Paris with the rest of Europe. In the old paintings, Paris is entirely organized around the river. For the past one hundred years, the city pulled back from the river and put its highways and factories along the river's edges. But Paris is now reconnecting with its source and finding its pleasures in, on, and near the water.

Paris Plage, a summer festival that turned the riverside highway into a beach, was one of those manifestations of the return to the river. I have a tendency to imagine something French using American images. The first time Bob and I rented a house in France, the advertisement said it was 1500 meters from shopping. I pictured US Route 1/9 in New Jersey, a garish, car-dominated non-place, *non-lieu* as they say in France. What I found was a country village with all the pleasures of taking my *panier* and walking down a country lane to one of the two bakeries to buy a freshly baked morning croissant.

So it was with Paris Plage. On the way down the ramp to the beach, there was a misting spray that cooled me off and I was instantly Some Place Else, a place designed by Cartier and Chanel, outfitting the new beach with top-of-the-line chaise lounges for sunbathing, showers for cooling, rocks for climbing, music for listening, and art for amusing. Paris Plage lounged in all its elegant ease along the great river, which was coursing under the bridges and lapping at the stone walls that formed its sides. In that way that people have, the Parisians immersed themselves in the pleasure of the space. They flirted, skipped, teased, ogled, meditated, painted, got wet, and got dry. There by the Seine, the city had created a space of sufficient size and elegance to lift people from the *quotidien*—the everyday—so that they could return to it with new spirit and joy. It was a space that was out of place and time, ephemeral, enchanting, and enriching.

Barbecue by the river

Lots of people can think about cities, but few bring to that task the infinite imagination that Cantal does. It's rare that he tells a story in which someone proposes something more outrageous than what he has suggested. But here is one such wonderful story.

Cantal got a call from a tenants association. The caller said, "Monsieur, we need some help, but we worry that you are too expensive for us."

Cantal replied, with equal solemnity, "Monsieur, my fees can be substantial if I take you on as client. But perhaps you might invite me to dinner with your neighbors? In that case, we might chat and perhaps resolve your problem. I am a connoisseur of wine and would ask only that you serve a potable vintage."

On the appointed day, Cantal arrived. He looked around the buildings and noticed that in one corner there was a much-used barbecue made from the frame of a concrete mixer. He was shown to the largest apartment, where the neighbors had assembled a potluck dinner, each contributing their specialty. They were proud of the wine they served, which he found delightful.

Over dinner, they got to talking about the problem: the city was proposing some renovations that the tenants didn't like. "I see you have a fine barbecue downstairs," Cantal said.

A silence fell over the group. That was the issue. They loved their barbecue, but the city plans would eliminate it. They were afraid to speak of it, in case it was illegal. You see, this was a group of immigrants from Africa and they were not entirely certain about French policies on barbecues.

Cantal nodded. "I will be happy to help."

He got maps of the area and began to work on a plan. He noticed that there were lines on an old map that indicated a river. He started to ask around and soon found an old-timer who remembered that, indeed, there used to be a river there, but it had been put underground. It was called the Rivière aux Dames, or the Ladies' River.

Cantal explained to the tenants what he had learned. "That's wonderful," one said. "A river!"

"Oh my goodness!" said another. "We could make a park like a river bank, with sand and trees. Wouldn't that be great?"

A chorus of assent went around the room as people caught the vision of a riverfront park by the barbecue.

Cantal was astounded. He would never have dared to suggest such a thing, although he loved the idea. He drew the plan, carefully respecting the barbecue, and the city built it. "That," he told me, "is a triumph of the imagination."

Getting complexity

There is another reason Cantal wanted me to understand what was big enough to organize the city: he wanted me to begin to appreciate the complexity of the city. "I'm an urban ecologist," he said, "though, of course, that's meaningless because there's no separate ecology of the city: there's only one ecosystem."

He wanted me to think about the city's water, food, light, air, living creatures, structures of roads, bridges, dams, buildings, education, transportation, and disease management simultaneously. This is what he called "urbanism": the science of the city, the most profound of his many contributions to my thinking.

But complexity can be overwhelming. Cantal's next great contribution was a way to manage the masses of information urbanism requires. From 1998 to 2010, Cantal was professor and chair of the department of urbanism and the environment at the National Conservatory of Arts and Trades in Paris (CNAM is the acronym in French). The papers of Benjamin Franklin are there, he told me with great pride, and he joked that he would send his papers to Columbia University to restore balance in the universe.

He loved CNAM's library, which used to be the refectory of the monks of St. Martin of the Fields. It is housed in one of the oldest buildings in Paris, a building of the age of the great Sainte-Chapelle. During one of Cantal's visits to the library, he found an old copy of the first encyclopedia, made in the eighteenth century by the Enlightenment philosophers known as encylopedists, a group whose work helped lay the foundation for the emergence of the modern era, with its technological advances and belief in individual liberty and human dignity (Diderot and d'Alembert 1751–72).

Cantal was astonished to find that the library's copy contained a foldout page that had been lost in copies that were in circulation. That page told the story of the manner in which the encyclopedia was organized. Every contributor was asked to address three aspects of the topic: *Memoire*, *Raison*, and *Imagination* (memory, reason, and imagination). Cantal found that this structure had a remarkable resonance with Sigmund Freud's (1961) triptych of the symbolic, the real, and the imaginary.

Cantal also pondered a third triptych, the Borromean knot of Jacques Lacan, in which the overlap of three circles helps us to find the "trough of desire." Cantal named the Lacanian circles using the encyclopedists's memory, reason and imagination (Figure 3.4). This triptych, he proposed, is the fundamental tool of urbanism because it both organizes data and leads to a solution, a path forward from the current situation to a better future. Cantal demonstrated its use during a consultation in Orange, New Jersey.

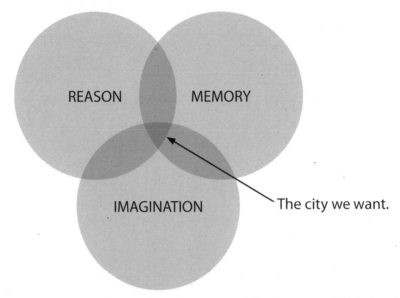

Figure 3.4: Memory, reason, and imagination reveal the city we want. This is the triptych that Cantal developed.

Drawing by Sarah Schell, after an original by Michel Cantal-Dupart.

Love on Elm Street

Orange, New Jersey, is my hometown. Like many another egghead, I got bullied all through school. "Just because you get all A's, that doesn't mean you're so smart," the kids jeered at me. I left town in 1967, limiting my subsequent exposure to quick visits once or twice a year. In 2007, on one of those trips, I went on a tour led by Pat Morrissy, head of the local community development corporation, HANDS. We went a few blocks and the bus stopped. We all got out. A substantial Japanese maple with wine-red leaves gave balance to the sparkly blue of the sky. A set of well-cared-for wooden homes flanked the street. We stood on the sidewalk while Pat explained that the neighborhood had nearly been swallowed by the devastation of the drug scene.

"There was one house in particular that was wrecking the block. My coworker Wayne and I called the bank that owned the house to offer to buy it. An appraiser came out to see the house with Wayne.

"The appraiser was driving a Jaguar, I mean a new Jaguar. It was getting dark. Wayne said, 'You can park there. It'll be OK.' The guy looked at the house—and knew that it was a crack house he was looking at—and he looked at his new Jaguar. 'What do you think?' he asked Wayne, '$35,000?' '$30,000 tops,' Wayne replied. The guy said, 'Sure,' and jumped back in his car and drove away."

HANDS rehabilitated the house and sold it to a stable family that had never owned a home before. Rehabbing that home led to other investments by HANDS and then the people who lived on the block took heart and started to repair their properties. They formed a block association and got control of the activities on the block. In a few years, the block had emerged from crisis and was a stable place to live and raise a family. "HANDS has pursued this kind of strategic targeted investment, fixing the worst properties, the ones that are on everybody's mind. When you fix one property like that, you unleash a whole block," Pat told us.

I never thought I would like Orange, but in those few minutes on Elm Street, I fell in love with my hometown (Figure 3.5). Although we didn't know it at the time, my daughter, Molly, felt the same call to home that fateful day. We both started working with HANDS, and eventually she joined the staff as a community organizer and I joined the board of directors.

As I began to work in Orange, I learned that I was not the only one who thought ill of the town. When I told someone I was working there, she said, "I don't know much about the Oranges, but I know there's a good one and a bad one. Where do you work, the good one?"

Orange, the working-class city inhabited by people of color, is, by all the rules of redlining, the bad one, and as such, the whole city has been wrapped in an invisibility

Figure 3.5: Love on Elm Street. Pat Morrissy explained how the block had been stabilized by renovating a key abandoned house. Both Mindy and Molly felt a call to return to Orange to work.
Photo credit: photograph by Howard Heyman, courtesy of the CRG Collection.

cloak provided by high-speed roads, a train that rolls past, and a plethora of "do not enter" signs that scare those who try to peer in. People don't go there so much as land there by accidents of fate, similar to the one that brought my mother there in the 1950s or the one that brought me back in 2007. I learned from Pat that in 1995, one in ten houses in Orange was vacant and deteriorated, a total of 392. By 2008, that number had been driven down to 49. HANDS's program of strategic investment and community organizing around the issue was the main ingredient. Over the years, HANDS had acquired sixty-six of the most problematic properties, the ones that were holding large areas around them hostage. Just as it had worked on Elm, this intervention worked all over the city.

I started wandering around Orange. I noticed that the city had, in its 2.2 square miles, the whole story of the sorted-out American city. I joked that Orange was a university, which got everyone laughing.

"Where's the quad?" asked one.

"Party in my dorm this Saturday!" proposed someone else.

"I'm going to be the head of athletics!" said Pat. "I want bocce, rock-paper-scissors, and ultimate Frisbee to be our school sports."

One joke lead to another, and that is how our free people's university, the University of Orange, got founded in 2008.

Once we had the concept, Pat reflected, "I think we could get a planning grant from the state for a second neighborhood revitalization project, like the one that's evolving the arts district in the Valley section of Orange. We'll use the grant to engage residents, business owners, and youth to come up with a vision and details of a neighborhood-wide, comprehensive plan, all under the banner of the University of Orange."

"Great idea," I replied enthusiastically. "I would propose that we make a plan for the center of the city, around Main Street. It includes the area cut up when the highway went through. Main Street is strong, but the bleak, half-empty streets around it remind me of Sore, a city in France where Cantal did some work. He tried to convince them that the main commercial street would thrive if the area around it were strengthened. They didn't go for it. When I visited Sore in 2000, the main street had stores going out of business. I think this central section is key to making the city whole and Main Street strong.

"And let's invite Cantal," I added for good measure. I knew that Pat and Cantal shared a *goût*, a taste for the city, and would get along famously. Cantal and his wife, Marie-Dominique, came at the end of March 2009. Molly, as the person in charge of HANDS's Heart of Orange Plan, led the effort to organize his visit.

Molly and Cantal

Molly had traveled with Cantal since she was seventeen, and her roots in urbanism derive from those trips. Her first foray in using Cantal's tools took place at Hampshire College, a liberal establishment with a high drop-out rate. Molly and her friends were suffering. They were suffering passively, however. They were all engaged in analytic work to decipher the roots of their collective problem. I found it interesting, in talking to them, that each person had a remarkably detailed and often brilliant analysis of the problem, but no two people had the same analysis. The question was: How might we get to 1) the real problem, whatever that meant, and 2) a shared understanding of the real problem?

I was working with Terri on teach-ins in the Hill District at the time, so I proposed we have a teach-in. Molly and several of her friends organized the first day-long session, gathering a substantial crowd for the investigation. Matt Phillips painted a map of the campus on his bed sheet, and we spread it out in the pit of an amphitheater. Everyone gathered around, and we began to look at the realities of how life was lived on campus. Some startling facts leapt out at us. Most spectacularly, the freshmen lived and ate in one corner of the campus, while the older students resided in the other three corners. There was also no central place in which to congregate, get a cup of coffee (my complaint), or shoot the breeze.

Once we had established a common sense of the problem, the search for solutions took on more direction, most notably, creating physical and social centers to ease the harms of isolation. Molly proposed that, as students, faculty, and staff all felt the burdens of isolation, it would be good to gather for a party. The Red Barn, she concluded, after exploring the campus, was an expansive, gracious space, just right for mingling. She searched the restaurants of Amherst for the right mix of food. She got Hannah Pearl Walcott to make the first of many event posters. And she walked the campus day after day with a clipboard and a lot of enthusiasm. The Student-

Faculty-Staff Cocktail Party was a hit, not least of all because everyone had a cocktail, and an important precedent was established for campus parties. This is not the least of the accomplishments she shares with Cantal.

Over time, the students developed a central space, the Bridge Café, and a set of ritual social events helped to assemble people on a regular basis. With these bulwarks against too much aloneness, Molly and her group were able to dive into their intellectual work and complete college.

At Hampshire College, the students elect the graduation speaker. As she approached the completion of her Div III, the last of the college requirements, she began to consider whom she would like to hear. To my great honor, she decided she'd like to hear *me*. Her classmates agreed, and I was elected to give the 2002 Commencement Address. For my speech, I tried to decipher the meaning of a story about Justin Lowe, an artist who'd rung the graduation bell until his hands bled. It was, I concluded, a testimony to their passion for justice. I told them how lucky America was that they, with their good hearts, keen critiques, and unrelenting commitment, were now ready to become leaders of our society. And I gave them all mini bells to ring anytime they needed to remember who they were and what they were about.

Molly's urbanism was sharpened by two major travels with Cantal. In 2005, she directed our film *Raccommodage: Mending Our Destiny* (Kaufman 2007a). We traveled for three weeks at a crushing pace and everyone in the film crew—with the exception of Cantal and Molly—reached a breaking point. Molly loved charging around cities with long stops for lunch and dinner and fun conversations with people on the trip or people we met as we moved from place to place.

In 2007, she traveled with Bob, Lily, and me to Cantal's wedding, the ultimate Cantalian adventure—three days of costumes, scene changes, and a cast of hundreds. Again, she proved that she had the imagination and the stamina to keep up with Cantal (see Figure 11.1 for a photo of Molly in her costume for Cantal's "Come as Your Favorite Movie Star" wedding).

When Molly started to work in Orange, she explored intensively. Pretty soon, she pointed out that the city was not only a regular, full-service city but also a fun place to be. She led visits to all the restaurants, shops, bakeries, historic places, and public spaces. She invited the youth of Orange and her friends and interns from nearby universities to explore with her. Molly asked elders like her grandmother Maggie, the first black city councilman Ben Jones, and retired developer Walter Barry to look around with us. Out of those explorations emerged a moveable feast that involved many generations and a lot of laughs.

In 2009, with Cantal on his way to help with the neighborhood revitalization project in Orange, Molly was prepared. She knew urbanism, she knew Cantal, and she knew Orange. She organized to host his visit for the Heart of Orange Plan.

Is this a welcome?

My assignment, during Cantal's visit, was, appropriately, the academic one: I was to show him the area and support his investigations with my own readings and library. He and I drove around, following what he'd studied before coming and my explorations of local sites that I knew would interest him. We had a great time at the home of Thomas Alva Edison, the great inventor, who lived and worked in West Orange. We located nearby golf courses and the ritzy suburbs that he'd identified on Google Earth. We admired the town's war statues and walked Main Street.

I showed him my childhood home on Olcott Street and the nearby park. Cantal was intrigued by a peculiar observation I'd made. The park was partially fenced, as it was when I was growing up. Crawling under the fence to get into the park was an important ritual of my childhood. What I realized on my return was that the fence was erected between the park and the black neighborhoods that existed then. On the sides where there had been white people across from the park, there was no fence.

On the second day of the visit, the formal events started. Molly had organized a Cantalian series: a luncheon at one of the area restaurants, a tour, a party, a placemaking conference, and a Monday morning quarterback session. City officials lunched with us, and afterwards, they presented Cantal with a proclamation that it was "Michel Cantal-Dupart Day" in Orange. Pat had prepared a speech in French and pulled it off with aplomb. It started to rain while we were dining, so John Rappaport, director of the Orange Police Department, called for a bus to take us around.

It was Cantal who led the tour of our city. Our first stop was the historic First Presbyterian Church. We stood amidst the colonial era graves and Cantal said, "I brought you here because of this tombstone, which

Is **this** a welcome?

Figure 3.6: Cantal explained that the train station was the trump card for the revitalization of Orange, New Jersey. He used his hands to gesture to the area around the train (shown in the photo at the top) and asked, "Is this a welcome?" In the photo on the bottom, we can see that he continued to hold the dramatic gesture while Pat Morrissy listened to Bob Fullilove's translation. When Bob got to the punch line, Pat looked at Cantal, looked at the scene, and got the message.

Photo credits: Mindy Fullilove.

reads 1745. That was a key year for cities around the world. In that year, cities were opening themselves to the world. Orange is part of that.

"I love Orange," he said, "because I love the word 'orange.' It's an international word."

We laughed.

The tour went next to the train station. "This," he said, "is what made the city. Thomas Edison lived there, in Llewellyn Park, because he could take the train from here. This train is also your modernity, your passport to the future. Pat, I'm speaking to you. This is critical to the future of the city.

"But," and he turned to look at the area around the train, "is this a *welcome*?"

We followed his sweeping gesture, taking in the vast sagging parking lot that encrusted the foreground, seeing with the eyes of a newcomer descending from the train (Figure 3.6).

The discoveries continued. We went next to Orange Park, where Cantal talked about the fence. He said to city planner Valerie Jackson, "We who are old have a responsibility. We have lived this history of exclusion. We must fight it."

The fourth stop was at the site of the Orange Memorial Hospital, the local community hospital that closed in 2004. "You have a chance here because you have a remarkable amount of open land near the train station. I argue that no place in the New York metropolitan area has such a potential asset. But don't waste it simply on real estate. Cities are more than square meters for rent or sale—they have history and culture. In Europe, places for wellness are very popular. That would work here."

The final stop was on Main Street in front of the library. "This is the Garden State. That's what is on all your license plates. Where's the garden?"

Again, he gestured with his hands and our eyes followed, agreeing that there was no garden to be seen. "You must plant trees, one tree every day."

He jumped into the street and showed us where we could put a tree without taking away parking. "Here! Put a tree here!"

Valerie protested that she didn't have money to take care of the trees and laughed. Cantal gave no quarter. "There must be trees in the Garden State."

That evening, there was a party at the gracious home of the Wells family, where Karen Wells, a leader of our effort, has a remarkable collection of art and antiques. In addition to wonderful food and a capacity crowd, Cantal got to explore the historic artifacts all around. He quickly zeroed in on some historic maps, pulling out a magnifying glass and studying carefully. Brad Harrington, our program officer from the New Jersey Neighborhood Revitalization Tax Credit program, assisted him.

We held a placemaking conference on Saturday, at which local citizens got to weigh in on their concerns for the Heart of Orange Plan. The conference was held at the First Presbyterian Church and benefitted from its gracious spaces. We all went to see the city, teams going in different directions and coming back with their observations of pleasures and trash.

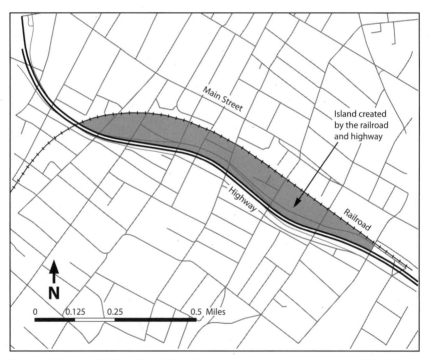

Figure 3.7: Beautify City Island. Cantal annotated a map of the Heart of Orange to suggest that we think of Route 280 and the train tracks as rivers that create an "island" in the center of the city (shown in gray). The revitalization of the area focused on: 1) beautifying City Island, and 2) strengthening its connection to the north and south of the city through lighting the area's many bridges and tunnels.

Drawing: Redrawn by Sarah Schell from an original by Michel Cantal-Dupart. Courtesy of the CRG Collection.

It was Shirley Torho's birthday, and so we celebrated with a cake from Sanitary Bakery. Kiara Nagel led a spirited discussion of all we had seen and compiled everyone's ideas for Cantal's examination.

Meanwhile, Cantal studied maps and books all weekend, preparing for the final presentation at the library. There, he offered an overview of urban history, explaining the particular challenges and solutions he saw for Orange. He presented his triptych so that we could all appreciate the history, function, and imagination that we'd unearthed together.

We all knew that the highway had torn the city apart. What Cantal showed us was that an early twentieth-century shift in the train tracks had caused major changes in the city. Like the highway, the elevated train tracks were left raw, a non-place, *non-lieu*. Between the train and the highway was a little island of space (Figure 3.7).

"Think of the train and the highway as two rivers," he urged us. "This space in the middle is a kind of island between two rivers. In Paris, we have exactly the same thing and we call it *Isle de la Cité*—City Island. Your City Island is dirty and neglected. This serves to dissuade the visitor.

"What is needed is to turn this around, to beautify it, to light it up! And what better way to shine a new light on the city than to light the bridges and tunnels that connect City Island to the rest of the city. I propose that you hold a design competition. Let the Museum of Modern Art sponsor it for you. Let artists design dazzling light displays. Then the passersby will look in wonder and say, 'That's Orange!'"

Memory, reason, and imagination in Orange

Cantal gave us more detail in a written report. His history of Orange emphasized the railroad, which arrived in Orange in 1832. The three east-west streets, Central Avenue, Main Street, and Park Avenue, defined the urban core. Near this center, Llewellyn Haskell, a pharmacy magnate, created Llewellyn Park, one of the first garden cities, which was built in the 1850s. Its proximity to the train gave it easy access to Newark and New York. It attracted interesting people, which is why Thomas Alva Edison moved there in 1886 and built his "factory of invention" and factories for production nearby.

The evolution of the city followed these tropes: interesting well-to-do people seeking each other; factories following trends and inventions; and transportation evolving with time. Whatever the changes, Cantal noted, "the city always left its heart to the poorest citizens."

Cantal divided "reason" into that which was not functioning and that which was. "Not working" opened with the observation, "The cut made for the railroad, repeated by the cut for the highway, created a trench that forms a physical and psychological barrier." The center of the city, with streets named Oakwood and Hickory, was nearly barren of trees. The bleak landscape presented a deplorable image from the train. Old signs of segregation—like the fence in Orange Park that only faced the former black ghetto—had not been erased.

But the city had much that was working: 32,868 residents, a substantial infrastructure, a busy main street, and other smaller commercial streets. The city had a remarkable amount of open land in walking distance to Orange Station. Orange also had a second train station at Highland Avenue, built to serve the wealthy homeowners in the southern end of the city and the industrial section of the Valley. Cantal wrote, "Profiting from two train stations, it's a city of modernity because it offers an excellent alternative to travel by automobile. One finds the spirit of Llewellyn, the developer of Llewellyn Park who profited from proximity to the train back in the 1850s."

Cantal also emphasized that there were seven bridges to reknit the north and south, as well as a vacant hospital with its historic smokestack, to transform.

Cantal then began to imagine a city on the move. He urged us to find the spirit of Edison, who invented the future only a few blocks away. Orange was once the hat-making capital of the world and deserved its own hat museum. Given that there were once two major hospitals, might Orange capitalize on this history of hospitality and become a wellness center?

It was essential, he wrote, to get started immediately. He proposed five activities:

- A civic day to clean up the Heart of Orange;
- An international music festival to celebrate the many ethnicities in Orange as well as Edison's invention of the phonograph;
- A competition, run by the Museum of Modern Art or the Guggenheim, to light the bridges and tunnels;

- The creation of a hat museum; and
- The development of a plan to make Orange a paradise of fruit.

Cantal's triptych helped me hold together hats, trains, cars, phonographs, segregation, hospitals, trees, music, toboggans, museums, trash, bridges, tunnels, the Revolutionary War, churches, the cemetery, the garden city, mountains, a paradise of fruit, and more. Cantal offered us the complexity of the city, but threaded the pieces into history, reason, and imagination, a manageable threesome that retains the essence of complexity.

With the city in mind, we could proceed.

CHAPTER FOUR

Element 2:
Find What You're FOR

> There was a miller who left no more estate to the three sons he had than his mill, his ass, and his cat.... The eldest had the mill, the second the ass, and the youngest nothing but the cat. The poor young fellow was quite comfortless at having so poor a lot.
>
> The Cat... said to him with a grave and serious air:
>
> "Do not thus afflict yourself, my good master. You have nothing else to do but to give me a bag and get a pair of boots made for me that I may scamper through the dirt and the brambles, and you shall see that you have not so bad a portion in me as you imagine."
>
> —Andrew Lang, "Puss in Boots"

"Oh no, not that story again!" I used to say every time my dad started to tell the story of the cat, the fox, and the programmatic tree. Forty years later, when we were starting the University of Orange, I insisted that our mascot be the "Programmatic Cat." I thought of him as Puss in Boots, a magical cat we'd inherited that would help us make our fortune.

My University of Orange cofounders had read the book my dad, Ernie, and I had written, *Homeboy Came to Orange: A Story of People's Power* (Thompson and Thompson 1976), and knew the story, but as our faculty grew, it became important to retell the tale. "The cat and the fox," I told them, "were discussing what to do when the dogs came. The fox said, 'I have a lot of tricks—I'll do my tricks.' The cat said, 'I only have one trick—I go up the tree.' Then one day, the dogs came and the cat scooted up the tree. From his perch, he watched as the fox did his tricks. The dogs were not fooled and tore him to pieces. The cat shook his head and said, 'It doesn't pay to know too many tricks.' And, at the end of the story, Ernie would always say, 'We have to be like the cat and go up the tree—the Programmatic Tree.'"

Of course, after I'd told this story a few times, my granddaughter Lily started to say, "Oh no..."

But Molly, who was working as a community organizer, understood the admonition to stick with one's program. Crises, attacks, and unexpected problems may divert attention or raise issues, but it is essential to refer back to one's program in response to problems and to relocate one's direction. A program of action arises from people's needs and a desire to fix the deep structural problems we face in the city. A program is a compass through the thicket of urban life.

Find what you're FOR, the second element of urban restoration, leads us to three considerations. The first is that we have moral, humanitarian, and pragmatic reasons to include everyone in the conversation that creates a program. The second is that the program must address the restoration of the sorted-out city. If a vision plan fails to move us towards this goal, it will aggravate current conditions of separation and inequality. The third is that the program needs to have technical guidance that calls on the art and science of urban restoration to help people achieve in space what they imagine in relationships.

Find what you're FOR, the second element of urban restoration, involves:

- Including everyone;
- Addressing the sorted-out city; and
- Using the art and science of urbanism for restoration.

Including everyone

My dad, Ernie, got active in Orange in 1957 and developed the New Day Platform in 1958. He was immersed in the life of the ghetto where we lived. His favorite listening post was the Harmony Bar, which had a modest bar, some wooden booths, and some tables. Its big window overlooked Central Avenue, one of the major thoroughfares, and Orange Park. While not as bright as outdoors, the Harmony was open and welcoming. The men of the neighborhood dropped by in regular rhythms and talked about all the things working-class black men talked about in a bar in those days.

The black community in Orange had no political life at that time, but my dad changed that, first, by desegregating the schools and then by leading a campaign for Dr. John Alexander to be elected as a city commissioner. As part of that campaign, he and others put together the New Day Platform. Because it was written for a citywide election, the platform addressed the problems of the city in a manner infused with hope and dignity. It celebrated character and beauty in a city that was commonly seen as lacking both. It looked at issues as mundane as the water supply and as lofty as representative government. In its thorough, comprehensive look at the city, it offered a model of urbanism (Figure 4.1).

This "New Day" platform guided my dad's organizing in Orange until his death in 1971. While helping him with his book, I noticed that most of the work he had done over the years was on education. The other points of the platform had gotten much less attention. "I knew from my work with the union," he explained, "that manufacturing was in rapid decline. What were the unskilled workers going to do for jobs? They would have to have skills. That required much more education than they were getting in the Orange school system. I realized that, without education, they were doomed to die: inadequate education was a policy of genocide. I focused on that part of our program and we made great progress. We were one of the first cities in the nation to start a Head Start program and we made many other innovations in teaching and learning. We fought for the new high school—the powers that be were not going to build that school and we would have lost our accreditation, further dooming our children. When you work in a programmatic way, it is a means of focusing your attention and your energy towards the goals that you think are most important."

Making the just and beautiful city

New Day Platform

I. REDEVELOPMENT AND RELOCATION

1. The partial redevelopment plan now under consideration must be implemented to include other sections of the City in order to increase ratables and improve the character of the city.
2. Study future water needs based on the projected plans.
3. A Citizens Committee be set up to work side by side with the City Commissioners to bring in private housing capital and industry.
4. Seriously examine the need to replace the ancient City Hall.

II. UNEMPLOYMENT

1. Problems resulting from the current recession and shops leaving our City must be vigorously met by the City officials.
2. Unemployment Compensation should be extended and increased immediately as was done in the state of New York.
3. Federal taxes should be immediately reduced to increase the purchasing power of consumers and relief to business.
4. Maximum distribution of federal surplus food supplies to the unemployed and others in need.
5. The maximum use of local labor forces in the Redevelopment program and other government projects should be mandatory.
6. The efficiency of the Welfare Department and its service to the people should be studied for maximum benefits to be obtained.

III. FREEWAY

1. It should be the policy of the City Government, which is not now the case, to provide all aid and assistance in relocation of the displaced families.
2. An official city committee should be established whose duties it shall be to provide relocation and assistance.
3. Depress the Freeway to protect the properties and beauty of the City.

VI. SCHOOL SYSTEM

1. Discriminatory school lines still in existence in Orange and all other forms of discrimination in the school system should be wiped out.
2. Federal funds should be sought for the purpose of improvement of the physical plants.
3. Adequate pay for teachers and other city employees.
4. Strengthen the school system by amending the charter to permit an elected Board of Education.

V. CIVIL RIGHTS

1. The City of Orange should have a functioning Civil Rights Committee.

VI. RECREATION AND JUVENILE DELINQUENCY

1. Develop and implement a year-round recreational program thru-out the City.
2. Establish a special division in the Police Department manned by trained personnel to develop a program to prevent and manage Juvenile Delinquency.

VII. REPRESENTATIVE GOVERNMENT

1. The future of Orange is contingent upon achieving these objectives through representative government made up of Negroes and Whites.

Figure 4.1: The New Day Platform was developed by Ernest Thompson for a 1958 city-wide campaign in Orange, New Jersey. The platform is reprinted from *Homeboy Came to Orange* by Thompson and Thompson (1976, 62).

What is the character of a city?

How do we support the local labor force?

How can the displaced be helped?

How do we make the city beautiful?

How do we end educational inequality?

How do we establish civil rights committees?

How do we ensure representative government?

Design Sketchbook page by Sarah Schell.

In 2008, as Pat Morrissy, Molly, Karen Wells, and I launched the University of Orange (U of O), we pulled out the New Day Platform and began to study it. We were struck by the timelessness of its seven themes. We also noted the way in which "the more things change, the more they stay the same." We happened to be at the beginning of another recession so the comments about how to manage an economic downturn rang a bell. The old city hall was still the old city hall. The freeway, although it had been depressed, had not been adequately integrated into the urban fabric, negatively affecting the city's properties and beauty. And construction at a number of sites had been stopped because the city needed to upgrade its water system to be in line with the demands that would arise from the new construction.

We realized that the New Day Platform was a holistic plan for city development that focused on making Orange just and beautiful. Following its lead, we established U of O's mission as, "Making Orange, NJ, *the* urban village of the twenty-first century, a just and beautiful city." We subscribe to the belief that any city could start to think about its future using the New Day Platform.

But, like Ernie and his coworkers in Citizens for Representative Government, citizens must start with a common understanding of the problems in order to move to the correct solution. My second contention is that it is essential to see the ways in which the sorting process has injured and is injuring our cities and our citizens.

Addressing the sorted-out city

We need to know what we're *against*

In the sorted-out city, we are divided by race and class and our separation is reinforced by spaces that lie between our neighborhoods. It is nearly impossible to see the problem of the sorted-out city from within a neighborhood. That is why Cantal, in his first visit to Pittsburgh in 1998, urged us to find the rivers. It was in getting out of the neighborhood—looking for those larger structuring forces that shape the city—that we might begin to see the characteristic landscape of the sorted-out city: that of

How sorting injures the city

Injury	How it works in the sorting system	What to look/listen for
Unequal Investment	Policies of differential investment of public and private resources according to the status of area residents, reminiscent of the redlining protocol, lead to markedly different outcomes in viability of infrastructure and of the social organization dependent on that infrastructure.	Lots of building and repair in one neighborhood, collapse and neglect in another.
Borders	Marking the edges between areas of different status inhibits passage and limits "mixing."	A wall, an impassable expanse of land, a place people say, "Don't cross."
Invisibilization	Using geographic marginalization renders some areas "invisible" to passersby and limits "mixing."	A detour around a land mass that is occupied by people.
Spatial homogeneity	Assembling people to live and work in areas according to class/race/sexual orientation/age or other markers of sorting creates social groups that have little variation.	People of certain groups in one area, and people of other groups in another area.
Exclusion from governance	Using "divide and conquer" strategies so that people believe themselves to be separated creates antagonisms that eliminate most people from decision making.	Low voter participation, expression of racial or other kinds of hatred.
Draining the spirit	Making people feel helpless because they cannot influence the larger structures within which they are embedded leaves them immobilized, politically apathetic, and angry/afraid.	Listen for people who say, "You can't fight city hall."
Serial displacement	Policies that push people out of their neighborhoods destroy community function and feed inequity.	Look in the landscape for markers of the social groups that have lived in a space, listen to people's stories for the history of their journey.
Social disintegration	Policies of constant upheaval break social ties that help communities function.	Listen for focus on one's self and one's group as opposed to interest in larger wholes.

Figure 4.2: This table shows the kinds of injuries that one can see or hear in the sorted-out city.

crumbling ghettos and prospering suburbs in the process of transforming into prospering urban neighborhoods and crumbling suburbs.

In addition to the difference between urban and suburban places, there is a landscape of separation, of borders that make crossing from one sector to another a scary and difficult act. A magazine writer once wrote about visiting Morrisania Neighborhood Family Care Center, where I was working in the South Bronx, as "crossing the great divide" (Simon 1986). In terms of systems therapy, that is the great work of urban restoration. I have found eight characteristic injuries that the careful observer and attentive listener can identify (Figure 4.2).

Unequal investment, which was codified in redlining and accentuated by planned shrinkage, marks the landscape. It is not difficult to discern places of investment and places of disinvestment in any American city. The whole system is unstable, as today's poor place could be tomorrow's irresistible investment. Flipping real estate, a term that refers to purchasing property to sell quickly at a profit, is a fundamental part of American capitalism, representing its tendency for "creative destruction." Applied to communities, this is destructive for both the located and the serially displaced people. The sorted-out city is fundamentally damaging to the society and to the whole range of peoples of which the cloth of society is woven.

As some neighborhoods are going up and others are going down, there are *borders* that develop between these increasingly divergent places. The fracture lines, whether inscribed with walls or with highways or simply understood as a matter of local usage, define passage in the city according to the rules of apartheid.

All methods of inscribing fracture create *invisiblization* (Bishop and Harrington 1997). This works on both sides of the line. The poor have strange fantasies about the life of the rich and the rich have equally lurid ideas about the poor. They can't and don't visit each other to find out what's really going on. To see invisibilization one has to go to a place that is hidden. In public health, this is often discussed as the problem of the "hard-to-reach." As the hard-to-reach are usually standing on the street corners of the invisible zones, the real problem is crossing the border into "dangerous" and "unknown" territory.

It is a universal—and probably genetic—trait that most animals, including people, don't cross into the unknown if they can help it. The

San Diego Zoo, which avoids fences, uses the optical illusion of impassibility to contain the animals that reside there. Only the bold will go past the boundaries. Caroline Parsons Moore, a student in the Columbia University master of public health program in the early 1990s, was famous among her peers for her explorations of forbidden space. One day, she came to class and described walking down a street in Harlem, then very much out-of-bounds. She passed a decrepit, abandoned house. She told the class, "I was thinking, what would a two-year-old think if she passed by that house and saw the door open? She would think, 'I should go in.'

"So I did. And then I wondered, what would the two-year-old do if she saw the broken stairs up to the second floor? I thought she'd probably go up and so I did."

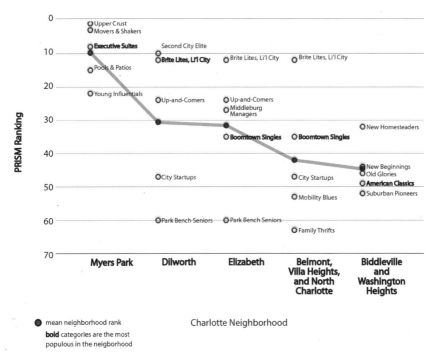

Figure 4.3: Charlotte neighborhoods as viewed through PRISM. PRISM is a system of 66 sociogeographic rankings, with 1 as highest and 66 as lowest, and each group given a catchy name. This system was used to examine the Charlotte, North Carolina, neighborhoods that were the focus of Thomas Hanchett's (1998) book, *Sorting Out the New South City*. In this graph, we show who lives in five Charlotte neighborhoods, by PRISM name and rank. See also the maps of sorting in Figure 1.4.

Analysis: Molly Kratz; Graph: Sarah Schell.

The story went on like that. The class was terrified, as if they were watching the moment in a horror movie when the heroine is ready to open the closet door and wanted to scream, "*Don't!*" Many in the class spoke to me afterwards and told me I needed to control Caroline. But Caroline was her own person and wanted to see the world. Most of us are not so bold, and so the invisibilization effectively hides much of the world from our sight.

When people live in sections with only others like themselves, it creates *spatial homogeneity.* Tom Hanchett's (1998) exquisite analysis of how Charlotte, North Carolina, was sorted by race and class helps us to understand how this unfolded. A student in my 2011 Urban Space and Health class, Molly Kratz, used the PRIZM system of "geodemographics"—a system that helps identify where different types of people live—to look at what Charlotte's like today.

The PRIZM rankings identified Myers Park, originally built as an exclusive suburban neighborhood on the southern side of Charlotte, as the top of the socioeconomic ladder in the city (Figure 4.3). In the middle were the adjacent neighborhoods of Dilworth and Elizabeth. Both started as suburbs of the city, but had become increasingly mixed as time went on. Belmont-Villa Heights and North Charlotte, on the city's northeast side, were originally built around factories and the isolated communities of their workers. In 2012, an increasingly diverse group of people was moving in, but the neighborhoods were still quite poor. The poorest and most predominantly black areas, Biddleville and Washington Heights, were found to the northwest of the city. All in all, Molly Kratz's analysis demonstrated that Charlotte's sorting by race, class, and lifestyle meant that there was minimal diversity within neighborhoods and little overlap among them. This constricts the opportunities for social bridges to develop that might knit the city together.

In the sorted-out city, power is concentrated in the hands of the haves, while the *have-nots are excluded from governance.* Those in power construct a narrative of being providers and producers whose taxes are consumed by the have-nots.

While this seems to be a system that favors whites and the well-to-do, in fact, as I have noted, stagnant, even paralyzed, communication actually undermines civic vitality and general problem solving. Issues that we urgently need resolved cannot be managed. We are all trapped in the dysfunction of the fractured city, and *the fracture and paralysis drain the spirit.*

The constant movement of money from established places to new sites of investment is a feature of the system that aggravates fracture and flourishes in it. David Harvey (2003) has linked the concentration of wealth to the dispossession of people, proposing that there is a fundamental system of "accumulation by dispossession." The constant movement of money is accompanied by the *serial displacement of people,* which is the source of many of the worst problems we see. It is the serial displacement of people that makes life so miserable. People have an ability to get by on very little money if they have dense social networks, the kind that operated in Simms I, the period from 1930 to 1960. But people are helpless and afraid when those social networks are gone, which feeds the dysfunction of Simms III—the period after 1980—a dysfunction an informant so cleverly named "unexpectancy" (Fullilove and Wallace 2011).

Social disintegration follows on the heels of serial displacement, as social ties are broken and people lose the ability to work together (Leighton 1959). Small groups composed of people who share strong ties of family, race, religion, or residence form. These groups have little contact with others who are "different." When the weak, bridging ties are lost, society becomes paralyzed in the stand-offs of identity politics, which, to the detriment of all, replace programmatic politics.

OK, that's what we're against, but what are we FOR?

Carl Redwood and Bonnie Young Laing, leaders of the Hill District Consensus Group, shared Ernie Thompson's perspective of fighting for economic justice for all, especially the most disenfranchised (Figures 4.4 and 4.5). They saw the sorting process at work in the Hill District and proposed to counter the "money power" of developers with the "people power" of organized groups. The goal was to prevent displacement and other forms of economic oppression and to achieve shared prosperity. That's what they were FOR.

In a report called *Organizing for Economic Justice: A Model,* Carl Redwood and Bonnie Young Laing (2012, 1) wrote, "Economic justice organizing calls for using tactics such as broad coalition building, defining

Figure 4.4: Carl Redwood at the One Hill Demonstration.
Photo credit: Rich Brown, used with permission.

Figure 4.5: Bonnie Young Laing.
Photo credit: Rich Brown, used with permission.

community wants and needs then codifying those wants and needs into principles that can be translated into law and/or social policy such as master planning documents, zoning law and/or local development plan approval processes."

According to the report, as early as 2005, the Hill District Consensus Group had formulated a list of questions designed to show the extent to which proposed developments were going to further economic justice or not. These questions were:

1. We support community ownership. What is the nature and percent of community ownership?
2. We support hiring neighborhood residents as the first source for construction and ongoing jobs. What is the nature and percent of these jobs for local residents?
3. We require a financial contribution to the community from developers. How much are you going to contribute to the Community Improvement Fund?
4. What was the public subsidy for this project? What percent of the public subsidy is your contribution? (Redwood and Laing 2012, 7)

These questions helped to push an understanding of inequity and how it worked. This is a fundamental part of addressing the sorted-out city. In the process of sorting, some neighborhoods are designated for investment and others for disinvestment. In attacking the disinvestment of the Hill, the Consensus Group was helping to restore connection and unity in the whole of Pittsburgh.

In 2007, the Pittsburgh Penguins began to hint that they would leave the city if they did not get a new arena. The state, county, and city agreed to come up with hundreds of millions of dollars in subsidy for the arena. In April 2007, the Consensus Group launched the One Hill coalition, an attempt to create an umbrella coalition that might bring together the two major groups in the Hill: those participating in the Consensus Group and those organized around the smaller, less transparent Hill District Community Development Corporation. By July of 2007, One Hill had developed a coalition of one hundred organizations and had begun to create a list of demands for a Community Benefits Agreement.

Like Ernie, Carl and Bonnie understood that starting a program was a way to stay on course. Working in a programmatic fashion is a manner of working that begins with naming what one is FOR and then finding the ways to achieve those goals in the setting of the city. Ernie organized the East Ward—the Orange ghetto—because he thought it was right that the people who lived in the neighborhood should make decisions about how it was run. But, he wrote,

> it was not sufficient for the growing machinery of Black control to sit idling in the ghetto. To solve the problems of the ghetto, it was necessary to go into the central arena, to go where decisions are made. Just as General Electric and General Motors are not controlled in the ghetto, neither are school systems. If we wished to improve the school system, to guarantee that our children would be prepared for the world of work, we had to fight for representation on the Board of Education. In moving out of the ghetto, we knew that we had to multiply our strength, to find allies. In every struggle, we emphasized coalition. (Thompson and Thompson 1976, 200–01)

It was Ernie's view that successful coalition building involved both attention to organizing one's own base—the sole force with which one moves into a coalition—and the identification of common cause with other groups. Ernie wrote, "If a coalition succeeds, it is because each of the groups within it succeeds as well. In the fight for education, we fought for all children… We raised our battle cry for a good high school because we believed that every person should have a right to dignity and a place in this society" (Thompson and Thompson 1976, 200–01).

One Hill, Carl proposed, had to develop its program by getting people to express their needs in open meetings and envisioning sessions. He insisted that leaders be held accountable to the residents, rather than function free of them. In *Homeboy Came to Orange*, Ernie wrote about much the same struggle. He reflected,

> The power we acquired in Orange through control of the Democratic Party in the ward and through Citizens for Representative Government was mainly in the hands of the working class. It was just and reasonable that the working class, as the majority, should be in control of

the machinery. The workers knew what discipline, exploitation, and struggle meant; the middle class did not. At the same time, we tried to use the skills and training of middle-class Blacks to maximize their contribution. Our leaders were sensitive to this problem and struggled to prevent the middle-professional class from taking control of the movement. (Thompson and Thompson 1976, 200)

One Hill, with its work style of inclusion and representation, developed the *Blueprint for a Livable Hill Proposal* (Laing, n.d.). The program proposed in the blueprint included:

1. Master Plan to Build a Livable Community
2. Livable Hill Community Improvement Fund
3. Family Sustaining Jobs and First Source Career Opportunities
4. Community Grocery Store/Economic Anchor
5. Community/Multipurpose Center
6. Historic Preservation and Green Space
7. Policy Commitments for a Livable Hill

The organization of One Hill and the development of a shared platform were both part of the solidification of the base within the Hill District. At the same time, One Hill understood that it could not win the battle with the city, county, state, and Pittsburgh Penguins without the help of others from outside the Hill. A major partnership was forged with Pittsburgh United, a union group that had foundation funding to support community benefits campaigns. As Bonnie Young Laing (2009) put it in a paper on the challenges of coalition building, Pittsburgh United had been funded for the work One Hill was doing, which made the situation both provocative and unstable. Yet, the leaders of the One Hill Coalition recognized that Pittsburgh United had skills in negotiation and mobilization that would benefit One Hill, were it possible to share them. These problems were eventually resolved, and the partnership was able to function.

The struggle for the Community Benefits Agreement (CBA) was a hard one. At one of the early negotiating sessions, a second group, the Hill Faith and Justice Alliance that was composed of a few area ministers, a former councilmember, and others who opposed One Hill, claimed to be the true representatives of the Hill. The presence of two groups, each claiming to represent the community, derailed the negotiations for months. It took intense political strategizing to get the Hill Faith and Justice Alliance to step back and let One Hill lead the process. Then, at the point at which the government was willing to reopen negotiations with One Hill, the Pittsburgh Penguins refused to participate.

As luck would have it, the Penguins reached the Stanley Cup Finals in 2008. Rather than face protests with the spotlight of world attention on them, the Penguins returned to the negotiating table and the CBA was completed. As reported on May 11, 2008, by the *Pittsburgh Tribune*:

> The deal would have the city and county hire a professional to develop a master plan for the neighborhood, according to the One Hill Community Benefits Agreement Coalition. It also would keep the Penguins, who have development rights for the property, from submitting their own plans until the master plan is finished.
>
> The agreement would commit the Penguins and the URA [Urban Redevelopment Authority of Pittsburgh] to contribute $1 million each to attract a grocery store to the neighborhood. It asks the team to help attract corporate sponsors to pay up to $500,000 a year for community development and various services, in return for state tax credits.
>
> It also includes measures to create jobs, including having new businesses give hiring preference to Hill District residents. (Houser 2008)

The CBA brought direct benefits totaling $8.3 million to the community. It also brought indirect benefits, such as First Source Hiring, a clearing-house process to hire local residents, and the recognition of the Hill District Consensus Group as the community table. The establishment of a community table meant that people from outside the neighborhood could—and, more importantly, needed to—"come by the house" to discuss proposals for the community with the community. This is a massive shift towards equity in inter-neighborhood relationships. Despite these gains, the Consensus Group was keenly aware that the Penguins—a private corporation—had received $750 million in public subsidy. The answer to the question, "What percent of the subsidy is your contribution to the community?" was 1.2 percent, a pitiful amount given the needs of the Hill.

Hard as it was to win the CBA, the even harder part was fighting to make the agreement meaningful, to create change in the lives of people who had been marginalized and left to die. In the teeth of a fierce and unrelenting recession, that was a tough proposition. One of the first fruits of the agreement was the funding of a community master plan. The goal of the Hill master plan was to propose how this marginalized neighborhood might get on its feet. This meant bringing in planning professionals who would be interviewed by the community and who would work on behalf of the community in thinking through the issues of economic justice and neighborhood revitalization.

This leads to the third consideration I proposed: that the program needs to have technical guidance that calls on the art and science of urban restoration to help people achieve in space what they imagine in relationships.

Calling on the art and science of urban restoration

Knowledge in service of the common good

Because my 2004 book, *Root Shock: How Tearing Up City Neighborhoods Hurts America and What We Can Do About It*, dealt at length with the story of the Hill, I had standing to be a consultant in the master plan process set in motion by the CBA. Three teams, when asking if I would work with them, said they would gather information, hold envisioning sessions, and then develop a master plan. It was not clear what principles would guide the outcomes. While community involvement was guaranteed as part of the contract, I kept asking myself the question, "What does this group *mean* when they say all that?"

Ken Doyno was part of the fourth group that contacted me. He first introduced himself to me over the phone, explaining that his firm was submitting a proposal for the master plan contract and wondering if I might consult with them. Then he said, "I believe in the inherent worth and dignity of every human being."

I was startled, as that is one of the seven principles of my religion. I said, "Excuse me. Are you by any chance a Unitarian Universalist?"

"Yes, I am."

"I am, too!" I replied. It isn't such a large denomination that this is an everyday occurrence. The pleasure was twofold: a member of my tribe and the application to planning of a principle I hold dear.

He then went on to say that his group, Rothschild Doyno Collaborative (RDCollab), had designed The Legacy, then a brand-new building on Centre Avenue in the Hill. Terri had gushed with enthusiasm when she first told me about The Legacy and she took me there as soon as I got to the Hill. We examined the outside of the building and she explained the limestone panels with names of great jazz musicians. "I love the jazz-inspired art in the lobby," she said with pleasure. "It was all made by local artists."

We walked slowly through, soaking in its sunny space and remarkable art collection. "I can't believe it's here—on the Hill," Terri said with satisfaction.

As soon as Ken said that was his firm's building, I thought they should be awarded the contract, and, as I got to know about the principles employed by their organization, I became even more enthusiastic in my support. RDCollab's thesis was that a vision, initiated by the community and then supported by the government and investors, would initiate a cycle of upward investment. The firm believed that the community's role in starting the process was crucial to lay the basis for inclusion, to prevent the imposition of top-down strategies that often led to displacement, and to ensure that every member of the community was protected as development went forward.

Underlying this proposition was a set of observations that were less obvious. The parties in the development process had different, and sometimes quite contradictory, goals. Investors, for example, were trying to make money, community people were trying to have a better life, and the government was trying to be all things to all people with far too little money to do any of it. For RDCollab, without analyzing economic, social, and physical problems at the same time, it was impossible to find the interventions that could meet the needs of all parties. They had titled this search for the solution their "ESP" framework, which stood for simultaneous economic, social, and physical analysis.

I didn't really understand what RDCollab meant by ESP in the brief presentations that I got to hear during the master plan competition. That day, they showed an image of their work for Brick Towers in Newark, New Jersey. They simply said that they had worked to find a win-win in a difficult situation.

At a later date, I went by Dan and Ken's offices in the Strip District and got a fuller explanation. The first corollary of using ESP is that you have to have the ability to listen to all the parties. This is something they routinely codify in Design Sketchbook pages entitled, "What We Heard."

"Brick Towers," Dan said when we had a chance to discuss the story in greater detail, "was a symbol, depending on how you looked at it. For the thirty-two squatting families that had refused eviction notices, it was an example of failed public housing policy. For the Newark Housing Authority, it was an impasse to future redevelopment of the Central Ward. It needed to be knocked down. An impasse of years had resulted—nothing was moving. Councilman Cory Booker moved in to show solidarity with the squatters—he lived on the fifteenth floor with no elevator. He became mayor and told the Newark Housing Authority, 'You've got to come up with a solution.'

"My first meeting was with five residents, two lawyers, and two staff members from the Newark Housing Authority. Upon noticing the lawyers in the room, the Housing Authority staff got up and left. They were without legal representation. I called the director and asked if I should leave, but I was given permission to stay. We returned to the table. I opened the conversation by saying, 'I've been asked to come up with a solution, but I don't know the depth of what you've been through, so I'd like to listen to what's been going on.' For the next two hours, they told tough stories about their life at Brick Towers. It was as if they were physically vomiting bile and hatred. Every time a speaker would stop, I asked, 'Anything else?' And more would come. In the end, I said, 'That is *terrible*. How are we able to go from *that* to a shared wish for a win-win solution? All I've heard is win-lose, lose-win. If the two parties can commit to search for a win-win, then we'll stay in the game until the win-win is reached.'

"The mission statement that we came up with—the shared vision—was that the solution had to be a positive catalyst in the *surrounding* area—it had to be timely and it had to be an economic catalyst. It was the connection to the surrounding area that created the possibility for resolution."

The second corollary of ESP is that the social, physical, and economic must connect at the point of intervention, as they did in Brick Towers. The solution that Dan proposed had two parts. The first floor of the public areas would become retail and start-up space, thus oriented to welcoming the public. In addition, the space between the towers, which had been a private space elevated from the street, would be transformed into a public square with a farmers market, public concerts, and other activities that would bring the neighborhood to life.

"After that proposal was made, the squatting families signed a document to move under certain conditions. It was a win-win situation. The ability of the project to look outside itself to the surrounding neighborhood was crucial. There had been no similar discourse up to that point, all the conversation had been about renovating the buildings, the flooring, or the style of kitchen cabinets."

Linking the social need of the embattled tenants to the economic needs of the city and the physical need of the neighborhood is the kind of linkage that creates real leverage and unleashes an upward spiral of community repair.

A third corollary of ESP, Ken emphasized to me, was that, "Good design exudes respect and celebrates humanity." He elaborated by saying, "Some argue that design is simply about beauty. I believe that design has to do more than that: it has to help us live together and be a good society."

Joys undreamt

Sometimes, looking at the full extent of all the destruction, I wonder, "How can we ever repair all this?"

That is when, I have found, the urbanist's leadership is so critical. One morning, I was driving with Ken through Braddock, a semi-abandoned steel town. I was looking at the vacant lots while he was explaining all the plans for rebuilding. "You're not paying attention to the vacant lots, are you?" I asked him.

"No," he answered. "People love this place, and we will rebuild it *with* them."

Cantal has, on many occasions, expressed the same optimism about places that struck me as beyond repair. When I first saw it, I thought of Bagnolet, a small city on the edge of Paris, as too fractured to be repaired, yet Cantal was not particularly impressed by the problems. He could feel the citizens's love for their city and see the solution. After Hurricane Katrina had driven black people out of New Orleans and there were clear plans to keep them out, I called Cantal in my frustration at this turn of the wheel of sorting-out the city. "Don't worry," he said. "They will return."

While I am often caught off guard by the calmness of these urban designers, it is true that they know and do things that are out of my competence and experience. I know about the love people have for their places, but I do not know about making buildings, roads, and parks.

Cantal helped the French city of Montauban build a dike. One summer, we visited a site along the river where there were bulldozers moving earth. I watched for a long time as they shaped the safety net that would protect the city in the event of floods. I've never told a bulldozer, "Go, push the earth!"

Watching that huge machine recreate the terrain, I realized how much the city is ours to make. It doesn't happen on the time frame of this week

Figure 4.6: Machines for Montauban. In Montauban, heavy equipment made massive changes in the city to protect it from floods.

Photo credit: Mindy Fullilove.

or even this year. It is a long time frame, and even a generational time frame. I am reminded that Rome, destroyed by barbarians, rose again to become the most beautiful city in the world, but it didn't happen in a day—it took *centuries.*

Therefore, making the city is something we must do with our children and our children's children. My father helped to make Orange a better place and we have inherited his Programmatic Cat. It is in that fashion, guided by our love of place, our dream of the just and beautiful city, and our wish to pass those heartfelt emotions on to generations to come, that we will push the land into forms as yet unimagined and into joys as yet undreamt.

CHAPTER FIVE

Element 3:
Make a Mark

One evening, after thinking it over for some time, Harold decided to go for a walk in the moonlight. There wasn't any moon, and Harold needed moon for a walk. And he needed something to walk on. He made a long straight path so he wouldn't get lost. And he set off on his walk, taking his big purple crayon with him.

—Crockett Johnson, *Harold and the Purple Crayon*

In 1996, when we were invited to Cantal's country home in Saugnac, a small village south of Bordeaux, for our first visit, I didn't know much French. Shortly after we got on the highway, we came to a sign that read, "*Bayonne bis*." I'd seen the word "*bis*" on a house, and it was explained to me that when two houses had the same number, say the number 2, the second one would be called "2 *bis*." I reasoned that the road marked "*Bayonne bis*" would work just as well as the road marked "*Bayonne*." Véronique Héon-Klin, who is half French, finally called Cantal and got the real instructions.

We were forgiven for being hours late for lunch in the large dining room. I couldn't follow all of the conversation that went on during the many hours of the meal. I passed the time looking at the strange paintings, one of a burning church and another of a Cantal-looking guy crazily riding a bicycle. I also reflected on the intriguing collection of boxes, books,

A village in the woods in the world

Figure 5.1: Cantal made a series of posters to highlight the story of Saugnac as a village in the pine forest and in the world. In the photograph above, we can see one of the posters in place in Saugnac. Opposite, we can see the reproduction of a poster that explains how the local river, the Leyre, linked the village to the area and the Atlantic Ocean. As part of animating the village, Cantal showed the film, *Gone with the Wind*. "The Civil War made this place rich," he said, "because the English couldn't get pine products from the American South, so they came here."

Photo credit: Mindy Fullilove.
Scan of the original poster, used courtesy of Michel Cantal-Dupart.

medals, lace doilies, silver dishes, china, games, and maps that beckoned from the shelves and atop the wardrobes.

After lunch, I took my camera and went out the creaky front gate. I looked around the grassy verge that served for parking. Across the road by the church, I saw a sign. It told how the church had served the village, but had been closed in recent years as the population diminished. I looked again at its façade and up to the iron filigree that held the bell. Just a little bit away was another sign that told me that Saugnac was situated along the Leyre, a river that runs through the region and empties into the Atlantic Ocean. Its waters had provided the energy for a mill.

I was excited to tell Cantal about the signs I had discovered. That particular smile, which I came to know over the years we've been road trip

buddies, was his indulgent pleasure in my learning the world, his sense that his newest pupil was really starting to learn. "I made the signs to bring the village back to life, to let people know that small as this place is, we have a place in the world [Figure 5.1]. This village sprang into prosperity during your Civil War, because the Northern blockade of Southern ports meant that Europe couldn't get the pine products it needed for its ships. Suddenly, Gascony's vast pine forests were a rare resource. People became rich overnight. Buildings went up everywhere, my house included. This house was the apothecary. Come, I'll show you the shop and how it opened onto the street."

On dark shelves stood massive glass jars with their paper tags carefully lettered for the herbs they contained, some still full, some holding only the memory of medicine as homeopathic water does. The door from that room opened to a garden. In the back wall of the garden stood a ruined door that had once been the point of access for patients seeking their medicines. It was part of the past that Cantal was honoring with his signs.

As urbanists, we make signs to start a new dialogue between people and their spaces. Whether we are noting history or current events, beauty or horror, we are indicating that the space is important. Signs are the beginning of the change we need to make.

The third element of urban restoration, make a mark, involves:

- Shifting movement from going through to going to;
- Placing the mark in the right spot; and
- Bridging to the future.

Shifting movement from *going through* to *going to*

Taste for place

One day, in Barcelona, Cantal said those magic words, "I want to show you something." I hopped in the car and Cantal drove us down to the port. He parked on a sidewalk, and we crossed over to Christopher Columbus Tower. He was beaming as we got in the elevator. "From here," he explained, "you can see the whole of Barcelona—the port, the neighborhoods, the mountains. You will get the logic of the city."

The glass windows of the tower were etched to identify the landmarks. "This tower is set in a circle, and circles are important to cities. As a citizen, I know the form of a circle. When I see a circle, I feel included. If I get some place and I can't read the signs, I feel excluded. I lose my taste for the place. When we're working in distressed neighborhoods, we know that the residents have the sense that their neighborhoods don't work any more. We're trying to help people reconnect with the taste—*le goût*—for their space."

Le goût is something a Frenchman says with layers of meaning. Children are taught at home and at school to have a *taste* for smelly cheese, crunchy baguettes, organ meat, flaky croissants, yogurt, olives, and perfectly ripe fruit. They are expected to eat what is put in front of them and they are taught how to enjoy the sensations that pop up in their mouths.

French children are also taught about place. Once, when we stopped by her house in Nantes, Cantal's daughter-in-law, Christelle Nory, pulled out some brightly colored posters. Her face beamed as she displayed them to me. "I found these in an antique store—they are old classroom posters, teaching us to love the city. You see the house, the street, the port, the hospital, and the farm? These posters were displayed in our classrooms and helped us to learn to love where we lived."

The French are, finally, taught to link taste to place. Of this last, Cantal (1994, 68) wrote, "If you taste a vintage, on the site, in cellars or caves, regardless of the season, whether the vine is cut or in full bloom, your taste will never forget what happened at that time. All you have to do is taste the wine, no matter where you're drinking, to remember the spirit of that place where you first had it."

This visceral never-to-be forgotten pleasure of place, then, is what we are seeking to restore with these marks on the landscape. As Ken explained to me, making a mark is an important strategy for changing the sorted-out city so that the place outsiders *move through* can assert its claim to be a place outsiders may, and perhaps should, *go to*. One who *moves through* might be perceived as an enemy, a terrible consequence of the sorting-out system. One who *goes to* is a guest, and that is a status of honor and respect. The mark, like breaking bread, is a symbol of welcome. No matter its nature—happy, sad, angry—the mark shares the here and now with any who care to *go to*.

Art calls us

Terri Baltimore, the chief organizer of the Hillscapes project, is what people in Pittsburgh call "nebby," meaning always wanting to know what's going on. She combines that curiosity with a passion for improvement. Once she learns about a new tool for neighborhood development, she can't wait to see how it will work. One of the great joys of my relationship with Pittsburgh has been that she always takes me to see new projects—both her own and others—on every visit I make.

On one visit, she showed me a set of photographs placed in the windows of empty buildings. In New York, when the South Bronx was burning down from planned shrinkage, city officials cynically placed paintings of windows with curtains and window boxes along the train route, attempting

Figure 5.2: Jazz window. Photographer Ray Gerard made photos of local jazz artists and the Times Project put them in the windows of vacant buildings in the Hill District. The idea was to create the illusion that a jam session was going on.

Photo credit: Mindy Fullilove.

to hide the destruction from the commuters rushing home to the suburbs. There is no better illustration of *going through*.

Terri's windows were quite the opposite. Hallie Binder, director of the Times Project, a group that did arts projects downtown, wanted to do a project on the Hill and approached the Hill District Consensus Group, the Hill District Community Development Group, and the Hill District Community Collaborative looking for partners for a collaborative initiative that would open the conversation on public art. Artists from other communities came to support the effort. Robert Qualters, who made a remarkable set of paintings that captured the memories of the residents of Braddock for RDCollab's design for The Avenue, was part of the conversation (see Figure 8.7, Buildings as Neighbors). People talked about what they did, how they did it, with the hope of restoring a positive vibe in their community.

Terri saw it as a way to take back space on the Centre Avenue corridor. At the site of the West Funeral Home, and with the owner's permission, the project placed a set of windows called House of Jazz. Photographer Ray Gerard took pictures of famous local jazz artists and placed them in the windows and doors (Figure 5.2). The idea was to create the impression that the artists were just hanging out, having a jam session at a local joint. The windows were both reassuring and accusatory. They left a "So? What are you going to do about it?" hanging in the air. It was no surprise to me that architects as sensitive as Dan and Ken picked up that challenge and wove it into the fiber of The Legacy. In that way, the jazz windows made Centre Avenue a place to *go to*.

At other locations in the Hill, the art took other forms. Local artist Jorge Myers wrote "Wylie Avenue Days" on a door and installed art pieces there. Perhaps because they were so lovely, each time he'd put one up, it would get stolen. The last was bolted to the building, but it still disappeared. At another site, children helped paint a door with street signs, buildings, butterflies, and flowers. When the project was completed, the group had a wonderful party at the Kaufman Center.

I asked Terri what she thought these projects contributed. "Denys always says," she replied, "you can be in a community that's in transition and there can be beauty on many levels. Even now, there are people doing it all around the neighborhood in a similar fashion, creating placeholders for the beauty to come. It reminds us that art is part of the culture of the neighborhood."

My all-time favorite of the marks in the Hill was the brainchild of Jorge Myers and Stephanie Flom. They had two goals: to make something beautiful and to do something with a vacant lot. They took some gravel and a bench and transformed the space into the Magic Penny Garden (Figure 5.3). Because it was a large lot connecting two major avenues—Centre and Wylie—and it was on a slope, the path created a line of perspective, a

Figure 5.3: Magic Penny Garden. This garden, created by Jorge Myers and Stephanie Flom, was a pleasant place to sit to watch the crowds go by.

Photo credit: Mindy Fullilove.

sweep of connection, that I loved from the first time I saw it, peopled with Hill folk who were enjoying a bench as a place to soak in the sun and pass the time. They said I might take their picture and it is one I treasure. The bench was set in the middle of the park and off the street, but at a pleasant distance for people watching. "People were not afraid to sit, and people were not afraid to pass," Terri said.

She related, "What was really great was that the lot across the street also became active. One summer, students from Carnegie Mellon University built a stage. There was jazz, poetry slams, and singing throughout the summer. People would put their chairs in the Magic Penny Garden and enjoy the shows. Then the lot evolved into the Ujamaa Marketplace, an outdoor market that is open from mid-summer to early fall."

It was not just marks in lots by then, but actual buildings, including The Legacy and the new library at Centre and Kirkpatrick. This shifted the dynamic of the neighborhood. People who had spent their days at Centre and Kirkpatrick were forced off the corner. They settled into the Magic Penny Garden. That made it a place to be avoided, especially at night. Terri shared, "Ultimately, the community decided to shut it down. The bench was taken out, and the lot ceased to be a park."

"I'm not sure about that choice," I said to Terri. "How are we to unsort the city if we chase away the 'bad' element? Don't they have a right to the city, too? Not that they should make others afraid, but I think they shouldn't be excluded."

I told Terri a story about Cantal, who had faced such a situation in the plaza by the metro station Charenton-École, alongside the busy National 6 highway. The existing plaza was a classic *non-lieu*, a place for parking large trucks, where young hooligans had taken over the one bench. Cantal (1994, 62) wrote in *Merci La Ville!*,

If you're going to improve a square next a main road, you have to understand that a compromise is in order. Reconciling the heavily traf-ficked road with the plaza was straightforward: I depressed the plaza one meter, to create two phonic worlds, one for cars, one for pedestri-ans. To solve the problem of the young men who were monopolizing the bench, I put in 12 benches. These interventions worked.

Cantal and I stopped by the park at dusk one day on our way home from another project. "Let's take five minutes and see this place," he proposed. The park had a beautiful music kiosk at one end and a fountain in honor of King Henry IV at the other. We descended a short flight of steps to get to the large open space of the plaza that was surrounded by benches, placed all around the edge. We had the place to ourselves, and

we strolled around, appreciating the separateness from the street created by the grading of the site. "That fountain was a gift from the city of Pau," Cantal reminded me. King Henry IV served as a link between the two cities—one where he was born (Pau) and the other where he visited with his love, Gabrielle d'Estrées (Charenton).

I was sad when the Magic Penny Garden ceased to be a park, but I noticed that it did not return to being a lot. The path had been worn into the ground, a marker made by many feet. It reflects the light, carrying our gaze up the hill, even more intense now that the gravel has washed away and the bench with its interesting denizens is gone, too. You can't keep a good mark down: they have a life that is long and important.

And sometimes this life is transcontinental. I was sitting in Cantal's class at the National Conservatory of Arts and Trades one day during a set of presentations by his urbanism students. I was captivated by a series of photographs of the Cheshire Cat painted high on walls all over Paris. A pack rat by nature, I love series. I kept

Figure 5.4: That famous smile. Cheshire Cat in New York (top) and Paris (bottom). Photo credits: Mindy Fullilove.

looking up, but the Cheshire Cat eluded me. On a trip a year or so later, I happened to spot him, sitting enigmatically high above the street, around the corner from the Pompidou Center. A few years later, I was parking my car on West 18th Street, near the corner by Eighth Avenue. I was fiddling with something, which made me linger by a fence, which made me look closely at the fence, which me made look through the fence, and there was that famous smile. I ran around the corner to buy a disposable camera—I had the feeling I had to hurry before he disappeared, starting with his tail. And then one day, I was walking on West 26th Street and there *she* was, Cheshire Angel!

Placing the Mark

Stick it

In 2000, when I was in Paris for the summer to learn about cities, I would show up at Cantal's office every morning, a big grin on my face. He would give me projects to do: go to the Museum of the City of Paris, go to the Center of Documentation and get my book, *La Ville à Livre Ouvert*, go to the Loire (just get out of my hair—he didn't say that, but my mother used to in the summer when I was underfoot wondering what to do next). One day it was, "Go read about Sixtus V," as he handed me *Design of Cities* by Edmund Bacon (1974). Trivia fans will be interested to know that I know Roberta Brandes Gratz, who knew Jane Jacobs, who knew Edmund Bacon, who is the father of Kevin Bacon, giving me a Bacon Number of 4. Just saying.

The story I was to study was about Pope Sixtus V, who spent years in frustration as a cardinal, dreaming about Rome but powerless to make it better. When he became pope in 1585, he knew his time was short. The worried and ailing Sixtus was focused on bringing coherence to a pilgrimage route that included seven major churches in Rome. To create a system of movement among these churches, he strategically placed four obelisks. Over the succeeding eighty years, the development of Rome organized around these four points, emerging at the beginning of the Renaissance ready to claim its place in the pantheon of great urban centers.

Bacon (1974, 131), who served as the executive director of the Philadelphia Planning Commission for many years, noted that "Sixtus achieved far fewer actual architectural changes during the five years of his reign than any democratic city government could achieve today. It was the inherent power to his idea, not his political influence, that caused the chain of events which followed... the single point in space can become a powerful design force, bringing order out of chaos."

It was not until I started to study landscape design that I could really appreciate the point Bacon was making: that a single point in space might become a force in the world. I learned that it is literal, this shaping of space. I take a stick and I put it in the stream and the water goes around the stick. I have changed the stream, and maybe the world if the chaos theorists are to be believed. That is the power of the sign, the mark. When I know what mark to make and I know where to make the mark, I shift the world—I ease grief, I excite the visitor, and I relax the passersby. But I make that change because things are really changed as a result. Archimedes once said, "Give me a long enough lever and a place to stand and I will move the earth."

The urbanist just needs four obelisks to give the world its most beautiful city. But the obelisks literally changed the streaming of the city, making it flow towards beauty. That is why Cantal spends so much time walking the terrain, in search of the messages it is sending to him. We were hanging out at Saugnac one day, and he picked up a stick and started to walk around the yard, pointing it at the ground. "I am a dowser," he said in all seriousness.

"I know," I replied.

No more redevelopment

"It is the understanding of the site forces that helps us place the mark," Ken explained to me one day. Site forces are many—they include the terrain, the other buildings and objects, the way people use the space, the history of the space, and the hopes for the space. Forces are represented in math as arrows that have length and direction, and they obey the rules of the universe like the law of gravity. Architecture, which is rooted in physics, is fully cognizant of the implication of force acting on one's building.

Urbanism, equally rooted in physics and steeped in the wisdom of architecture, searches for the ways in which these forces act in the city.

The Hill's most enduring mark, made in 1968, reveals much about this (Glasco 2011). That is the year a billboard was erected at the intersection of Centre Avenue and Crawford Street (Fullilove and Baltimore 2012). As former Hill District Councilmember Sala Udin related the story to me, urban renewal had torn up the Lower Hill. Civil rights leaders had been told that the program would lead to real improvements, but they soon realized that whatever the improvements might be, the black community would not be included—the reality of "urban renewal is Negro removal" had hit home. And more "Negro removal" was being proposed, in the form of the demolition of the Hill up to Kirkpatrick Street, about sixteen blocks to the east.

Frankie Pace, a religious woman who sold gospel sheet music in a store one block east of Crawford Street, in the very next block to be demolished, started a campaign to stop urban renewal. She organized a billboard that was erected at an intersection that had once been nestled in the interior of the ghetto and was now located at its naked edge.

The billboard read, "Attention: No Redevelopment Beyond This Point!" But what is important is that no billboard would have been placed at that intersection prior to urban renewal: there was no distant viewpoint from which to appreciate what it had to say. A billboard is the object of a vista, and deep inside a dense urban neighborhood, there is no such sweep of the eye. It was the bulldozing of the Lower Hill that opened the perspective from downtown to the doorstep of the ghetto, now at Crawford Street.

A march was called. People assembled on the steps of St. Benedict the Moor, the church just opposite the billboard. They chanted, "Not another inch!" and marched in the face of death threats. Their fervent opposition defeated the extension of urban renewal and saved the midsection of the Hill from the bulldozer. The site of the billboard has since become the site of a civil rights memorial, called Freedom Corner. As of the writing of this book, it still served as an assembly point for all kinds of marches for peace, justice, and civil and human rights.

During our ongoing conversation about site forces, Ken and I discussed the pivot that I'd observed in Pittsburgh urbanism between 1997 and 2012. What had made that pivot? I was wondering. "We pivoted in

Figure 5.5: No Redevelopment Beyond This Point! This billboard was erected at the intersection of Centre Avenue and Crawford Street to protest a proposal for more redevelopment.

Photo credit: Billboard inscribed "Attention City Hall and U.R.A. No Redevelopment Beyond This Point! We Demand Low Income Housing for the Lower, Hill, C.C.H.D.R., N.A.A.C.P., Poor People's Campaign, Model Cities," at Crawford Street near the intersection of Centre Avenue, Hill District, 1969, by Charles "Teenie" Harris, American, 1908-1998, black-and-white, Kodak Safety Film, H: 4 in. x W: 5. in. (10.20 x 12.70 cm.). Carnegie Museum of Art, Pittsburgh. Heinz Family Fund. 2001-35.9463.

1968," he replied emphatically, "when the billboard went up at Centre and Crawford. That's the moment of triumph over old-style, top-down urban planning. The community stopped urban renewal, saved the city, and created the path we're on now."

Bridging to the future

In January 2000, Bob and I moved from Hoboken, a very urban city in New Jersey, to Englewood, one of the state's many modest towns. Six months later, in July, we left for Paris. Returning after fifty-six days of immersion in urbanism, I found I didn't want to live in a big suburban house. I had loved the tiny attic apartment in Paris, and I missed the ceaseless cacophony of Rue St. André des Arts. The deep quiet of Liberty Road seemed oppressive. In October, I celebrated my fiftieth birthday with a party that filled the house and its yards. It was a beautiful, warm fall day. We barbecued in the backyard while godchildren, grandchildren, and young friends played all around the yard, house, and porch. The kids then organized a play, and we all sat on the steps of the front porch to enjoy the spectacle.

After the play, we ate ice cream and cake, and I opened my gifts. I got many wonderful presents that day, but I especially remember that Sebastian Quinn, a leader in the organizing at Hampshire College, gave me our house number, 488, carved in mahogany and outlined in blue. By the time the party was over, I knew where I was, and I had taken the first tentative steps forward in creating a satisfying way of life.

In 2004, I enrolled in the certificate program in landscape design at the New York Botanical Garden. When I took my first design class in 2005, my yard was my assignment. The first exercise was to examine what worked and what didn't. It got me thinking about the space and how we'd come to live in it. We regularly had parties in the yard, and our guests spread out. Perhaps the great truth of my garden was that it was a subsidiary of that of my neighbor, the redoubtable Eleanor Harvey. In return for being part of the sweep of grass she liked so well, my friends and family could romp through her three-acre estate.

Nearly every time I've gone to study cities with Cantal, we've ended up at Saugnac. Cantal's approach to gardening was to compromise with nature, gently encouraging some transplants including a grapevine and a climbing rose, but also accepting the oak and the pine trees that had volunteered to be part of his yard.

I liked his studied casualness. I thought a lot about Saugnac as I was walking my own grounds, trying to imagine what I needed to do for the final assignment, when I was to present a garden design.

Suddenly, I felt a profound horror of the suburban garden.

I thought I knew what my teacher wanted me to produce, and I couldn't do it. On the last day of my class, I arrived with my plan scribbled on photographs. I watched my classmates unfurl their designs, beautifully drawn, carefully considered. My teacher was enthusiastic in her praise for their accomplishments.

My design—I am perhaps being generous in calling it that—had embraced what was. My teacher looked at me. "You did such a good job defining the problems," she scolded. "I thought you'd solve them in a much better manner."

The other students looked away, unwilling to meet my eyes.

But every gardener, Joe Eck says, has her own garden. I never fully realized the force of this statement until I visited the magnificent garden Wayne Winterrrowd and he created at North Hills. Martha Stittelman, my classmate from medical school, and I were roving the grounds with her granddaughter Anna when we chanced upon a man who beamed welcome at us. "Would you be Mr. Eck?" I asked, delighted that chance had created an opportunity for me to meet my hero.

"I am," he replied.

I explained that I was so inspired by *Elements of Garden Design* that I was writing a book about the elements of urban restoration. I introduced Martha and Anna. He was very happy that we had brought a little child to see the garden. Somehow, we started talking about chickens, and he said he loved all birds, all animals, and all living things. And that thought led to his reaching out to stroke a lovely plant just at the edge of the driveway. "This plant," and he kindly supplied its Latin name, "is very rare—there are only four in North America. It is endangered. Wayne and I got it when it was this big."

Figure 5.6: A greenhouse at North Hill. This is a photo of the lower greenhouse at North Hill Garden, created by Joe Eck and Wayne Winterrowd.

Photo credit: Mindy Fullilove.

He showed us with his hand that it had been about two inches tall, a little bitty thing. It had grown magnificently. "And in the winter?" I asked.

"Oh, it goes in the greenhouse, of course."

Sadness passed over his face. Wayne Winterrowd's death, not quite a year before, had been sudden and heartbreaking. Joe Eck was finding his feet, with the support of many plant and garden lovers, but, without his darling husband, it was hard. Standing with him, in his sorrow, talking about Wayne and their shared love of plants, I knew with certainty that I was in a garden of plantsmen.

The garden at 488 was something else, something I could not articulate in 2005. It was what I might now call a garden of diffusion, to acknowledge Eleanor's organization of our shared space and her reciprocal permission for us to spread out over her lawns when we gathered to celebrate the changing seasons. This joint yard was dominated by flowing lawns with occasional thickets of small trees and shrubs to provide variation and interest.

It was an amazing space for parties. Molly and I invented a fall fair with urban competitions like pumpkin-carving, autumn crowns, best schmoozer, and best bottle of wine for less than twenty dollars. We also had field games, like sack races and an egg toss. People proudly displayed their Fullilove Fall Fair ribbons and medals. I will always remember the year we went out after dark had fallen and discovered that a particularly spectacular set of pumpkins were grinning on the picnic table. Molly and I lit candles and got out the video camera. She made a dazzling movie of the spectacle of light flickering through ingenious eyes and mouths and noses.

Then in the spring, we would open our barn, shoo away the squirrels, and begin to decorate in the spirit of the season. Suddenly, on the special day of the Molly Rose Show, we were poets, musicians, dancers, and comedians. The barn rocked with laughter as we reveled in our homemade acts and modest talents. I mostly recited poetry, but one year, I ventured into camp songs Lily had taught me; I was overreaching, but Lily got me through. My Molly Rose Show trophies sit proudly in my office window where I can always see them.

These gatherings, in which about a hundred people spread across the lawns, were possible in the system of our garden—Eleanor's and mine—where lawns predominated and there were no borders. I did want a bit of screening from the one section of the road that made me feel too exposed to driversby. I found it was possible to extend the thickets where that was needed. I augmented one with a line of forsythia, designed to provide a very loose weave of green between the patio and Liberty Road. When I started to write this book in 2009, I installed myself on the patio. The lacy forsythia worked exactly as I had thought it would, creating a feeling of security that nourished my writing, while not creating more enclosure than the open plan, or my claustrophobia, could tolerate.

By then I had deepened my education in plants and I had developed a longing for the geometry of shrubs. I didn't know where to put them, though, as the density of shrubs could conflict with the open diffusion plan. I realized, while sitting on the patio wondering what the dickens to write about, that the sides of the buildings might be happily filigreed without causing enclosure. There, I might have hydrangeas, holly, spicebush, and a million other delightful plants. There is almost always a "yeah, but," and in my case, it was that both Eleanor and I had black walnut trees, a species that is jealous of its territory and produces a poison that destroys most other plants. So, the million possible shrubs were reduced to a handful, and even they struggled. I sigh when I remember the sad state of my beloved hydrangeas.

That was the last summer I spent on Liberty Road, as that was the year Bob and I ended our marriage. I was relieved to leave the quiet, sad to say goodbye to my forsythia, and happy to imagine life without a black walnut tree.

We sold the house in April 2010. The last thing on the moving truck was my sign.

I learned that if a sign opens a path to the future, it is a path of exploration and invention, a path that benefits from our openness to learning, and a path in which different ideas of full and tidy will meet in conflict and search for reconciliation. Just as I had to learn what "*bis*" meant, so I have had to study the many signs I've encountered, determine what is signed and what is signified, and decide which of the possible directions the signs offer might be best to follow.

As it turns out, Molly had organized our second annual Orange Place-making Conference to be held the day after that final move from 488. Cantal's proposal to light the bridges and tunnels, made a year earlier when he came to help us with the Heart of Orange Plan, was on our minds. Molly had worked with Mike Malbrough and Jody Leight on developing

Figure 5.7: Spray-chalking the just and beautiful city. Shirley Torho, who was celebrating her birthday, spray-chalking a tunnel in Orange, New Jersey, during the University of Orange's Placemaking II in 2009.

Photo credit: Mindy Fullilove.

activities that might begin to express that vision. Mike had proposed that we use washable spray chalk to enliven one of the tunnels, using a set of African symbols as the basic images.

Jody suggested that we tie streamers with messages on one of the bridges. Speaking with her authority as a lawyer, she said, "We write something on the streamers and then tie them to the fences of the bridge. That's an expression of our ideas—we have that freedom here in the US—and it's protected by the First Amendment."

Thirty people of all ages took part in the fun of making a mark. Our streamers, in their varied colors, waved gaily in the breeze of the bridge, with an interesting array of messages about life, love, and the city.

Our spray chalk amended the walls of the tunnel with yellow, pink, and blue words and symbols. The city planner, Valerie Jackson, hated what we'd done and sent painters to cover it over. Molly went by and told them how sad she was to see it go. One of the painters said, "We know. We are, too. But we're painting it white so that the next time you do it, it will show up better."

Tiny pieces of our spray painting were still there, three years later, untouched by rain or painters' brushes, serving as reminders of a day and an event that enlivened our city. Our first amendment—the change we made to the tunnel—will be followed by many more, and people will be excited to *go to* Orange.

That is the future towards which our signs point.

PART III

Create

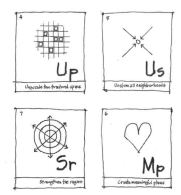

4 Up — Unpuzzle the fractured space	**5** Us — Unslum all neighborhoods
7 Sr — Strengthen the region	**6** Mp — Create meaningful places

CHAPTER SIX

Element 4:
Unpuzzle the Fractured Space

The magistrate shook his head, for he did not know what else to do, and after thinking a long while he said, "I won't decide this case."

"But you must," the neighbor began.

"No," the magistrate said, "instead I shall give you a riddle and whoever answers best shall win. Agreed?"

The farmer said, "Agreed," and the neighbor nodded. Both men were certain they could easily answer a riddle.

So the magistrate said, "Answer me this. What is the swiftest thing in the world? And what is the sweetest thing? And what is the richest? Return tomorrow to tell me your answers and this case will be closed."

—Eastern European Folktale, *The Clever Girl*

In 2004, the Community Research Group (CRG), my research team, started a project called "City Life Is Moving Bodies" or CLIMB. It was a project to increase physical, social, and economic activity in Northern Manhattan by building a hiking trail from Central Park through Highbridge Park. Every year, we held a party called "Hike the Heights," which started with hiking from various parks to the party site in Highbridge.

In 2005, I was a hike leader, and my mission was to get fifty children to the party.

That doesn't sound so bad, except that we had to cross one of those speedways owned by cars where crossing poses a risk to life and limb.

Across the speedway...

1. Molly: "We are going to hike through the woods to a party."

2. Everybody heads up the stairs to Edgecombe Avenue.

3. Molly: "We have to be very careful crossing this big street."

4. Going through the woods.

Figure 6.1: This series of photographs are from Hike the Heights 2 in 2006. We set off up a set of stairs from the bandshell at Jackie Robinson Park, north on Edgecombe Avenue. We paused for the light at 155th. Molly led the troop across while the rest of the adults formed a defensive line between the traffic and the children. We plunged into Highbridge Forest at 157th Street, the beginning of the Croton Aqueduct Trail. We emerged near the Terrace, where the children joined in the games and other fun.

Photo credits: Amelia Krales. Courtesy of the CRG Collection.

and through the woods

5. Molly and kids arriving.

6. The party!

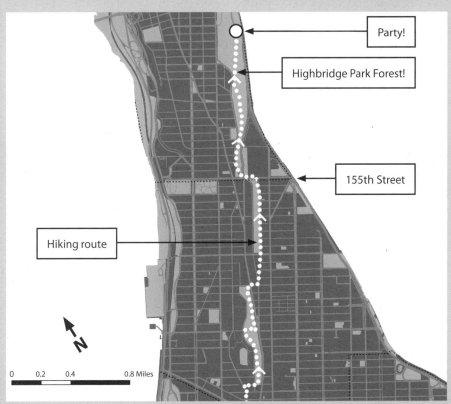

Party!

Highbridge Park Forest!

155th Street

Hiking route

N

0   0.2   0.4   0.8 Miles

The impassability of 155th Street might be the reason it has endured as the border between Washington Heights and Harlem. It is a street cut by highways on both ends and lined with ceremonial places, like churches and a large cemetery, that have few connections to the street. I once asked Harlem planner Lionel McIntyre what might be done with 155th Street and he just shook his head.

Of course, it wasn't just 155th Street that posed a problem, but also the intersection of that heavily traveled street with the access road to and from the Harlem River Drive. Here, cars traversed at top speed, using their momentum to pivot into the turn where we would be crossing. I consulted with Molly and the other adults with me. We agreed that we would put ourselves between the children and the traffic and hope for the best (Figure 6.1).

The next day, I told Lourdes Hernández-Cordero, a member of our CRG team and the leader of CLIMB, about the problem. After she had defended her doctoral dissertation and became *Dr.* Hernández-Cordero, she had gone to Paris to study with Cantal for two months. She called that time her "postdoctoral fellowship in urbanism." She traveled with Cantal to many cities. She also used her time in Paris to see all that was going on. She loved to tell us about a festival of music that occupied every street corner and performance venue while she was there.

So, it is no surprise that she responded to my story by saying, "Let's get Cantal."

There is a game Molly taught me to play. Each person has an object in her hand and says to the person next to her, "This is a ___" and names what's in her hand. Then everyone says, "A what?" And each person repeats the first sentence. This happens again. Then, the next time the statement "This is a ___" is made, each person passes the object she's holding to her neighbor while saying, "Oh, a ___." But the "Oh, a ___" names the object that she's just received, which was in her neighbor's hand previously. I found this game so confusing that I had to play it many times before I got the pattern and wasn't puzzled anymore.

"This is a puzzle."

"A what?"

"A puzzle."

"A what?"

"A puzzle."

"A what? Oh, a plan!"

Lourdes and I had a puzzle. What we needed was a plan.

In urban restoration, a plan that can unpluzzle the space is key to progress. The fourth element of urban restoration is to unpuzzle the fractured space. Three tasks are key:

- Opening the perspective so that we can see;
- Opening connections so that we can move freely; and
- Sharing resources so that we have equity.

Opening the perspective

Unpuzzling 155th Street

In February 2007, Cantal and Marie-Dominique came to help us with the puzzle of 155th Street. We hiked the whole CLIMB trail, up from Morningside one day and down from Dyckman Street the next. The second day was bitterly cold, and our stalwart group had to brave terribly icy paths.

"Nobody but us is crazy enough to do this," began Cantal, as he shared his reflections on our trail. "In the guidebooks, Europeans are advised not to go above 96th Street, except for the Cloisters. That museum is well known and greatly loved in Europe.[1] Your trail should go from Central Park to the Cloisters. Do you see how this helps to fill out the giraffe?"

He showed us how linking to Fort Tryon Park on the western side of the neighborhood gave the giraffe a real head (Figure 6.2) (See also Chapter Seven, 179-81). "You can make that trail easily enough—that's not the problem. The problem," he said, "is that the parks are disconnected from the surrounding city. In order to connect with the city, you have to have east-west connectors every five blocks or so."

Some of the connections he was bringing to our attention were obvious, even famous. The High Bridge, the oldest surviving bridge in New York City, was an historic structure that connected Manhattan to the Bronx. At 158th Street, there was another rotting staircase, the John T. Brush Stairway, given to the city in 1913 by the New York Giants. The team played at the Polo Grounds, located alongside Highbridge Park. Though barred by chains and fences, the John T. Brush Stairway was so useful to the

Figure 6.2: Cantal's giraffe. The proposal for east-west linkages to strengthen our north-south trail from Central Park to the Cloisters.

Plan: Atelier Cantal-Dupart. Courtesy of the CRG Collection.

neighborhood that people made their way around the barriers. They understood the magic that Roger Angell had described when it was a way to get to the Giants's stadium:

> It's the only ballpark built against a cliff—Coogan's Bluff—so that a patron could walk downhill to a seat. You came slowly down the John T. Brush stairs to the cool of the evening, looking down at the flags and the tiers of brilliant floodlights on the stands and, beyond them, at the softer shimmer of lights on the Harlem River. (Epting 2009)

We had also found buried stairs at the northern end of Jackie Robinson Park. One snowy day, we had gone exploring in this unused corner of the park and our tracks had been the first to be made in the fresh white powder. On other days, the traces of steps beckoned us to try it as a route to Bradhurst Avenue.

Cantal agreed that we had found important connectors, but he was talking about this as the core idiom of the CLIMB trail: east-west connections every five blocks, twenty or more over the course of the hundred blocks from Central Park to Dyckman Street. "The logic of New York City," he explained, "is to cluster in small neighborhoods.

People get their food, they find the subway, and they meet friends fairly close to home. They don't go for long treks. If they want to go to the park, they're going to go to the park close to home. Therefore, you have to bring every bit of the city into a close relationship with the park, with easy and welcoming access. You're counting on entrances at the ends of each park for people to go north or south, but that will only meet the needs of a small number of people. It's in the dense network of streets that you will really open the parks so that all the people can use them as part of their daily lives, getting the exercise and enjoyment of nature that you have in mind."

It was a lot to digest.

E. B. White, perhaps most famous as coauthor of *The Elements of Style*, had written an essay called *Here Is New York* (White 2000). He had made the point that New Yorkers live on their block. Moving two blocks, he observed, put one in an entirely different neighborhood. It was the micro-organization of the city that Cantal was calling to our attention. Each small nugget of the city needed to be attached to the parks in order for our Long Trail to work.

"Cantal," I asked, ever mindful of the little children that had to cross 155th Street, "what do we do about getting the children across the intersection?"

"Instead of taking the upper roadway, go under the highway and up the stairs. At least you eliminate the most dangerous leg of the crossing."

"Why didn't we think of that?" I asked Lourdes.

"Because it was a puzzle," she replied, "and he solved it for us."

To riff on that sentiment, Cantal *unpuzzled* our space for us.

The massive fractures had disoriented us, the vacant spaces scared us, and the invisibility left us with no clear idea of what to do. Cantal could see the parts in ways that we couldn't. He did us the great favor of showing us how the pieces fit together.

The triumph of Vaux-le-Vicomte

One Sunday in July 2000, while I was in Paris for my urbanism immersion, Cantal called to say my favorite words, "I want to show you something."

On the way to the surprise, he told me a story. "There was a man named Fouquet who managed the affairs of Louis the XIV, the famous Sun

Everything is in the perspective...

Everything aligns with everything else.

Figure 6.3: The garden at Vaux-le-Vicomte is organized along lines of perspective. But not everything is revealed. The long sightline to Hercules on the horizon makes it appear that one could walk directly there. But a canal, at a lower level, transects that line and makes the path quite different from what one thinks while looking at the perspective from the vantage point of the château.

Photo credits: Mindy Fullilove.

SURPRISE!

Canal is invisible at a distance.

As you get closer the canal is revealed.

King. Fouquet wanted to create a château for himself that would delight the world. He called it Vaux-le-Vicomte. Fouquet recruited the world's best architects, sculptors, and landscape designers to help him achieve this vision. The man who developed the garden was André Le Nôtre. He had some new ideas that were just being tried in France and he was given carte blanche to design the garden using these innovations. When the château and gardens were finished, Fouquet invited the king and the court for a party. The magnificence of the château and its park awed the guests: they had never seen anything like it.

"Louis XIV was furious that his finance minister had a better house and garden than he had. He sent D'Artagnan and the Musketeers to arrest Fouquet in Nantes. Fouquet spent the rest of his life in prison. The king then hired André Le Nôtre and the other artists who'd worked on Vaux-le-Vicomte to create Versailles, a grander but not more beautiful, version of what Fouquet had achieved at Vaux-le-Vicomte. Today, we are going to see the original, Vaux-le-Vicomte."

As we started to walk through the garden, Cantal said, "What I want you to understand in this garden is the use of perspective, the directed gaze. Look—off in the distance—you can see Hercules at the top of the rise. Our eyes are drawn to that spot by the organization—very precise—of the landscape."

We walked a little further, and he pointed back to the château. "This edge of the garden matches precisely with the window, and that edge is matched precisely with the edge of the house. Every single item in this garden is in a precise alignment with other parts of the garden. His original drawings were lost, so we don't know how he did it." He shook his head in disbelief at this achievement. "We do know that at every point in this garden, we are in the perspective." As we proceeded around the garden, he pointed over and over at the linkages that had been made between every here and every there.

Vaux-le-Vicomte is a place of visual wonders (Brix 2004). Stables flank the entrance to the château. As one advances into the garden—on the other side of the château—the distance between the stables and the château closes until the stables appear to be wings of the mansion, tripling its apparent mass. In the other direction, this advance into the garden takes one closer and closer to the statue of Hercules in the distance.

Or so one thinks.

Suddenly, there is a sharp drop, invisible from just a few feet back, and a canal cuts across the garden, wide enough to row a boat, wide enough that the walk to Hercules must be rerouted to the left or right. And then you have to trudge a ways to get around the water. "It is essential to understand that the secret to perspective is *not* to show everything," Cantal emphasized. "That would be boring. The secret is the dance of the obvious and the hidden, that's what makes it such a pleasure."

As we marched through the garden, Cantal showed me wonder after wonder. He did not stop to admire the carefully clipped parterres or the legendary lion statues. He focused on the spaces of the garden, carefully noting distances and connections among the elements. I had not been on many tours like that, tours of form rather than content, garden contra dancing in which we twirled to see the perspective from every possible angle (Figure 6.3).

Perspective is often associated with the imposition of imperial will on territory (Orsenna 2000). This quality is derived from the opening of a long view that permits the lord of the land to indicate the extent and power of his domain. Or shoot a canon. At one point, Cantal pointed up to the window overlooking the garden. "In such a garden, the king could look out the window and see all the women: they all belonged to him, *droit de siegneur*, the king's privilege."

OK, that was gross.

But Cantal's larger point was that André Le Nôtre's use of perspective had a property other than the display of power and subjugation. Perspective was a method for bringing the parts of a landscape into relationship with each other.

Perspective was a point that Cantal, having so carefully taught me, emphasized all the time. He was always thinking and working to create perspective, to open perspective, to be in perspective. At the heart of his urbanism is perspective. It speaks to our desire to be here and there at the same time, to be nurtured by the foreground and beckoned by the distance. To be safe and to be free in Western society are the two great goods. Cantal believes that inscribing them in the landscape by the use of perspective helps people to live that way.

When things are in perspective, we can see clearly.

Opening connections

In 2005, Bob and I took a group of family, friends, and coworkers on a Cantalian voyage of discovery, out of which we made the film *Raccommodage: Mending Our Destiny* (Kaufman 2007a). We visited nine cities in three countries and filmed in three languages. Molly, as I have mentioned in Chapter 3, was the director. How lucky were we to find the trilingual and widely traveled Frederic Colier to be our editor?

During the filming, Cantal took us to visit a cooperative housing complex in Marseilles that had massive problems. Joining a class that was visiting the project, we listened to extensive explanations of the renovations that were being made to the buildings. With the excitement of someone about to see a prizefight, I waited for Cantal to put in his two cents.

Cantal opened by telling a story about visiting there a few years earlier. He traveled to Marseilles by train and went to the taxi stand just outside the station. When he said the address, the taxi driver said, "I don't know where that is, maybe you better take the next taxi."

Cantal got furious because he knew the refusal had to do with the stigma attached to the area. After all, the taxi driver had a map of the city. He insisted that that man take him to his destination and lectured him on civility. "You don't know who I am. You are supposed to be an ambassador of your city, not someone spreading hate." In spite of this stern lecture, when they arrived, the man wanted to drop Cantal off outside the complex. "I don't know where the building is," he said.

Cantal was apoplectic by that point. "I am going to building 'H' and this is 'A'—we'll drive and look!"

When he got out of the taxi, he paid the fare, but said, "I will not give you a tip because your behavior was unconscionable."

In telling that story, Cantal set the premise for having the whole city in mind: the real issue, he made clear, was that the neighborhood had been so abandoned by the city that those key ambassadors, the taxi drivers, might treat it with contempt. Then he turned his attention to the buildings. He said with characteristic energy and insistence, "It's *not* the buildings."

As we had just listened to an hour of minutiae on the renovations to the buildings, this was quite a statement. "Look at the balconies on all these buildings—they're beautiful. You could have a contest for the most beautiful balcony. These buildings may need repair, but they are loved. The problem is the street. Look at the street—that's where the fracture is."

Molly and I went out to see. Across the street from the complex was a bit of old Marseilles, but a dense and disorganized parking lot and a narrow roadway marked a definitive separation between the city and the complex. In the area at the center of the complex of buildings was a blank, barren, and bleak space. The sea beckoned in the distance, but in the foreground, the earth was packed, white, and hot. In the rear, abandoned factories told a familiar story of lost work that matched all too closely with the lost people.

It was that and other visits to "problem neighborhoods" in Marseille that made him so upset when he looked at the "sack of potatoes" map (Figure 3.1). The callous disregard for people's feelings about their neighborhoods and the intensification of an already unbearable exclusion were intolerable to him. The map became a symbol of all that needed to be repaired in the sorted-out French city.

It was in Perpignan that Cantal had the fullest opportunity to repair the terrain of exclusion. Perpignan is a French city nestled between the Pyrénées and the Mediterranean Sea. It was an ancient capital of the kings of Majorca and shares the Catalan heritage and language with Barcelona, two hours to the south. The summer after the 9/11 terrorist attacks on the World Trade Center, Cantal had told me he wanted me to go to Perpignan to see a demolition. The destruction of the Twin Towers had been very painful for me, and I was quite sure I *didn't* want to see a building destroyed. "This will be different," he promised me.

The site of the demolition was an area called Clodion. We got there early and walked around looking at the ends of buildings that had been emptied of people, appliances, pipes, and windows. In one of the buildings, Mayor Jean-Paul Alduy stood by a model of the site. Cantal leaned over and whispered to me, "The mayor is an architect and has a profound understanding of urban issues. He is the head of the national program for urban renewal. Listen carefully—his explanation will be great."

We all gathered around as Mayor Alduy explained the problem. "You can see we are here," and he pointed to a building on the model. "The only way to reach this site is through one of the two small passageways under the train tracks. The neighborhood is locked in a cul-de-sac. That is always difficult for people. What makes it even more difficult is that a major road whizzes by a hundred yards from here."

He pointed to the layout on the model, and the sounds of traffic coming through the empty windows reinforced his words. "Our plan is to nip a bit off this part of the building—where we're standing now—and a bit off the building catty-corner from here. Then we will link the road that dead ends here to the major road going past. This will connect the neighborhood directly to downtown, freeing people to come and go." The French word he used was *desenclavement*—emancipation, freedom from slavery—which is a profound and joyous word for altering urban space.

Cantal looked over at me, beaming at the mayor's enthusiasm. Then, we all went out to watch. A massive machine lumbered up, a kind of crane with a mouth on the end, resembling an apatosaurus. We were all herded behind a fence: the moment had arrived. I tensed as the apatosaurus lifted its head, but what followed was not the crashing I had feared, but a very precise and gentle bite taken out of the wall. The apatosaurus put the materials in a truck and turned back to bite again. This went on for a few minutes, but was stopped because of high winds. I had never seen a machine eat a building before: it was tender in the care with which it did its job.

On our way out of town the next day, we drove past the site and stopped to take a photograph through the fence that cut the housing project off from the main road. "It will be different the next time you see it," Cantal promised.

A year later, in 2003, much had changed. First of all, it was a breeze to get there. We just drove right in on the new road and *voilà*—there we were. But the buildings had also been altered. The set of homogeneous buildings had been individualized with paint and architectural elements so that each had a unique *allure*. *Allure* is pretty much the same word in French and English, but because France is so much more *ooh là là* than the US is, their *allure* is more alluring. It's an important word in French. That the French make life alluring is partly why we Americans have so much fun there.

In short, when I went back in 2003, the neighborhood, which had been drab and trapped in a cul-de-sac, was freer and cuter, a place with a future. But Cantal and the leaders of Perpignan had much more in store. Cantal drove me around, as he did on our first visit, pointing out where changes would be made and listing his plans. "The football field, which is here, will go there. A community garden will go here, a road will go there."

My head was spinning at the end, trying, feebly, to imagine changes that I could barely list, much less picture in the landscape. I hadn't started to study landscape design, so it was only at the level of theory—reconnect the parts so people can move freely—that any of it made sense to me.

It was only in 2012 that I really got what they meant by *desenclavement*, liberation of the neighborhood. That was partly because I had learned a lot in my landscape design program at the New York Botanical Garden, partly because much of the change had already been accomplished, and partly because I got to go on a tour with Jean-Paul Alduy. His title had changed to president of the Agglomeration of Perpignan Mediterranée, but he was still the best articulator of urban change I've ever met.

I flew in on Wednesday morning, May 22, arriving with a group of potential investors. We got picked up at the airport and went to meet Jean-Paul Alduy and other leaders at Clodion. We whisked in via the new road, past the buildings with *allure*, and parked by a set of old stores that were about to be replaced. We got out of the car and started to walk around the site, and we immediately walked through an area that had previously been a field enclosed in a shabby fence. The field had been moved, opening flow and perspective. In its place were a connecting road and a park.

We walked around the second section of intervention, in which the concentration of buildings had been reduced; the plan was to create small houses. This would serve to knit the parts of the neighborhood together and to diversify the income groups who lived in the area. *Mixité*—mixing—is a major goal of French social policy to combat the sorting-out that they did in rebuilding their cities and accommodating new immigrants after World War II.

Although the French policy is often compared with policy in the US, I find that the two are different, perhaps because France has not pursued policies of serial displacement with the avidity that we have in the US. The French love their cities, invest heavily in them, see them as the launching pads for the future, and protect people's places in those cities with strong laws against displacement. Furthermore, while they certainly struggle with their history of colonialism and racism, their revolution was based on the doctrine of natural rights—that the rights of man are held to be universal and valid in all times and places—which became the foundation for the Declaration of the Rights of Man and of the Citizen and a strong commitment to human rights and antiracism. In the United States, by contrast, we were influenced by the same Enlightenment philosophers, but bowed to the power of slaveholders in creating our nation. Among other concessions, we inserted into our Constitution the idea that slaves were to be counted in the US Census as three-fifths of a person, creating a foundation of inequality from which we have yet to escape.[2] These foundational differences influence our two nations today and were part of the process I was witnessing in Perpignan.

We went to a second set of housing projects after our visit at Clodion. That area had been even more difficult for me to imagine. I had walked the grounds a number of times with Cantal, and I know that he had searched for many days to master the terrain and understand its logic. In that area, there were two sets of housing projects, locked in and obscured, as thoroughly separated from the city as anything might be—a profound realization of geographic marginalization.

There, too, the city had cut a new road. This one had just opened weeks before our visit, so I had never seen or driven on it before. It had created a new entrance, one that linked directly to major roads and made the entrance to the housing complex fluid and transparent. One of our guides, Alexandra Souleyreau, proudly called it a *rambla*—in the sense of the great street in Perpignan's fellow Catalan city of Barcelona—for its wide and inviting walkway. We parked alongside the housing complex and went in to see the three-bedroom homes that were being added to the site. Then, we walked around the whole area. A new garden, just nearing completion, created a space of serenity in an interior courtyard. As in all of Cantal's gardens and parks, the perspective was maintained in all directions.

Jean Paul Alduy introduced me to the investors of the housing project. "Madame is writing a book about Michel Cantal-Dupart. I met Cantal as part of Banlieues 89, the project President Mitterand initiated to ameliorate the connection between massive new construction and the existing cities. When I became mayor, I asked Cantal to accompany me on this journey of urbanism. We have been working together ever since. So a book about Cantal is, forcibly, a book about Perpignan."

We walked further, returning by a road that was perpendicular to the new entry road. The last time I'd seen that road a massive building had been blocking the way. I asked Jean Paul Alduy about it. "We just took that building down," he said. "It took longer than we hoped to get that done."

Whatever the delay, the obstacle was gone and the vista was revealed just as Cantal had foreseen. I stood there, taking in the feeling of the space. I had first seen it in 2002, before any of the work had started, then midway through in 2010, and now, in 2012, with the whole new vision realized. The shift in sensation was powerful. Before, I had the sense of being in an old Western town with a stout stockade around it to keep the Indians out. It had felt very off to itself, and this somehow had made me feel as if I were an outsider. I hadn't been sure where to move, and I had trotted close to Cantal's heels.

Instead of those feelings, I felt like I was in a normal city neighborhood. I could see my options, I was obviously allowed to be there, and I could relax in the way I do in any vibrant city neighborhood.

Later that day, Alexandra Souleyreau took me back to Clodion for a more leisurely visit. I got to walk around the park, where women in North African garb were watching their children play. The park's curves and grading pleased me mightily. As I had at Paris Plage, I felt the precision and elegance of French design. I've seen many a park placed in a poor neighborhood in the US, and very few were fine. This park was fine.

We continued over to the community garden. Alexandra Souleyreau pointed out the mural that youth in the neighborhood had painted and signed with their names. A woman, also in North African garb, was tilling her garden. She grinned at us. We asked how it was going. "I'm thrilled," she said. "Here I can be outside, growing things—otherwise I'd be inside, watching TV."

I made a mental survey of all the US neighborhoods I'd seen remade in such a delightful fashion. A few were meant to serve the people who had been there before—a HOPE VI project in Seattle came quickly to mind—but most were meant to create beauty for people of substance who would be lured from other places. The beauty was a goodbye to the old-timers and a hello to newcomers. By contrast, that happy woman in the community garden at Clodion was reveling in something created for her. She could breathe freely.

Connected, open, and beautiful

Connected

Open

Beautiful!

2002

2012

New road.

Figure 6.4: In the section of Perpignan called Clodion, Cantal worked with the city to create connection, openness, and beauty.

Plan: Courtesy of Michel Cantal-Dupart.
Photo credits: Mindy Fullilove, 2012 "New Road" courtesy of Michel Cantal-Dupart.

BEFORE

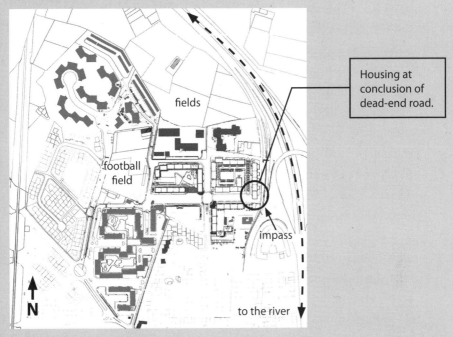

fields

football field

Housing at conclusion of dead-end road.

impass

to the river

N

AFTER

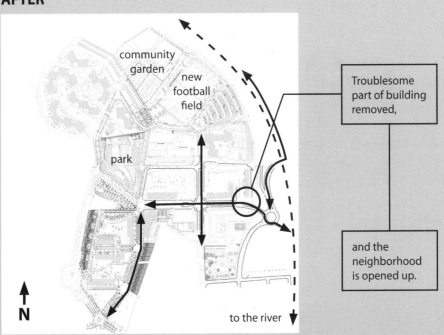

community garden

new football field

park

Troublesome part of building removed,

and the neighborhood is opened up.

to the river

N

During that visit with Alexandra Souleyreau, I again found my body relaxing. We encountered open and beautiful vistas with each turn, and my eyes and brain, it seemed, could expand out toward the horizon. The pleasure of this was so profound that I realized I'd expected to be closed in, a very uncomfortable feeling for someone with the kind of mild claustrophobia I have. The place had previously been so oppressive, in fact, that my body had remembered it from those early visits. I had tensed in anticipation of reexperiencing the earlier constriction, but instead I had encountered space to breathe.

On the way back to the hotel, we passed by the Perpignan train station, which Salvador Dali had declared the center of the world. Then, Alexandra Souleyreau dropped me off at my hotel.

I didn't feel like I could go inside, so I looked around for a place to unwind. I remembered that there was a bench just a few paces away, at the foot of a grand staircase that ascends the wall to enter the old city. I had been speaking French all day, and I couldn't even think of any words in English. I was filled with the sensation of expecting constriction and finding freedom. As I walked toward the bench, I saw that someone had been there before me. On the bench it said: "Tr↑p."

Creating equity

People in Pittsburgh agree that the urban renewal carried out in the East Liberty neighborhood was an unmitigated disaster. Designed to stop the loss of business to the burgeoning suburban malls by imposing a pedestrian mall at the center of the business district, the massive interventions in the neighborhood only succeeded in destroying what had been one of the busiest shopping districts in Western Pennsylvania. Even the planner, Robert Pease, could only shake his head. "It looked great on paper," he remembered.

At the heart of the devastation was the creation of Penn Circle, a one-way traffic loop that encircled the perimeter of downtown and was encased in parking lots. The massive urban renewal had triggered contagious housing destruction that brought the surrounding neighborhoods to their knees. There was a deep distrust of the space because, after all, who wants to drive around in circles? Getting rid of Penn Circle was essential, but the terrain was so distorted that the path to restoration was not obvious.

RDCollab, known at that time as Rothschild Doyno Architects, took on this puzzle in 2002 (Rothschild Doyno Architects and Brean Associates 2004). The firm worked with community leaders to assemble a consortium of property, citizen, developer, and government groups who wanted to improve their understanding of the shared path forward. The result was a type of "treasure map for unpuzzling," where individual projects could work together to reweave the center of the neighborhood with the major thoroughfares from the surrounding communities that ran through East Liberty. This included the articulation of development guidelines for each thoroughfare, instilling a different personality for each. There were suggestions for sight lines, green spaces, parking, building types and heights, and uses for the subunits of the area that had arisen from the participants, the pieces that needed to work together, and the real paths and destinations that would emerge.

Ken once asked me how Cantal worked. It was an interesting question. Cantal believed that the foundation of intervention was careful study of the site, to which must be added detailed examination of maps, consultation with history books, visits to libraries and museums, and examination of old photographs. He was interested in understanding the history of monuments and fountains, the destinations of roads, the sources of money, the history of ceremonies: in fact, everything about the city—that is to say everything—was interesting to him.

Ken worked in much the same way as Cantal, constantly cultivating his understanding of the city and then deepening that understanding by finding design solutions for specific problems. It's possible the biggest difference is that Ken worked in one city, while Cantal worked in many. But, if you had to pick one city to which to devote a career as an urbanist, Pittsburgh was it. Its complex topography, myriad neighborhoods, dense history, and knotted personal relationships require a lifetime of study. During my 1998-9 Falk Fellowship at the University of Pittsburgh Graduate School of Public Health, I spent a lot of time with Phil Hallen, then the president of the Maurice Falk Medical Fund. He, too, loved to say, "Want to see something?" Then, he would drive down some strange alley that looked like a street but suddenly became a set of stairs. "Not a good

I can see clearly

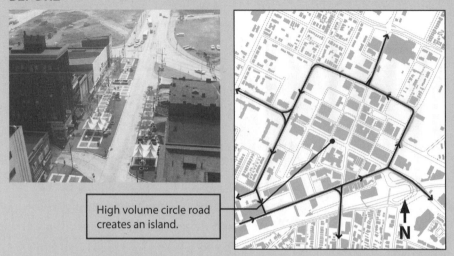

High volume circle road
creates an island.

Figure 6.5: Above, we see a photograph of the center of East Liberty, transformed by the ring road. In the plan, we see how the ring road dominated the movement of traffic, forcing it around the downtown. In the photo on the opposite page, we see the perspective to the Target logo. In the "after" plan, the ring road is eliminated, and a denser system of movement has been created.

idea to do this if you've been out drinking," he would quip, bringing to the imagination horrible pictures of cars in mid-staircase. Like Ken, Phil was from Buffalo, New York, and had spent his career as an urbanist in Pittsburgh.

Ken approached the East Liberty project with the utmost respect for the people and the mystery of the remnants of the past and their value to the future. He was just starting to tackle urban problems after years of work in architecture, and he was in full discovery and learning mode. The study of the ruined terrain, and his own need to learn urbanism, required all of his enormous capacity to focus his attention. He shared with me that he went to Penn Circle often, stopping by on his way home from work to spend a half an hour checking out an idea. He walked and drove the streets until he could decipher the secrets of the disconnects and the imperatives essential to making an aligned and connected center. He talked to people

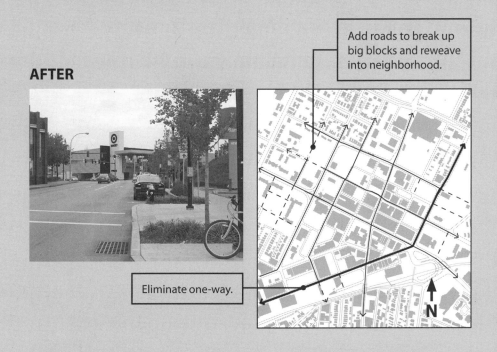

AFTER

Add roads to break up big blocks and reweave into neighborhood.

Eliminate one-way.

N

Plans: Courtesy of Ken Doyno.
Photos: Left, photographer unknown. Right: Beatrice Spolidoro, used with permission.

to understand how the history had been lived on the streets: What had they been? How were they remembered? What might they be?

This is how intensely East Liberty is lived: When Terri and I were studying the East Liberty Development Guidelines, she named every single building that was shown there and related the story of the role it had played in her life. There was the building where she had shopped with her beloved great-grandmother, the building where she had her first job, the building with a wonderful candy store, the building with the best clam chowder, the building where the movies played, and on and on.

I know that in other cities people are attached to their places, but there is a preciousness to the life people have in Pittsburgh that must be met with awareness. Ken brought that to the task at hand, keeping his own ideas out of the way so that other people's issues, loves, desires, peculiarities, successes, and ghost stories might find their way to the surface.

The first part of the project was to decipher the state of affairs and find the solution to the puzzle. It goes without saying that the one-way loop had to be restored to normal and that the parking lots had to be returned to urban use. But many streets had been disrupted and the sense of connection had collapsed from contagious housing destruction.

It would be possible, Ken found, to restore function by teasing out a series of east-west streets: a regional connecting street, two main streets, and neighborhood streets. These brought the right mix of function and flow to the scene. Main streets, I have found, work best when they cut through a dense core of activity, and that is what Ken proposed. These streets established the warp of the design, the threads that run lengthwise. Figure 6.5 shows the before and after of these streets.

Cantal once told me that perspective is the warp of the city, and, indeed, Ken placed key lines of perspective along the streets. One of the urban-site-force guidelines dealt with sight lines and indicated a landmark element at the bend in Penn Avenue. Target opened a store on that corner and put their highly branded two-story glass lobby and entrance there. For the other sightline, Target put their big logo, a massive target symbol that is visible from quite a distance. Ken pointed out to me how Target had been able to leverage the guidelines for their purposes, while simultaneously advancing the goals of the community. "Not quite Hercules," Ken observed, alluding to the statue on the horizon at Vaux-le-Vicomte (see Figure 6.3), "but the Target logo does draw the eye."

It was also possible to overlay other systems of connection, create greenways, and upgrade secondary systems of movement for pedestrians. These systems were particularly important for amplifying the north-south connectors and strengthening the woof, the crosswise threads. In Cantal's system of the city as weaving, these crosswise threads enable solidarity, and fundamental to solidarity is the free system movement in the city. Jane Jacobs (1991, 71–72) noted,

> Sidewalk public contact and sidewalk public safety, taken together, bear directly on our country's most serious social problem—segregation and discrimination. I do not mean to imply that a city's planning and design, or its types of streets and street life, can automatically overcome segregation and discrimination.... But I do mean to say that

to build and rebuild big cities whose sidewalks are unsafe and whose people must settle for sharing much or nothing, can make it much harder for American cities to overcome discrimination no matter how much effort is expended.

The second part of the East Liberty project was to present the solution in an alluring manner so that people could adopt and advance the vision. Cantal often talks about *appropriation*, by which he means that the people take ownership for a space or project. In English, appropriation is defined as, "[t]he action of taking something for one's own use, typically without the owner's permission." In Cantal's usage, it is the first part of the definition that is important: taking something for one's own use. And he is specifically referring to the taking of public goods for one's own use, as in taking a walk in the park and feeling that one is an owner, along with the whole rest of the society, of the park. Without this appropriation, projects do not succeed.

Appropriation has little to do with law or rules and everything to do with people's understanding at highly symbolic levels. How does it fit within the system of meaning that people hold? Cantal says people ask themselves, "These public spaces, how are they for me? They look to the space for answers to that question. Are there signs of welcome? Are there signs of exclusion?"

As I have already tried to suggest, there is not one system of meaning in the sorted-out city, but many, and the conversations that might bring the multiple systems into coherence are themselves impeded by the sorting-out process.

The solution RDCollab employed was to create a document that was legible, connective, and alluring. By including both plans and photographs, the designers created multiple points of entry. The captions by the photographs added a third way of making meaning. By pointing all of these systems in the same direction, RDCollab contributed to the healing of the mind politic and created the strongest possibility for appropriation of the plan. When this plan was presented to the East Liberty leaders, the head of the Community Design Center said, "It's the first time I no longer see Penn Circle."

During my visit to France in May 2012, Cantal took me back to Sore and we strolled the whole village. They had attempted to follow some of the ideas he had put forward more than a decade earlier, but had done so, he thought, without professional help. While they had given a bit more structure to their village, they had not achieved the full force of interventions that used the warp of perspective and the woof of solidarity. A few weeks later, however, on another visit to Sore, Cantal was surprised and touched to encounter a man who said, "I am on the city council, and I remember vividly what you told us twelve years ago. We have been following your advice ever since, slowly and not perfectly, we know, but with great belief that what you told us is right."

East Liberty, like Sore and many other places, has been inconsistent in following the guidelines. On the one hand, a new library was built that cut off one of the east-west "green links" that would connect flow in the southwest corner of the area to the center. This was an oversight that, in 2012, appeared to impede progress on the no-man's-land that still existed between those two areas.

On the other hand, a pedestrian bridge that opened in 2012 made a major contribution to the sidewalk flow. This was made more remarkable by its landing on a private development that had to integrate a public stairway and a public elevator. The bridge was the first in a city of bridges to be designed by an artist.

It is at this point that a curious fact emerges: unpuzzling is tightly connected to unslumming, which I examine in the next chapter. In fact, the two are so closely related that we might ask: which is the chicken and which is the egg? I have put unpuzzling first, but really what happens is a kind of unpuzzle-unslum-unpuzzle dialectic in which one leads to the next. I think that East Liberty—and Sore—will unpuzzle a bit, then unslum a bit, then unpuzzle a bit more, gradually emerging as vibrant places of the twenty-first century.

When we can see how the pieces fit, the world opens up to us.

CHAPTER SEVEN

Element 5:
Unslum All Neighborhoods

[B]ut Max stepped into his private boat and waved good-bye
and sailed back over a year
and in and out of weeks
and through a day
and into the night of his very own
room where he found his supper waiting for him.

— Maurice Sendak, *Where the Wild Things Are*

M y mother, Maggie, tried to get a fair deal for everyone she met. When my brother Josh was a young musician, she met a lot of trumpeters, saxophonists, guitarists, and drummers. She helped each of them, but, perhaps most important, she let them occupy her living room, turning it into a den of very loud sound. She rushed home after work to turn down the sound before the neighbors called the police.

At her memorial service in Orange on March 10, 2012, a man grabbed my hand and said, "You won't remember me, but I lived on Olcott Street in the 1970s and I hung out with Josh and all the fellows. I remember watching your mother, coming home in the evening walking down Olcott Street. It was a like a change in the atmosphere. A peace would descend on street, touching all of us as she passed by."

I finally made my way through the throng of mourners and into the Parish Hall, where my brother was playing with many of the men whose teen years were spent in the cacophony of my mother's living room. Having grown up to be internationally renowned musicians, they rocked the hall for her.

I saw hope bloom in the faces of the people jazzed by the sounds and the rhythms and the memory of Maggie's engagement with the city. Pat Morrissy was glowing with pride to have been part of Maggie's life. Kathy Grady brought the beautiful quilts she'd made for the fiftieth anniversary party—that fateful day in 2007 when Molly and I were called home to Orange—and she, too, was glowing. Members of our congregation beamed to see our little church jumping and shaking.

Later that day, Lourdes's six-year-old son, Diego, told her, "I like to help people, so I am Maggie's grandhelper."

Jane Jacobs (1991, 71), in *The Death and Life of Great American Cities*, observed, "Lowly, unpurposeful and random as they may appear, sidewalk contacts are the small change from which a city's wealth of public life may grow."

Maggie was not only rushing home, but also participating in the life of the neighborhood. Her kind and welcoming presence contributed to the street, and the street contributed to the world, and the people who lived that experience were able to pass it along to a young boy who'd only met her once.

Maggie's contributions to her city are the heart of unslumming: making a modest city more important by the investment of her time and her love (Thompson 2011). What drives us from places, I believe, is the lack of connection to others. It is in connection that we build safe, functional cities. Unslumming is a constant reflex, coaxing us to connect and improve wherever we are. It is the recognition and support of this natural process that could make our cities better faster.

In the stories of unslumming that I relate here, I want to emphasize that the rebuilding is mired in the weight of the past. It takes steady pressure to achieve gains, but these gains are easily lost in new rounds of the sorting process. Unslumming *can* work, but we must protect the new connections with all our hearts. In particular, unslumming, which occurs because of many small individual decisions to invest in the here and now, remakes the weak ties that are broken by upheaval and sorting, flourishes as confidence is restored, and generates energy for the larger social, economic, and political tasks of working for a just society.

Unslum all neighborhoods, the fifth element of urban restoration, involves:

- Acknowledging the pain of unexpectancy;
- Reknitting weak ties; and
- Investing in the places where we want to stay.

Acknowledging the pain of *unexpectancy*

For eighteen years, I had offices at 513 West 166th Street in New York City, on the "wrong" side of Broadway. On our side of the block, next to our building, there was a small office building that was barely used, which had once been the home of the Institute of Human Nutrition, where I got my master's degree, and which I remember with great fondness. After that, there was a parking garage and a boarded-up building whose use I still can't fathom. As if that weren't desolate enough, the parking garage was cloaked in scaffolding, creating a dim and foreboding section of street. Across the street were several apartment buildings, one of which housed the biggest crack dealer in the area. When there wasn't snow on the ground, we could walk from the corner to the side entrance over the satisfying crunch of the little plastic vials that the crack was sold in.

Our building was strangely walled off from the street. The whole first floor was used to store records. A couple of guards were inside, keeping the records safe, but, otherwise, there was no traffic in or out of that storage area. It had no windows overlooking the street. Above the storage unit were clinics and research offices, all of which opened about nine and closed about five.

Opposite our building were two lots, one was an official parking lot, where I parked my car, and the other was a semiofficial parking area, untended and usually full of litter. The winter of 1994 had eleven freeze-thaw cycles and incessant snowstorms. All during that winter, the fire hydrant near the main parking lot dripped on the sidewalk that nobody shoveled. The water would nearly instantly freeze, creating an ice pack that got to be three feet high before the spring came. There were many measures of the desolation, but one has particular importance to my story: Coffee carts abounded on the other side of Broadway, but our corner was too desolate to provide enough trade to sustain such an enterprise. If we wanted coffee—and I don't remember why we didn't have a coffeemaker in the office, but we didn't—we had to walk three blocks or hope that one of the few students brave enough to come see us would pick up a cup or two on the way. Sara Booth, our intrepid filmmaker, always arrived with two coffees.

The desolation was not empty, but rather was filled with many kinds of violence. Washington Heights led New York in the number of homicides early in the 1990s, just as I arrived from San Francisco. In the first month I was there, thieves stole a bag from my car. "I was robbed!" I moaned to my coworkers. "They took my camera and the dress I wore for my wedding."

One replied, "At least you weren't robbed at gunpoint. Let me tell you what happened to my cousin."

All of this is to say that the sorted-out city became the geography of everyday life for everyone in our office for the eighteen years we occupied that space. The small and large indignities of difference were engrained

Figure 7.1: Girl with banana. The girl walking through a police bust while eating a banana became emblematic for us of the accommodations people made to life in a neighborhood awash in violence.

Photo credit: Lesley Rennis. Courtesy of the CRG Collection.

in my sensibilities, my awareness heightened by having as my team a top group of ethnographers who enjoyed peering into the ordinary and bringing back its secrets. In 1996, we conducted a study of violence in Washington Heights. Our first task was to photograph the neighborhood. Three members of our team drove around documenting the area. Lesley Rennis spotted a massive bust going on and hopped out of the car to get a shot of the scene. In the center of the action was a girl calmly eating a banana. We called it "Girl with banana" and we gave a copy of the photo to our doctoral students when they finished their studies (Figure 7.1). We were all like that girl: "Oh yeah, danger."

"Oh yeah, danger" does not imply that we were oblivious, but rather that we had made accommodations to protect ourselves. One woman we interviewed said, "If I see my neighbor, I don't stop to talk. It's too dangerous." Another described how she moved a filing cabinet in front of her window in case there were shootings in the night. Our interviewees explained how they had changed their patterns of movement to avoid problems in the streets. They used telephoning to alert one another to danger. They moved quickly and did not linger outside. They avoided the open spaces and parks and kept their children indoors.

People in the neighborhood surprised us when they explained what they saw as the source of this terrible problem. They said it wasn't the drug dealers, who were the obvious bad guys, but the whole structure of unequal opportunity that existed for immigrants and for people of color that was to blame. And people from the Dominican Republic, who were the majority in the neighborhood, shouldn't face blanket condemnation for the misdeeds of some. Our interviewees named racism, colonialism, classism, sexism, and abandonment of poor communities as the source of violence that was exploding in our faces.

For the most part, colleagues and students didn't come to our offices. We learned that fear creates and maintains the sorted-out city. One day, I got a visit from a young Scottish doctor whose accent had led me to expect someone white and short. He was neither. He explained how his family got to Scotland and was a little annoyed as it must have been a question he answered all the time. I asked, "Would you like to see what disinvestment has done to our neighborhood?"

He agreed, a bit reluctantly, and we set out. We walked down my block and then continued on 166th, which doglegs at Amsterdam before continuing to Edgecombe Avenue. The buildings were in poor shape, and the block was five years behind the return to safety that was well underway in my own. A group of guys were gathered at the edge of some scaffolding and they looked us up and down. My guest, dressed in a fine suit and good shoes, thought they might attack or rob us. I nodded to the men and said hello, and we kept going. I was interested in pointing out the buildings around the corner that had been abandoned and burned down, the beginning of the process of contagious housing destruction. But that topic did not compete with the possibility of mayhem that had caught his attention. By the time we got back to the office, he was thoroughly annoyed with me for exposing him to danger and not at all reassured by the fact that nothing untoward had happened: it *could* have.

And he was right. *Unexpectancy* is the nature of Simms III. "Oh yeah, danger" is a sign that we have adjusted to the presence of the horrible and the untoward in our daily lives. Outsiders help us to remember that this is *not* the way we should have to live.

Reknitting weak ties

Restoring peace

In Washington Heights-Inwood, as in neighborhoods all over the US, people slowly won back the public space. In our area, I date the beginning of the recovery to establishment of what we called the "Rice Truck." This was a cooking van that was operated by several Dominican women and stationed alongside the parking lot near our office building. The quality of the rice and beans and chicken created a stir, and people began to stop by. Suddenly, our desolate little strip was peopled with livery cab drivers and others who knew how to police the street. The ladies of the Rice Truck did more than their share, contributing a cheerful serenity and an aggressive tidiness.

Around the same time, the storage place closed. Suddenly, the theretofore carefully guarded files were thrown into big dumpsters and carted away. We said goodbye to the guards, and the floor closed for renovations.

When it reopened, it was a clinic, with windows on the street and a great bustle of people seeking care.

At that point, what had been an unimaginable thing happened: we got a coffee cart on our corner! Martin, a Dominican man interested in having his own business, established his cart on our corner and prospered. He tamed the area, keeping án eye on all the people and telling those who got out of line that they needed to behave. His friends would stop by and chat with him, so there was usually a crowd of strong men around his cart. Though no one had a friendlier smile or kinder manner, there was no doubt that he could enforce peace on the streets. Martin knew all of his customers and prepared your coffee before you even asked. That was one less burden in the morning, not having to say, "Coffee please, milk, one sugar."

I don't want to overlook the work of law enforcement in restoring order and returning the streets to the people. The arrest of the crack dealer who dominated the area was important to our little neighborhood. Equally important was the opening of the temporary headquarters of the newly created 33rd Precinct on a lot around the corner from us. The coming and going of police cars helped in securing the safety of the neighborhood.

The expansion of the Columbia University Medical Center, in contrast to the help from the police, undermined the recovery. The Medical Center, which is constantly extending its territory, started to expand across Broadway as the violence ended. The buildings that got put up were in the style that architect and urbanist José Camilo Vegara (1995) identified as "defensive architecture," which flourished in the crack era. In that style, buildings were ringed with ribbon wire, surrounded by fences, or built with blank walls at the street level. The Medical Center's buildings were minimally open in the direction that faced Broadway, but presented fences and blank walls on the side that faced Audubon, that is, the neighborhood. As my office faced this rear view, I had the unpleasant sensation of a having a great white back side shoved in my face (see Figure 8.7). The buildings were both bleak and hostile, fortresses against the community rather than citizens of it.

CRG ♥ Highbridge

One day, Lesley, Lesley's son Anthony, Arelis, Lourdes, and I entered the forest in Highbridge, at a point about twelve blocks from our office. A

Exploring Highbridge

Figure 7.2: Highbridge Park includes a small forest. CRG explored the area and helped to advocate for its restoration. Clockwise from top left: The CRG team on the Croton Aqueduct Trail; Highbridge Tower, viewed from the Trail; Looking through the gate to the High Bridge; Rodrick Wallace taking the bottom right photograph; Lourdes leading a group of students through the forest.

Photo credits: Mindy Fullilove, except "Looking through the gate to the High Bridge," by Rodrick Wallace, used with permission.

broad path, muddy with spring rain and arched with trees, beckoned. Not knowing where we were going, and, even more fun, not knowing if it was safe to go there, we strolled along. The path ran along the eastern side of a rocky outcropping that formed a wall between where we were and the city (Figure 7.2). We lost sight of the buildings and found ourselves immersed in a new playground. Lourdes and Anthony immediately started to climb the rocks, while I started to take photos of the wild beauty all around me. It was the beginning of a love affair between the Community Research Group (CRG) and Highbridge.

Highbridge Park, including its wonderful forest, was in a peculiar state, sorted into "kept up" and "not so kept up" sections. In 2004, as we started to explore the park, we found a line of demarcation. In some places, the line was an actual fence, but in others, a low bar. To the west of the line, the park was maintained, its grass cut and paths tended. To the east, it was a largely abandoned territory claimed by the forest, which we learned had about 175 different species of trees. The paths through the forest were littered with glass and hypodermic needles and condoms, detritus from the users who went into the park to carry out activities that needed to remain hidden.

Highbridge had a history that was important to us as public health workers: it was part of the path of the Croton Aqueduct, which brought the first clean water to New York City back in the 1840s. Interestingly enough, the water was to be sold, which meant that only the wealthy could get clean water. It was soon discovered that the city could not contain the terrible epidemics of cholera and other infectious diseases without making sure that clean water reached everyone. This story had great meaning for our own work in making sure that the resources of our society are available to all. This is fundamental to addressing inequity as the cause of disease.

As part of the system of the Croton Aqueduct, there is an actual "High Bridge," which brought the water over the Harlem River and into Manhattan from the Bronx. For more than a century, the High Bridge was a pedestrian path from the Bronx to Manhattan. There is a very dramatic painting of Edgar Allan Poe crossing the bridge in the teeth of a pelting rainstorm. Allegedly, in the 1970s, some youths threw stones off the bridge and these landed on the Circle Line Tourist boat passing underneath. As a result, the bridge was closed to pedestrians. When we started to explore the park, the doors locking the bridge were draped in heavy chains. We could peer through the hole to see the bridge stretching off to the Bronx, but it was impassable, or nearly so, as a group of enterprising youths on their way to the Highbridge Pool demonstrated to us. The plaza that was meant to welcome people to Manhattan had fallen into desolation. It was a lonely site. Only a few ever passed that way. We loved hiking there because it was so empty and forested. At parts of the trail, I had the feeling that, though I was not four blocks from the hustle and bustle of Broadway, I might have been in the Adirondack Mountains. And the spectacular moment when the stone water tower emerged from the canopy of trees and jutted up into the sky was one we loved. On an autumn day, or in the snow, that was a special sight.

One day, a student climbed to the top of the water tower and took a remarkable photograph that shows the line of demarcation indicated by a

Figure 7.3: Line of demarcation. A stout fence created a line of demarcation between the more maintained part of the park and the less maintained part of the park.
Photo courtesy of the CRG Collection.

fence. To the west are carefully tended clipped lawns, while the forest, in full spring glory, lay to the east. We could also see some of the great and enchanting variety of trees that were beyond the fence and out of reach of the paths of the vast majority of park users.

Hike the Heights

When she was a doctoral student hanging around 513 West 166th Street, Beverly Xaviera Watkins thought that it would be a good idea to have aerial photographs of Harlem. That is how two enormous views of central Harlem came to be part of our office décor. It was interesting to study them. One of the photographs included the southern end of Highbridge Park and the northern end of Jackie Robinson Park. I would often find myself standing in front of that photo longing to pinch the two parks together. One day, when the violence was down and it was really safe to go for long walks, I set off to see this intriguing spot. In bear-climbed-over-the-mountain fashion, I checked out that connection and then got interested in looking at the connection between Jackie Robinson Park and St. Nicholas Park. They weren't quite as close—there were two blocks between them—but not so far either. After that, I got interested in the Morningside–St. Nicholas connection and then, finally, the Central Park–Morningside connection.

At the time, I was serving on two national committees looking at the benefits of exercise. One of the committees was a joint committee of the Transportation Research Board and the Institute of Medicine (both components of the National Academies); it was examining the intersection of health, physical space, and exercise. That committee pointed out that our society, through the use of cars, elevators, escalators, and laborsaving devices of all kinds, had engineered activity out of daily life. The brute physical activity that had helped our ancestors stay healthy just wasn't a part of our lives anymore (Humphrey 2005).

I often sat next to Dr. Steven Blair, a researcher at the Cooper Center in Texas, a leading exercise research center. He told me over and over, "The data show that people who exercise are healthy, whether they're thin or fat. People who don't exercise aren't healthy, whether they're thin or fat. The question we have to answer is: how do we get people to exercise more?"

The other committee was the National Task Force on Community Preventive Services, a task force that examined the evidence for public health interventions. One of our task force members, Dr. Ross Brownson, was a leading researcher on the benefits of exercise. He led a wonderful series of studies on interventions to get people to exercise, as Steve Blair had urged. Our task force recommended interventions in the local environment:

> These interventions attempt to change the local environment to create opportunities for physical activity. Access to places for physical activity can be created or enhanced both by building trails or facilities and by reducing barriers (e.g., reducing fees or changing operating hours of facilities). Many of these programs also provide training in use of equipment, other health education activities, and incentives such as risk factor screening and counseling. Several programs reviewed were conducted at worksites. (Task Force on Community Preventive Services 2002, 71)

When I learned how useful trails were for increasing exercise, I started to say to my friends, "Couldn't we make a trail from Central Park to Dyckman Street? We can go through the parks and connect via the streets."

Urbanist Marshall Brown got what I was describing. He took me to the Museum of Modern Art to see the 2005 exhibit of the plans for making the defunct railroad track, known as the High Line, into a park. Marshall also created a map, a name, and a logo for my hiking idea, the modern equivalent of a leaflet and button, which my dad joked were the fundamentals of starting an organization. The Center for Children's Environmental Health agreed to sponsor the first "Hike the Heights." We started small, hiking only Highbridge in our first year. We laid out a series of hikes around the Tower Terrace, where we planned to hold a party. We had about a hundred people that first year, and everyone had a splendid time on the Terrace and walking around the area.

We make the road by walking

We built the project slowly as we sorted through the obstacles, like how to cross 155th Street, which I described in the previous chapter. In 2006, Rod Wallace came by a CLIMB meeting to help us think through the challenges presented by the area around 155th Street. Rod opened his remarks by observing that behavior is part of a language, and language is part of our epigenetic inheritance and part of learning that is passed on. He explained the observation, made by sociologist Mark Granovetter (1973), that populations are connected in two different ways: strong and weak ties.

"The strong ties are disjunctive, they separate us into groups," said physicist Rod, "but the weak ties are non-disjunctive, that is, they connect us. In a well-functioning city, we have strong and weak ties, and that makes the city work. Serial displacement breaks the weak ties. In their absence, the strong ties become stronger, and the groups become hostile to each other.

"Violence is one of the important signs of the breaking of weak ties. Violence will fall off after a while, but it will be a much longer period before we start to see the full range of positive behaviors that make communities healthy. In New York City neighborhoods, we saw a rise in violence and then a fall. But it's ten years since the violence began to decline and people still don't have library cards and they don't vote. We have not returned to what we were before, and we will not. We will go forward from this point.

"This is the principle of 'path dependence.' We are on a path that is determined by the manner in which we treat each other. When we commit acts of violence, as when neighborhoods are ripped apart by serial displacement, we destroy the weak ties and undermine the foundation of our society. We have to go forward from that point of destruction. We can leave people alone and they will recover in fifty years or so. If we repair it through community organizing, we can recover more quickly. But we can never erase that destruction from the history of behaviors that we will pass on to our children and their children and their children's children.

"To relate this to what you are doing, the psychology of place teaches us that there are movements of certain kinds in certain places. You can make it easier, but that doesn't mean that the rules of the place will allow people to participate. Linking up the pieces to make the 'giraffe' requires synergism between making it easier and selling it to people as a new and useful way to move in their environment. Increasing the probability of contact leads to coalescence. But that challenges the existing psychology of place. You have to help people learn that it makes sense to go up the parks, that it's one big giraffe."

Lourdes asked, "So what we create has to make sense in the existing behavioral language?"

"Yes," Rod replied, "and we can think of that as making a new word or linking two existing words."

"At 155th Street, we have four quadrants and they are socially distinct. Does that mean that there are different behavioral languages in each?"

"Probably. So you have to make it easier to get across, but this is not simply a mechanical process because of the behavioral language underlying the patterns of movement."

Trish, one of our public health students, asked, "Am I right that you said we can accelerate the time for healing by paying attention to this problem of the psychology of place?"

"*Yes*," Rod answered emphatically. "Reverend Martin Luther King Jr.'s nonviolence—community organizing in the US sense—can cut the period of recovery. Nonviolent, spiritually based action can help. The black churches, for example, can play a role in this if they can reach outside of their denominational strong ties, as King did. Remember, King was killed while he was helping to organize the garbage men in Memphis. That was not an accident. It sent a message, 'Stay in your group.' It's that fear we have to overcome, it's King's broad outreach to people *not like himself* that we have to emulate."

Lourdes nodded. "I get it. The park is considered a terrible and dangerous place. The ghosts of all the bad things linger there. We have to exorcise the park, and to do that, we have to find what that means to people. And we can't wait for them to find their way to the park, we have to take them there."

Rod agreed. "That will work," he said. He flashed a big smile. "It's my night to cook!" he announced. "I'm going to get some wine and put some of it in the sauce and some of it in me!" He gathered his cameras and hurried out.

Lourdes implemented "walking meetings" in the parks. Highbridge, because of its size and terrible condition, was our central concern. We often walked the Croton Aqueduct Trail because it took us so far from the city and, due to its terrible condition, made us feel the full impact of disinvestment in the sorted-out city. Highbridge was not an asset of the city, but a reservoir of problems that could jump out into the neighborhood at any time. People who walked with us started to imagine, as we did, the positive things that might happen in that forested cliffside space. Rock climbing, nature classrooms, and forestry school—we had strange dreams while trying to avoid falling on the broken glass. I always had terrible images of someone getting cut on the massive piles of broken glass—the trash from parties that took place on the isolated trails—and bleeding to death just blocks from the hospital.

Lourdes kept saying to one and all, "Hike the Heights is a pot luck party, and whatever we put into the pot, that's what the party will be." Archana Negraj, who had done NYC RECOVERS with us, got the idea that her children's art group, Creative Arts Workshops for Kids, could link the trails with art. This developed into the "giraffe path," an annual installation of giraffes. There is nothing quite as powerful as a papier-maché giraffe, made by kindergartners, to bring an abandoned woods back into the sphere of the city.

Maudene Nelson, my buddy in nutrition school with whom I coauthored a thesis on neighborhoods and food, helped us think through the challenges of the menu (Thompson and Nelson 1976). Some argued that what our guests wanted was the standard party food: hot dogs, hamburgers, fried chicken, and potato salad. As we were in a school of public health, the "eat right" folks argued for more vegetables and fewer empty calories.

Figure 7.4: Papier-maché giraffe. A beautiful giraffe creates a new atmosphere in the park. The creation of the Giraffe Path became a tradition of the annual Hike the Heights celebration. The Children's Art Workshop taught classes all over northern Manhattan in giraffe making and then the giraffes were displayed on the trails and at the party site. Photo credit: Mindy Fullilove.

How Highbridge Park changed

Figure 7.5: These photos show how the park has changed with new investment. The two top photos show the Croton Aqueduct Trail, before and after it was covered with asphalt. The two bottom photos show the stairs between the Tower Terrace and the High Bridge landing before and after the staircase was rebuilt. CRG was especially happy to realize its dream of rock climbing, made possible by REI, the sporting goods store.

Photo credits: top left: Robert Fullilove, used with permission; top right: Mindy Fullilove; bottom left: Rodrick Wallace, used with permission; bottom right: Mindy Fullilove.

This argument went on for a few years, as the planning committee sorted through a reasonable amount of change. We didn't go from fried chicken to tofu burgers in one leap, but the pressure to provide wholesome food moved the menu annually.

Evelyn Joseph, for many years the administrator of our research team, had an annual vision for the T-shirt design. "I see yellow amidst the green trees," she said one year. Another year, "I see blue. A vibrant blue." Designing the logos for the T-shirts was another major activity during the months of planning.

Partnership for Parks gave us crucial support by providing the initial links to the New York City Department of Parks and Recreation, which helped us get permits, special clean-up support, and access to the Highbridge Tower, which was a special treat for our hikers. They connected us to the US National Park Service, which provided consultation on the development of our trail. Hike the Heights is held on the first Saturday in June because that is the Park Service's National Trails Day.

Most years, some group showed up to provide entertainment, but one year the promised show fell through. A little boy, who'd been eyeing the stage, walked up to Lourdes and said, "Could we have a dance contest?" Suddenly, kids became engaged in the competition. It was spontaneous and joyous and great.

Every year as the party grew, more and more people contributed more and more ideas. Having a great party is, of course, a goal of our urbanism. But this is a story about building the wealth of cities and encouraging the accumulation of small interactions in the public space. In our case, we had to extend the field of movement and lift the terrible blight caused by the abandoned park. We introduced people to the riches lying at their doorsteps and asked, "What could be done with this?"

The answer was certainly a growth in investment in the park (Figure 7.5). But much more happened. People who worked together on Hike the Heights also called on each other to solve other problems. The strengthened networks were able to compete for grants and support schools. They took the idea of the "walking meeting" into their daily lives, looking around to see what else needed to be tended. A neighborhood in that way takes charge of itself, identifying and prioritizing its problems and opening the search for solutions.

In the model of urban restoration that I am proposing, it is this collective capacity to identify and solve problems that is the real goal. The sorting-out of the city destroys this capacity. Urban restoration puts us on the path toward regaining this collective efficacy, our ability to work together as a community.

Creating the places where we want to stay

Raising the Big Top

The Valley Arts District, launched in 2001, evolved from a two-year planning process (2003–04) to revitalize the forty-block Valley neighborhood surrounding Orange's old industrial core. HANDS, the nonprofit organization that led the effort, was skilled at real estate and community organizing. "But what did we know about creating an arts district?" Pat Morrissy reminisced. "We organized ValleyArts and tried to get artists to come give us advice."

The goals of the Valley Revitalization plan included enhancing educational achievement, creating new career opportunities for youth, expanding recreational offerings, beautifying the neighborhood, and promoting a host of physical improvements in the area. HANDS secured a large multiyear grant to help launch the revitalization and brought in partner organizations. One partner was a well-regarded youth arts group that hoped to collaborate with the Orange school district and work with at-risk, high school-age youths who had an interest in art. ValleyArts, Inc., a collaboration of artists, community leaders, educators, and nonprofits formed to create a community arts organization that would link the arts and the aspirations of the community, was launched in 2005 at a community celebration called the Bigg Event.

The original youth arts organization collapsed, but the engagement of youth in planning for an arts district remained a central objective important to Pat. He wanted to get youth involved in planning their own program. This got off the ground in the spring of 2008 with the participation of five local high school students who brought a mix of skills to the table. One of the objectives for the group was to envision the ways in which an old industrial building might be reorganized to serve the youth. The young people in the program met with architect John Alford and visited the building, considered the programming of the space, and poured over blueprints to create a design that would work. They also named the program. Ironworks Studio was the front-running name, but that domain name had already been taken. Alternatives were considered, and Outreaching to the Next Generation Ink (ORNG Ink) was finally selected.

A summer program followed, with enough money for thirty youths to participate. One group worked with a sculptor to make a mosaic that would eventually go on the walls of Ironworks. The other group worked with Mike Malbrough, or Mike Mal, as he is usually known. That group began to make T-shirts, create a website, and develop ideas for future programs.

In 2009, Molly started to get involved. Her experience with CLIMB Summer and the CLIMB filmmaking project, which she had co-led with Kiara Nagel, had been the basis for the development of a very conscious program of youth urbanism. She and Kiara articulated the view that youth, because of their particular location in society, had a deep knowledge of the local that far surpassed most adults. In the liminal space between childhood and adulthood, they understood the whole lifespan as no one else could. This body of wisdom was crucial to society. It was a wellspring of healing and fun. As Molly got to know the youth around ORNG Ink, she started to search for ways to liberate their insights.

One of the first opportunities was a project called [murmur]. Pat had connected with a Canadian group that organized digital storytelling. He handed Molly a list and said, "These are the stories we want to get."

Molly said, "No. We have money from the Kenworthy Swift Foundation to run this as a youth program. The youth who are hired to work for the project will choose the stories."

Pat was uneasy about this, he told us later, but acceded to Molly's leadership.

As I saw it, the teens on the [murmur] crew were as surprised and uneasy as Pat to find themselves in this position of leadership. They were tentative and awkward at first. But roving the city with a microphone, editing stories on the computer, and making a jolly map of the city boosted their confidence. By the time [murmur] was launched, their good spirits were soaring. The great work they had done was widely acknowledged.

It was a great birth of youth urbanism. Molly and Mike became coleaders of the emerging program, their shared confidence in youth serving as the foundation for their partnership.

ORNG Ink moved into Ironworks, which was white and vast. Mike had the idea that it would stay clean and spare, but almost immediately it veered away from that future. Mike started a mural with the goal that everyone who joined the program would contribute to part of it. At its heart was a startling lime green creature with lots of legs, but there was little logic that I can discern in the evolution of that piece. The room soon filled with stuff of all kinds: art supplies and equipment, chairs and tables, a huge printing press, an industrial sewing machine, and a record player with, among other records, Michael Jackson's *Thriller*, which was played nearly continuously throughout the first summer.

The semi-chaotic filling of the space energized the program that began to take shape as a porous and welcoming place for youth. The early success of the T-shirt line fed the hopes of the higher administration that ORNG Ink would be an entrepreneurial wonder, making enough to support itself, maybe enough to support the whole ValleyArts organization. This did not happen.

A collision of visions ensued. Mike and Molly thought the growth of young artists was evidence of their success, while the skeptics thought the chaos and clutter were evidence of their failure. Mike was fired by the ValleyArts Board, the youth program collapsed, and Ironworks became tidy and empty.

A confluence of events resulted in an unlikely breakthrough. First, a couple of Mike's adult supporters confronted Pat over the fact that this unilateral action by the ValleyArts Board was antithetical to the assurances of youth influence over the program. At the same time, the board was becoming concerned that too much of their director's time was taken up with youth programming at the expense of building the ValleyArts organization and raising funds. Then, the director left and the position was vacant for a period of six months. ValleyArts was, in effect, leaderless.

In this leadership vacuum, it was proposed that the University of Orange take over the youth programming, while ValleyArts would continue to pay Mike's weekly fee and provide free space, thus allowing ValleyArts to continue the program, but with no day-to-day responsibility.

There was some board resistance around the fact that ValleyArts would lose control over the content of the program, but others on the board encouraged them, saying "not to worry, anyhow we have more important priorities right now."

While ValleyArts leadership concentrated on long-range planning, fundraising, and building relationships to propel the ValleyArts District, ORNG Ink and an expanded Ironworks program began to reshape its own future with no outside influence, direction, or control. As Pat told me, speaking about himself and other board members, people who might have meddled were preoccupied with other challenges.

The University of Orange, by contrast, was full of educators who understood the "open door" model that Mike and Molly had instituted. Those educators could guide them as they struggled to balance the possibilities of entrepreneurship with the varied skill levels of the young artists, some whose work still belonged on refrigerator doors and some who almost immediately were ready for galleries.

Why be porous? Mental health professionals have known for a long time that adolescents from poor families, piled high with stress and destabilized by a chronic lack of resources, respond best to low-demand environments. The Door in New York City is one of many famous examples of how splendidly this works. The Door demonstrated that letting youth come and go at will, always sure of a welcome and not obliged to perform in any way, was the best way to support fragile young people as they encountered their early independence. The Door also showed that these youth needed such support well into their young adult years, as their parents, beset by demands and worries, were often unable to provide support to their young fledglings. The faculty of the University of Orange took on the challenge of nurturing the ORNG INK program, carefully following the tenets of decades of educational and mental health experience.

Pat contributed the idea that made Ironworks the central tent pole of the Big Top: he said, "Let's build an outdoor, communal oven where people can bring their bread and bake it."

Stephen Panasci, a young landscape architecture student, had actually helped build such an oven and knew how the mud was to be shaped. Jon Foster, who was finishing a master's degree in urban planning, designed the housing for the earthworks. David Mitsack, who knew about mud, took

Patricia Rogers and Mahlin Mehta to a construction site with the right kind of clay soil. They filled a truck with good dirt and took it to Ironworks. Molly called the volunteers, and the actual process of work began.

Sometimes ideas flop and sometimes they work and sometimes they work beyond our wildest dreams. The earth oven was in that last category. The first bread out of the oven was so delicious, people could only dream about having more. Ironworks's oven instantly became the place to celebrate a birthday or other special occasions. The crowds arriving for homemade pizza created new tracks to the small, out-of-way building on Tompkins Street.

At about the same time as the oven was drawing new crowds, the whole of Ironworks was opened to the youth program, which the crew dubbed "a studio for emerging artists." Youth, aged twelve to twenty-five, gathered to share arts experiences and care for one another. A time of fervent and productive creativity ensued. Ironworks was likely to be open in the morning for administrators to meet, in the afternoon for the afterschool program, in the evening for video games projected on the studio wall, and in the middle of the night for the young painters preparing for a show. Everyone who came went someplace else in the neighborhood. Maybe they went by the Laundromat to drop off clothes and take advantage of the very low prices. Maybe they went to Hat City Kitchen, HANDS's restaurant, for a drink or some music. Maybe they went to the hardware store for supplies. Maybe they went to the corner store for soda. Maybe they went to my house to watch TV. Wherever they went, it increased the energy in the neighborhood, building the wealth that Jane Jacobs tried so hard to explain.

Slums, she said, were places where people didn't want to stay. Places that were "unslumming" were places where people had decided to stay. They were using their savings, their sweat equity, and their dreams to make the home they wanted. Ironworks became a center of unslumming, a place in which people were investing for the future they wanted, using whatever came to hand, whatever was freely given, to make their dreams come true (Figure 7.6).

Anj Ferrara and Stephen Batiz were two of the young artists who became part of the unslumming process. When ORNG Ink made a schedule for the gallery for the spring of 2012, they asked Anj and Stephen to prepare

Raising the Big Top

Figure 7.6: Ironworks is an arts space, redeveloped by HANDS from an iron-working factory. ORNG Ink, the youth arts program housed there, has led many activities that energize the reemerging area. Clockwise: Mike Malbrough doing live painting, a popular performance art at Ironworks, during VAMP 2012; Molly Kaufman, Patricia Rogers, Ray Sykes, Jermaine Sutherland, Peter Mawalo, Clifford Pierre, and Tyree Huey at the Orange City Council to talk about the work of the program; Patricia Rogers, Karen Wells, and Molly Kaufman making "Junkyard IPA" beer; the ORNG Ink regulars, ready for the start of VAMP; and Terry Boddie, Sandra Diaz, Patricia Rogers, and Molly Kaufman making the foundation for Ironworks's Earth Oven.

Photo credits: Mindy Fullilove, except "Beer Making," by Maulin Mehta, used with permission.

a show. As young painters, they were ready for such a challenge, having enough control of their media to make the paintings that were in their heads. The point was to actually do it. Hence, the late nights painting away, the lights visible through the garage doors, illuminating the emptiness and filling the void. They named their show "Transverse Megabirth" and created an advertisement that was a marriage of a face painted by Stephen and a forest created by Anj.

On Saturday, March 31, the show opened. Just before the show. Salam, a twelve-year-old who works on his novel at Ironworks, showed me the video of the making of the show. Each piece unfolded in its own time and space, and the videographer captured the fine work of the brush, Anj's pause to strum her ukulele high on a ladder, and the laughter and seriousness of working day after day to bring a vision to reality. Salam watched with great intensity. "You'll really like this part," he kept saying to me. "Tyree, the filmmaker, speeded it up—it didn't look that fast in real life," he explained of one section. He shared some of his Chinese food with me. "I'd like to have a gallery when I grow up. I'd eat Chinese food and paint and have artists over."

That was before the rush: one hundred and fifty people came to show. Neighbors, young artists, and friends of Ironworks came, drawn by the growing energy coming from the building. Stephen had observed what worked and what didn't from other shows and had carefully organized the flow of the space, opening some doors and closing others. The band created a second center of activity and the oven a third. People roamed, ate pizza, admired the art, met each other, and thought they were cool. "I don't know of any other space like this in New Jersey," said one of the young artists. "Most galleries are just art people. But here, it's everybody. I love this. I'm coming back tomorrow."

Unslumming

Jane Jacobs (1991, 271) wrote, "We need to discern, respect and build upon the forces for regeneration that exist in slums themselves, and that demonstrably work in real cities."

She described, in the introduction to *The Death and Life of Great American Cities*, two visits to the North End of Boston. On the first visit, she saw a neighborhood that was battered by poverty.

When I saw the North End again in 1959, I was amazed at the change. Dozens and dozens of buildings had been rehabilitated. Instead of mattresses against the windows, there were Venetian blinds and glimpses of fresh paint.... Mingled all among the buildings for living were an incredible number of splendid food stores.... The streets were alive with children playing, people shopping, people strolling, people talking. Had it not been a cold January day, there would surely have been people sitting. The general street atmosphere of buoyancy, friendliness and good health was so infectious that I began asking directions of people just for the fun of getting in on some talk. (Jacobs 1991, 9)

What is that magic key? "The foundation for unslumming is a slum lively enough to be able to enjoy city public life and sidewalk safety..., slums where the streets are empty and frightening, and one is unsafe, simply do not spontaneously unslum" (Jacobs 1991, 279).

It is important, I think, to understand that the path of unslumming is literally a path—the ways in which we walk around a neighborhood must feel fun and safe. What helps streets, which have been unsafe, to start to feel safe? As we learned in Washington Heights, the people of the neighborhood can take back the streets, but it also helps if some of the most egregious problems in the environment are removed and some bright spots installed. Ironworks is literally a bright spot—its big doors providing a focus for eyes on the street in an area that needs more help—and its growing traffic puts more people on the streets, providing people with their eyes on the street.

Just as with The Legacy on Centre Avenue in the Hill, Ironworks was acting like the massive tent pole that holds up the circus Big Top, a single building working to bring the neighborhood to life, what Ken called a "point of light." "When there are enough points of light, the whole neighborhood will be bright," he said. "That's the way to do it."

CHAPTER EIGHT

Element 6:
Make Meaningful Places

They walked on, thinking of This and That, and by-and-by came
to an enchanted place on the very top of the Forest called Gal-
leons Lap, which was sixty-something trees in a circle; and Christopher Robin knew that it was enchanted because nobody had
ever been able to count whether it was sixty-three or sixty-four,
not even when he tied a piece of string round each tree after he
counted it.

—A. A. Milne, *The Complete Tales of Winnie-the-Pooh*

Some of Cantal's stories I like so much that I make him tell them to me
over and over again. One of those stories is the story of the Princess
and the Medina. Cantal started his career in Tunisia, as I have mentioned.
He got a position in 1970 with the United Nations Educational, Scientific
and Cultural Organization (UNESCO) as the urbanist for the first urban
world heritage site, Carthage/Medina. The project was directed at saving the
archeological site of Carthage and the Medina, the historic center of Tunis.

At the time the project started, the modernization of Tunis called for
the elimination of the Medina so that efficient roads could be installed.
The Medina was a maze of small streets, byways, and dead ends accumulated over twelve hundred years of constant building and occupation. It
looked old and rundown, and somehow signaled the old-fashioned, while
the new nation wanted the modern.

Cantal had a different idea. He saw the *Medina* as the *modern*. Its massive heritage of palaces, schools, *souks* (markets), bathhouses, coffee shops, and residences was the accumulated treasure of a millennium of living. Its narrow streets were the route to healthy people and healthy relationships. Like Jane Jacobs, he saw and felt the intensity of the sidewalk ballet in this living and hearty place.

Figure 8.1: The Medina of Tunis. This image was drawn by a young woman taking art classes near Dar Lasram. It was used for the poster for the exhibit of treasures of the Medina.

Drawing courtesy of Michel Cantal-Dupart.

The UNESCO team, he explained to me, was installed in one of the old palaces, named Dar Lasram. It was going to be renovated for new uses, but, before the renovations could start, the archeologists on the team wanted to carry out an excavation. While digging in the basement, the workers came upon a tomb. The archeologists were called and made a careful examination of the site. Seven stones had been set in ritual fashion to ward off the evil eye. Remains, determined to be those of a young woman, were the only contents of the tomb. After the examination of the body, it was reinterred in the site in which it had been found, and the team went on about its business.

One of the projects they had undertaken was preparing an exhibit at the palace of photographs and artifacts explaining the treasures of the Medina: all the wonderful historic buildings and exciting events that made the Medina such a fascinating place to be. Posters for the exhibit, "Treasures of the Medina," were on display all over the area. A young schoolgirl taking art classes across the street from the palace made the drawing that was used in the poster, and it has been the cover of Cantal's curriculum vitae ever since (Figure 8.1).

The morning the exhibit was to open, the police called the team to the door. A mob scene was going on outside. Word had spread through the grapevine of the Medina that the body found in the basement of the palace (of course, everyone knew a body had been found) was that of a princess, and buried with her was a vast treasure. It was this treasure that was on display. Everyone wanted to see the jewels that had once bedecked this unknown girl.

Cantal remembered that the line went on for blocks, and the police had to keep order. The team tried to tell people that only photographs were inside. "Yeah, yeah," people said. And so the team found that they had an astounding number of visitors, to each of whom they had the chance to show the real treasures of the Medina.

At the time, the story was in the newspapers and it caused quite a brouhaha. "You can't tell these people there's treasure," grumbled one cynic.

But Cantal and the UNESCO team did exactly that: they said there were treasures in the Medina. And maybe they *weren't* the jewels of an unknown princess—well, how often does that happen outside of stories?—but there were *treasures* and the people found them. And once found, people kept the treasures their history had given them. The Medina of Tunis was saved, and the world started to take a new look at all the Medinas in the whole Arab world.

"Everything about urbanism," Cantal said, "passes by way of memory."

A major part of the restoration of the fractured city lies in the transformation of the non-place into a meaningful place.

When we create meaningful places, the sixth element of urban restoration, we are involved in:

- Starting with memory;
- Restoring the center, the edges, and the connections;
- Respecting the many levels of place; and
- Doing all that with style.

Starting with memory

Dan Rothschild said to me, the first time I met with him, "It is not enough to just make places. It is essential to make *meaningful* places." This made so much sense to me that I immediately adopted the idea. But, like all concepts, it came to have more resonance as I participated in places that I thought met his criteria. One such place is the Rothschild Doyno Collaborative's office in Pittsburgh.

In early 2012, Ken Doyno invited me to join him for a community meeting in Homewood. I knew that stories of the firm's work were a key to the completion of this book, so I asked if he would mind spending an hour or so talking with me. He responded with enthusiasm.

On the appointed day, I arrived at the firm's Strip District office, and he gave me my choice of places to settle. It's a big office with a lot of options. "What do you think?" I asked, deferring to his insider knowledge.

He pointed to a modest table in an alcove by a huge window looking over the street corner. He sat opposite me and said, "I've been reading Thom Hartman's (2000) book, *The Last Hours of Ancient Sunlight*. It makes the point that access to oil runs out soon. Ancient sunlight—light transformed to leaves transformed to oil—has driven the growth of our species. We had better figure out how we will get along. The sky is full of 'oil,' but how are we to use it?"

I thought it was an icebreaker, although as I got to know Ken better, I learned that he plunges into conversations in medias res and you just go from there. At any rate, it took my mind off how nervous I was to talk to him about my book. I pulled out the stacks and stacks of papers I'd brought, including the Design Sketchbook I'd been accumulating. When he saw the big pile of sketchbook pages, he smiled with approval and said, "Excellent!"

Before he plunged into my pages, he asked what questions I had. I said, "I'm wondering about these elements of urban restoration that I'm proposing and how they relate to what has happened on the Hill, how these processes emerge over time. And I'm wondering about 1997—about the welling up of community opposition to more destruction. How did urban renewal in Pittsburgh turn toward reweaving?"

I knew he took my questions seriously because a very large and expansive quiet emanated from him and enveloped me while he plunged into my pages. He examined each one, asked questions, and shared his experience. I clarified my ideas, considered his. It went back and forth in that way. At some point, I started to make a sketchbook page that related the elements to a timeline. After that, we went back and forth between our various ideas and this master page.

"What do you mean by 'public space'?" he asked me, indicating what I was using as a title for one of the elements.

"What Jane Jacobs talks about—that the exchanges in the public space are what create the social capital of the society. And, therefore, we have to attend to the social welcoming in the streets, sidewalks, parks, and plazas."

"My experience is that people connect with people. If you talk about this from the perspective of what the people are doing—not what the space is—I think people will understand it better. Why not talk about making a mark? That is something people do to get the public space working."

There's nothing more reassuring than when another person's experience is offered as a guide to right action. Ken also gave me the gift of his absolute attention. He never strayed from the work at hand, looked at his phone or his watch, let his gaze wonder, or hopped up to solve an office problem. In the calm he created, the exchange of ideas transcended time. I don't know that I'd ever sunk as far into a conversation as I did at that place and time.

Just as absolute as Ken's attention was the nurturing offered by the office. There was permission to collaborate: the space was designed for that task with multiple nooks and crannies for exchanging ideas. When we spoke of public space, we talked about what we could see from the big window at which we were sitting. When Ken was explaining the modern-day economics of redlining, he described what it had been like to buy a building in an old industrial area.

On the outside and inside walls and on rolling panels in the office are displayed their Design Sketchbook pages that are like real time maps, an open and transparent process that shows the progression from site forces to ideas to buildings. These make it clear that collaborating is a progression through a labyrinth. I could sink into the day because the process was there to guide to me to a fruitful conclusion.

Dan was a prominent part of this nurturing of collaboration as well. He was struggling with a cold and got to the office late that morning. He stopped at our table to say hello, then left us to the conversation. He returned a while later and said, "It's getting to be one o'clock, and at one, the Middle Eastern place up the street will close for midday prayers. Do you want to stop and go get something to eat or should I get you something?"

I was disoriented by the concept *go-outside*. Dan took all that in at a glance and quickly organized a menu, got the food, brought it to us with napkins and cutlery, and smiled at us benignly. "Wasn't that lovely of him?" Ken asked.

The firm had started as an architecture firm, but had evolved into a collaborative that was drawn to helping people—clients, communities, confused writers—develop and pursue their visions to make the world a better place. Coinciding with their move to the Strip District, they had a chance to do this for themselves. They had designed their offices for the purpose of collaborating. What does collaboration require? Recalling that day, I'd say really good coffee, yummy lunch, and Ken and Dan. I'd add: equity in the space, beauty, grit, hope, and a well-worn path from confusion to completion. The difference between a maze and labyrinth is this:

in a maze, you can get lost, but in a labyrinth, you follow a complicated but continuous path and you cannot get lost.

It—the work they do—is fierce and kind, supportive and nudgy, balancing and unbalancing, spiritual and profane. It deconstructs the known, creating the psychic demand that the collaborators find a new solution, one that lies in what the Taoist philosophers call the "space in between," neither yin nor yang, but the void that links them. The Design Sketchbook pages on the table were that *between*, the space of invention. At one point, the master page I was creating was oriented toward Ken, and I was writing upside down. He nodded approvingly, "A universal skill in this office."

Figure 8.2: Dan Rothschild and Ken Doyno by their office in the Strip District. Note the Design Sketchbook pages on the wall to the right of Dan.

Photo credit: Beatrice Spolidoro, used with permission.

The first time I had visited the Rothschild Doyno Collaborative's office, I had thought of it as a gracious and lovely reused industrial space with lots of raw elements softened by books, posters, and comfortable chairs. But the day I spent working there, I got to know the function of the light and the expansiveness. There was nothing wasted nor overdone, but neither was anything overlooked that could nourish that in-between space in which the collaborators were to do their work. It is, surely, the memory of collaboration that enabled them to create such a perfect space in which to do it.

The conversation glided to a close by midafternoon, and Ken proposed we go see the city. Jane Jacobs (1991), on the opening page of *Death and Life*, says, "The scenes that illustrate this book are all about us. For illustrations, please look closely at real cities. While you are looking, you might as well also listen, linger and think about what you see."

Like arithmetic class in grammar school, we left the office to check our work. Did what we'd thought on Penn Avenue make sense on Centre Avenue? Had the thinking gone astray? Or had the collaborative done

Restoration via connection

Figure 8.3: The plan for the ravine of Hédas is illustrated in the map, while the photos show the various ways in which Cantal opened the space and made it a successful center of restaurants and other city services.

Plan: Courtesy of Michel Cantal-Dupart
Photo credits: top left: Mindy Fullilove; middle and top right: courtesy of Michel Cantal-Dupart.

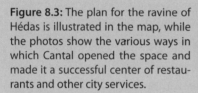

Wall was pierced to connect parts of the city.

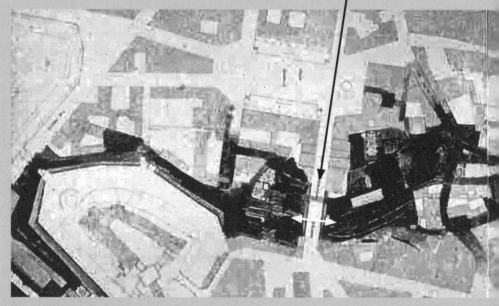

its work of keeping us anchored to the world, on track with sound solutions? We met Terri and went to see Cliffside Park, which she was helping to restore (Figure 10.2). Looking out over the Allegheny River and its

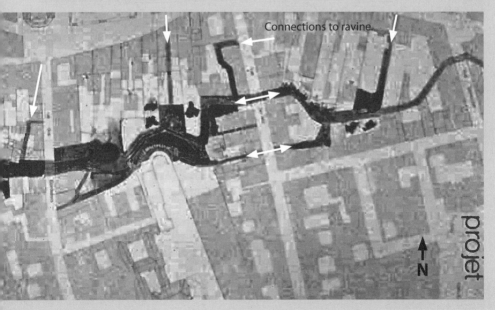

beautiful yellow bridges, my thoughts shivered in resonance to all that had been said, like an echo of rightness or a premonition from the future of how profoundly that day of collaboration would empower my work.

Dan and Ken, in designing their Strip District office, drew on the memory of collaboration. Thus, they created a meaningful space in which I could feel anchored during my visit and in my reflections on that time. I have only to think of the banal sunlit parking lot I watched through the window to have the memory of that experience return with the bursting satisfaction Marcel Proust described when he ate a petit Madeleine dipped in tea. That power to work, that challenging comfort: these are elements of meaningful places, the ones that we long to have, to visit, and to make.

Restoring the center, the edges, and the connections

Remaking the *non-lieu*

When Cantal started to work in Pau, a city in the Pyrénées, it was a place with nowhere to eat dinner after 8:30 p.m., a very early hour for dinner in France. One part of the city that attracted his attention was the ravine of Hédas, a *non-lieu*, a place where people dumped their garbage and old cars. It was so fearsome that the Germans wouldn't go there during World War II. Many plans to make the place better had only served to make it worse. "What I had to do," he wrote, "was to clarify the pathway and restore the bridges, fountains, and public laundries so that people could see the lovely brick homes that made the area picturesque" (Cantal 1994, 56).

Only a third of the projects he'd envisioned ever got done, but it seems they were the right ones: piercing a wall, opening some secret stairways to the public, making an old dying factory into a childcare center, and saving the fountain of Abdel Kader. It became a nightspot, with a skewer of restaurants. "For once, the Hédas had given a taste (*un goût*) to the city" (Cantal 1994, 57).

On a pleasant summer day, when blue skies and a light breeze made it fun to be out, I got to visit Hédas with Cantal. We walked down a long steep set of stairs and emerged in a central plaza that was anchored by a fountain. To my left was a parking lot, and beyond that lay a tunnel—cut by Cantal—through a huge wall. In the other direction was a charming small street, lined with restaurants and bars. People were walking briskly in all directions. We joined the traffic through the wall and emerged alongside a childcare center, with children playing outside and parents coming and going. We sat in the shade of palm trees while Cantal took a phone call.

We turned back to explore the other side of the ravine. Opposite the fountain was a public laundry, an urban facility that was popular throughout France in the late 1800s. The public laundry was a great advance for women, bringing their work from the riverbanks to communal locations indoors. They passed out of use with the invention of machinery for washing and drying clothes. The laundry was gated up, so I had to peer through the grate to see the facilities—according to the book I'd read at Cantal's house, the designs differed greatly from place to place. The old concrete slabs for rubbing clothes and the pipes for bringing water made me shiver in admiration of what it had taken women to keep their families clean. It was a story in placemaking, the public laundry, where stains told family secrets to colaunderers and women made their collective life.

As we proceeded up the little street, Cantal pointed out the inviting pathways that led up out of the ravine on both sides. I liked the bold sign on *Bar L'Imparfait* (Imperfect Bar). We exited at the end of street, mounting stairs back up the ravine's side.

Coming and going in the garden

Space, Cantal has taught me, can be an obstacle or an invitation: it has tremendous power to shape human behavior, a power we can use to advantage if we understand its rules and our needs. The anthropologist Edward T. Hall (1966) explained that the terms "sociopetal" and "sociofugal" can be used to describe spaces that, respectively, bring people together or throw them apart. Of course, in placemaking, what we need are places that do both and that do so at varying levels of scale, from the intimate to the regional. Cantal's work transforms sociofugal spaces into bifunctional spaces, drawing people together so that they can make the most of their city, but also facilitating their leaving when they're ready to go. This, in Cantal's view, is the spatial essence of freedom, so well served by the creation of perspective.

In the American experience, one of the great examples of such space is Bryant Park behind the main branch of the New York Public Library

How is this public space for me?

People sitting here feel exposed, alone.

Triangle Park. Orange, NJ

Here people can be part of something, but maintain privacy.

Van Vorst Park, Jersey City, NJ

Figure 8.4: This page compares the Triangle Park in Orange, New Jersey, with Van Vorst Park in Jersey City, New Jersey. In one park, the benches flank a central planter and face out, without screening from the street. In the other park, the benches are at the edge of a plaza, facing a central planter, with porous screening from the street.

Photo credits: Mindy Fullilove.

in midtown Manhattan. Some modifications to the park had cut it off from the street, making it an isolated and scary space. It had been taken over by drug users and homeless people. Other people cut a wide swath around the park, deserting the businesses, and even the library, out of fear. It was redesigned to connect to the surrounding streets. It was furnished with cast iron chairs and tables that could be moved around and grouped according to the needs of the users. It became a powerful attraction, and it restored vitality to the whole neighborhood and especially to the library. When I asked a class of twenty-five students how many had been to Bryant Park, twenty-two raised their hands.

In my hometown of Orange, New Jersey, a perfectly lovely grassy triangle that was used for children's play and neighborhood celebrations achieved the opposite result when it was landscaped in a sociofugal manner (Figure 8.4). Much of the space was cut up with pavers and planters. In the largest open area, a central planter was installed with two benches, one looking east and the other looking west. If two groups of people come to the park, they sit with their backs to each other. If a parent is there with a child running around, half the time the child is out of sight. The children run between the parent and the passing cars, which dads seemed to tolerate, but moms found quite stressful. I pass by the park nearly every day. There is rarely anyone there, and it turns out that mothers sit on the edges of the planters, to make it easier to watch their children.

I used to live in Jersey City, near Van Vorst Park, a lovely square block that has been made into a lush garden. Like the park in Orange, it has a planter surrounded by benches, but its benches are placed on the outside facing inward toward the fountain. The children who play in the circle are always visible to their parents. People sitting on separate benches have some distance, but they can still see each other, an effective organization of space that Cantal demonstrated in Charenton. I always saw a constant stream of people stopping on those benches, from homeless people who rested there, to mothers with children who wanted to run a bit, to families come to picnic. I often sat there, ostensibly to drink coffee and read my newspaper, but really to watch the ebb and flow of the park.

Van Vorst Park drew me with its many delights. I loved the lush plantings. From early spring to late fall, there was always something in bloom. I enjoyed watching all the animals: the dogs with their owners, the squirrels who cavorted through the trees, and the birds dipping in and out of the fountain. One day, as I was walking through the park, I came across a hawk hopping on the ground, his leg caught in a large plastic bag. I stood frozen in place. He quickly took off, flying awkwardly and landing in a tree, so vulnerable because of that tether on his leg. I watched for five minutes until he flew further away and I lost sight of him.

On another occasion, I had a few minutes to spare before picking up my granddaughter. I decided to go to the park, as it was just a block from my apartment. I was surprised to see a play in progress. Shakespearean actors were striding up and down the grass in cloaks and gowns, with fake swords dangling at their hips. I waved to friends in the crowd and sat on the grass. Fifteen minutes of Shakespeare gave me a good taste of poetry to take with me on my errands.

Cantal's work in space was designed to balance the sociofugal and the sociopetal, recognizing that people want to come to places, but they also have to leave. It should be easy to come and go.

I have often watched Cantal study space. He moves through cautiously, trusting senses other than his eyes: his sense of balance, his spatial sense, and his ability to divine flow come into play. As he searches for the deep logic, I know when he registers what works and what doesn't because I can see him twitch. The first time I saw this, we were in a square in Poitiers, once the largest city in medieval France, now a departmental capital, equivalent to a state capital in the US. We were walking through the cobbled central square, and he looked at the church ahead of us. He picked up the pace. He stopped at the door of the church and, clucking to himself, entered and exited several times. He knelt down and touched the lintel. He shook his head. We exited through another door. Only then did he speak, explaining to me that the side door was the *cagot*, the door for the lepers. He said nothing about his strange examination of the main door.

A few summers later, when he was many glasses of wine into a fine seafood dinner, Cantal turned to me and said, "You scientists are all the same. I know about you. You study the fish. You watch to see what the fish does, and then you watch to see what it means. I know you've been studying me."

He had me dead to rights, of course. I was watching his every move.

Like Thomas Edison, another man with a great gift who insisted that genius is 1 percent inspiration and 99 percent perspiration, Cantal is systematic and relentless in his efforts to understand the city. He visits cities all the time, taking in the places of interest and the local history museums. He reads history and the culture of cities. "Visit a city every week," he advised me. "I had a friend who played a game with me. Every week, we went to see a place in Paris, picked by one of us. We visited places that were amazing and wondrous—each of us wanted to outdo the other. I really got to know Paris playing that game.

"When I was working in Gafsa in Tunisia," he continued, "Steven Spielberg was there filming *Raiders of the Lost Ark*. I was invited one night to watch films with the crew. When it came to really important scenes, Spielberg would get up and stand very close to the screen. They said he watched two films a day when he was making a movie and four a day when he wasn't. It's that constant immersion in the medium that develops expertise."

Perpignan has a park called Square Bir Hakeim, after a famous World War II battle in North Africa. Square Bir Hakeim is not massive like Central Park, but it is substantial enough to provide that pause in nature that urban dwellers sometimes like, though they can be picky about when and where they take it. Jane Jacobs found that parks didn't work simply because they were parks. Rather, successful parks worked because they were carefully embedded in the flow of the city. If the city stopped flowing to and through the park, the park collapsed and became the enemy of the city. That is what had happened to Square Bir Hakeim.

Mayor Jean Paul Alduy asked Cantal to fix the park, which had fallen into disrepair. Asphalt had been spread over the surface so that it could be used for car races and parking. It had become so unattractive only clandestine lovers or people with large dogs sought it out. The neighbors wanted to wall it off in order to contain the danger.

"It's a garden," Cantal said to his team, "so let's make it a garden."

That meant reclaiming the park as a space for growing things. Asphalt was dug up and cars were pushed out. The garden was the site of spectacular old trees, and Cantal wanted to celebrate the symphony of the trees. Its many statues were all treated with care, restored as much as possible. The artificial lake was reorganized and extended so that it became a natural barrier dividing the square from the adjacent area. Cantal had the idea to think of the lake as a moat, with a drawbridge that could be pulled up in time of need. While I wouldn't have thought that would be necessary in a tranquil park, I learned differently. One day, I went to the park. The bridge was up and the square was off-limits because the *tramontane*, the strong, cold wind that sweeps along the Pyrénées to the Mediterranean, was at work.

The goal of Cantal's restoration was to make the square the heart of a city neighborhood. He achieved this goal with wide paths with open

A place for people

Parking encroaches on the park.

Tall fence blocked view to and from the park.

Park road used for car racing.

Figure 8.5: Square Bir Hakeim, in Perpignan, had been paved for car racing and was enclosed in a tall fence. Cantal pushed parking and car racing out of the park and created a new fence that allowed transparency. In the top left photo, we see how the park was used for parking, which extended up to the park's central fountain. After renovation, the parking had been pushed back, so that the fountain had a gracious

sight lines, convenient and frequent entrances and exits, a lacy fence that permits insiders to see the outside and vice versa, and a beautiful central place around a fountain. The gentleness is this: the trees, fountain, and path were all there, but they had lost their edge and their function. Cantal carefully peeled away the excess until it was renewed, and its function was restored. Everything about the renewal was in alignment with the flow of the city (Figure 8.5).

Square Bir Hakeim lies across the street from the Park Hotel, where I usually stay when I am in Perpignan. I love to get up early in the morning

Cars moved to periphery.

Fence lowered and made transparent.

Walking paths narrowed.

surrounding of lawn (top right). In the bottom left photograph, we can see the road inside the park and the high fence. The road was narrowed to a path and a new, transparent fence was created (bottom right).

Photo credits: Courtesy of Michel Cantal-Dupart, except top right, by Mindy Fullilove.

and head out to the park with my camera. If I am early enough, I can catch the coffee klatch of the dog walkers and the tai chi group. A little later, I am sure to see people going to work and others out for their constitutional. The park quiets for a bit after that, and I can explore the statues and study the trees. By late morning, the park starts to fill up again, and it is busy then for the rest of the day. Mothers come with children, lovers sit and drink to each other with their eyes, an occasional drunk staggers by, and women of a certain age gather to gossip.

After the renovations, the real measure of Cantal's work was not an abstract attractiveness, but this coming and going of people who leave wreaths, exercise on the lawns, wander off the paths, plan parties and ceremonies, and hold flea markets. It is their park, my park, our park, belonging to all of us who use it as we see it, making it a living and functioning part of the city. It was on Bastille Day 2008, when the center of Perpignan was flooded with tens of thousands of people, that I really understood what it meant that Square Bir Hakeim had been brought back to life. A frightening cloud of negative space would have inhibited and distorted such a gathering. The health of Square Bir Hakeim acted like a blessing for the fête of the French Revolution. .

Respecting the levels

Baby doll, middle doll, big doll

Rothschild Doyno Collaborative's office in the Strip District takes advantage of a fairly stable industrial district that has a strong urban form, long history, and present-day riches, like Salem's Market, the Middle Eastern restaurant, CJ's, the jazz bar across the street, and the Allegheny River, just three blocks away. Places are always nested in that way, and the work of the urbanist is to think at multiple levels of scale (Figure 8.6).

During Cantal's first visit to Pittsburgh, he introduced us to ways we might shape public space. In a memo called "Six Priority Issues for a Renaissance of the Hill District," he made a list of recommendations (Robins et al. 1999). Cantal knew our grassroots effort could win only by bringing the weight of the city into the equation, but he also knew that people had to make the right demands. His list focused on making strong public space that served many purposes: increasing ownership, enhancing pride, strengthening the grid, connecting to other parts of the city, and welcoming the world. His list paid attention to interventions at a number of levels of scale.

First, he directed his attention to the block, looking at building facades, sidewalks, and corners. At the block level, he noted, it is important to keep both the variety and the relationship among house facades. This gives depth and appeal to the streetscape, mirroring the joy of both difference and interaction. Uniform, predictable, and unvarying design is visually deadening and detracts from the public space (Figure 8.6, Box 1).

He also thought it was useful to add variation to places that were built without it. This is very helpful to housing projects, Cantal noted. Where possible, providing individual gardens was a way of creating a sense of belonging, a sense of community, and a sense that one's neighborhood was worth protecting and maintaining (Figure 8.6, Box 2).

In making strong blocks, Cantal emphasized, personal space needed to be demarcated from the public space of sidewalks, streets, and avenues. Some houses had stairs intruding into the sidewalk without the protection of a front yard. In some neighborhoods, these stoops served as assets, but in others, they were empty. On wide streets, it was possible to focus on creating more in-between space by widening the sidewalks and narrowing the road (Figure 8.6, Box 3).

After the block, Cantal turned his attention to the second level of intervention, the neighborhood. At that level of scale, he emphasized that it was essential to guard the corners of streets and avenues. The houses and stores on these corners had, he argued, a particularly powerful influence on a community, and their nature affected the whole community. Active and open uses cultivated social exchange and comfort. Hidden and closed uses had the opposite effect. In great cities, this is in harmony. Strong, well-designed corners protect the intermediate spaces and create an attractive vista. In this way, the private and public were always in a community-building dialog (Figure 8.6, Box 1).

Related to the need for strong corners was the need for market corners. One feature of urban life that gives neighborhoods great vitality is the presence of strong market centers. One obvious point of intersection was Centre and Kirkpatrick, while another was the cluster of stores near Hill

Getting the Hill on the road to restoration

1. Create a strong street facade.

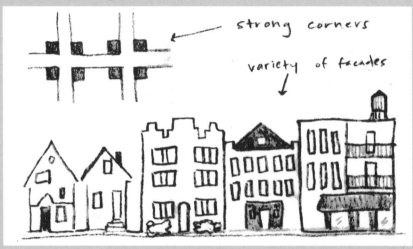

4. Create market corners.

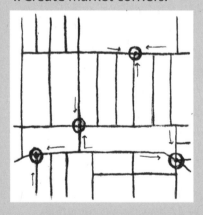

5. Restore access to the river.

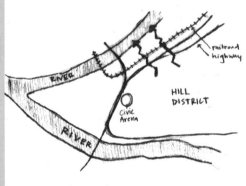

Figure 8.6: In these sketches, we depict the six ideas that Cantal put forward to begin the revitalization of the Hill (Robins et al. 1999).

Sketches: Sarah Schell.

Painting: Street Musicians, ca. 1939-1940, by William H. Johnson. Born: Florence, South Carolina 1901. Died: Central Islip, New York 1970. Serigraph on paper. 17 7/8 x 13 3/4 in. (45.5 x 35.0 cm). Smithsonian American Art Museum. Gift of Mrs. Douglas E. Younger. 1971.143

2. Personalize units.

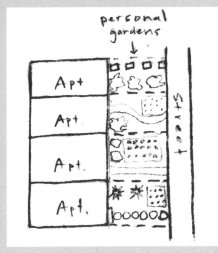

3. Separate houses from the street.

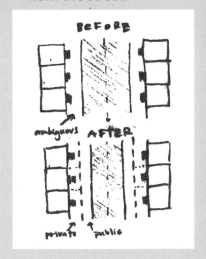

6. Attract people.

House at Centre and Dinwiddie. These and others should be developed, Cantal urged, to serve the community and attract people to visit. Housing should be close enough that market areas weren't left empty after the stores closed for the evening (Figure 8.6, Box 4).

Of course, Cantal's most critical assertion was at the next level of scale: connecting the neighborhood to the city. At that level, he argued, it was essential to create access to the river. The hillside down from Cliff Street was an ideal site for a park, for visual linkage as much as actual physical connection. That spot was crisscrossed with numerous traces of old stairs and trails. These connectors were cut off by the highway, which contributed to the isolation of the Hill from much of the city's current growth and development. Strengthening connection to surrounding communities in all directions was fundamental to the Hill's revitalization (Figure 8.6, Box 5).

Then, he turned to the international: the Hill should attract visitors from all over the world. Successful neighborhoods are magnets for international travel. What is it that would bring people to the Hill District? Cantal left this as a question. I have inserted William Henry Johnson's street musicians, used by Rothschild Doyno Collaborative (RDCollab) in imagining The Legacy (Figure 2.9), as they strike me as hitting just the right note (Figure 8.6, Box 6).

Cantal's style of intervention, like that of most urbanists I've met, is typically a "this and this and this and…" list of interventions that speaks to the complexity of the city that we are to have in mind. Cantal intends the bunch of interventions as a planned set that will act synergistically at a number of levels of scale, energizing the city and making it work again.

Cantal once made the point that the wheels of a mill have to intersect precisely in order for the water to power the grinding. What's involved in getting the wheels to work? Obviously, wheels, gears, shafts, and water are some of the components of such a machine. The city, conceived of as a mill of enormous complexity, has gears, shafts, and sources of power that must all be mobilized, repaired, and synchronized so that the city can function.

This brings us back to Cantal's (1993, 262) remark at *Colloque Triville*: "Doctors know that one can't cure a boil on the surface without treating the whole body. It's the same for the city: we can't resolve the problems of the neighborhood without treating the whole city."

We don't often think of placemaking in this way. We think of placemaking as the interior of a bounded area, as the inside of my house, let us say, or the interior of a great plaza. But Cantal is urging us to think about a place as working if and only if its connections and its setting also work. In this model, we are making the place, and we are making its surrounding place, and that is making the surrounding place, as if the littlest of the Russian nesting dolls could sculpt her larger sisters.

Doing all that with style

I've mentioned Dan and Ken's work on The Legacy, and I return to it here for a fuller exploration of how they made a building that contributes in a powerful way to the new main street emerging on Centre Avenue. They were asked to take on the design of a building to replace a senior housing building called Lou Mason, Jr. Apartments, after a notable African American leader of the Hill. The old Lou Mason building had been located on an isolated road up a hillside, but it was to be replaced by a new building on Centre Avenue.

One of the central facts of RDCollab's approach to the design of the new building is that they acknowledged the wrong of urban renewal. They wrote in the *The Legacy of Jazz*:

> The Hill District was once a vibrant community strongly connected to downtown Pittsburgh. In 1955, a massive urban renewal project was undertaken on the edge of the community. This planning decision leveled a large portion of the neighborhood and created a wasteland between the Hill District and Downtown. The demolition displaced 8,000 residents many of whom were moved to public housing projects on the outskirts of their community, separated from their main streets, houses of worship, retail, and community activities. The urban "renewal" that isolated the Hill District from Downtown brought on decades of social decline throughout the entire community, including a great loss of population. (Rothschild Doyno Collaborative 2008, 1)

RDCollab launched their study of site forces in order to answer the question: How was such a site to be helpful in reversing the urban planning mistakes made in 1955? Embedded in that question is my question: How does a central location solve connectivity problems at the edges of a community?

The answers to both questions lie, I believe, in the designers's broad perspective on what they were doing, their panoramic vision, or, as Ken and Dan say, their ability to "zoom out." They saw themselves as restoring hope and giving a gift to the community, interventions that challenged the demoralization and stigmatization of urban renewal by holding up the area's proud history. In the last chapter, I described how Ironworks, an art center in my neighborhood in Orange, acted like the central pole of the Big Top, lifting up the whole tent—RDCollab's building would be like that.

Furthermore, Ken and Dan were keenly aware of playing with main streets, as The Legacy was to sit between Centre and Wylie Avenues. Before urban renewal, as *Pittsburgh Courier* reporter Frank Bolden told me, Wylie Avenue was "the only street in America that started at a church and ended at a jail." It extended all the way to downtown and was an important connector. Its place in the neighborhood was celebrated in the famous film about the Hill District, *Wylie Avenue Days* (Bolin and Moore 1991). Wylie Avenue had been truncated by urban renewal, weakening its position in the urban hierarchy of streets.

The new building's strategic placement was further enhanced by its central location between Hill House and the corner of Centre and Kirkpatrick, the five-block heart of the emerging commercial section. Placing a new building on an entire central block on such a street has, in the philosophy of RDCollab, the potential to be a counterweight to decades of abuse. In particular, they have insisted that, as buildings are the "natural proprietors of the street," to use Jane Jacobs's term, buildings must connect with the street with maximum possible intensity. Buildings must be extroverted, that is, turned to the street. Buildings must amuse the street, lift morale, and affirm heritage. Buildings must be good citizens of the street. They set the standard for neighboring by the way in which they do their job. In Figure 8.7, I compare the approach to neighboring used by Columbia University Medical Center—a harsh, impenetrable white wall

Buildings as neighbors: making solid walls friendly

No way to connect.

Welcoming.

Figure 8.7: In the photo on the top, we depict the hostility conveyed to the neighbors in Washington Heights by the unrelieved solid wall of a Columbia University Medical Center building. By contrast, at The Avenue in Braddock, Pennsylvania, RDCollab was able to make a solid wall a friendly and inviting part of the environment.

Photo credits: Columbia University Medical Center building: Mindy Fullilove; The Avenue, photo by Rich Brown, used with permission.

turned towards the neighborhood—and that used by RDCollab to make a similarly solid wall a place of delight by installing art made by Robert Qualters in consultation with the people of Braddock.

In the *Lou Mason, Jr. Design Sketchbook*, Rothschild Doyno Collaborative's (2005, 12) musings about The Legacy are rooted in a page called, "Sense of Memory," on which they wrote, "This memory allows those of us fortunate enough to experience the rich and diverse community of the Hill and continue its growth as an experience, a place of comfort, a community, a Home."

These reflections continue on the next page, "Sense of Place," where they note,

> The Hill is not about one Moment, one Culture, one Race or one Belief. It is about all Moments, all Cultures, all Races, and all Beliefs. It is not about a building type or the placement of a function. It is about life and how each of these respond to each other, allowing the weaving of building functions. Each addressing all, giving this neighborhood a Sense of Place. (Rothschild Doyno Collaborative 2005, 27)

The four photographs on the Design Sketchbook page, "Sense of Place," substantiate this claim, depicting a swimming pool, a synagogue, the statue of St. Benedict the Moor that resides atop the eponymous church, and the Milk Station. This claiming of the Hill as a place of all races is both a true statement and a bold beginning of the design process. The process of sorting-out the city pushed whites out of the Hill and into other Pittsburgh neighborhoods, leaving an all-black ghetto. It has become reified as an "African American neighborhood." In the politics of ethnic cleansing that accompany serial displacement, change is likely to mean expulsion of all African Americans. Admitting the multiracial past is not a problem, but bringing that past into the present is fraught. RDCollab, having placed this complex truth on the table, must solve three problems at the same

Figure 8.8 (opposite page): Designing The Legacy: Jazz Fusion. In this Design Sketchbook page, Dan Rothschild took the jazz connection (diagram at right) and developed it via the concept of "Eckstinian Geometry." This allowed him to translate the rhythms of jazz into architecture. See also Figure 2.9, Designing The Legacy: Jazz Rhythms and Dissonances.

Credit: Design Sketchbook Page courtesy of Rothschild Doyno Collaborative.

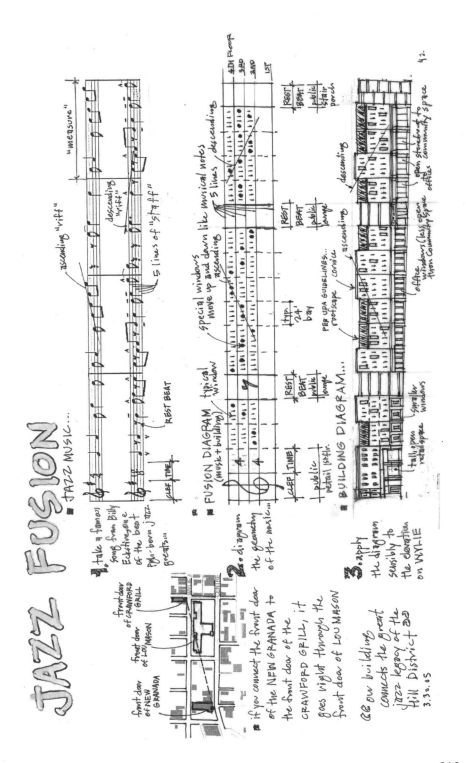

JAZZ FUSION

■ JAZZ MUSIC...

1. take a famous song from Billy Eckstine...one of the best "rhi-bourn JAZZ" Greats...

"ascending "riff""

descending "riff"

5 lines of "staff"

REST BEAT

"measure"

BEAT TIME

■ FUSION DIAGRAM (music + building)

2. diagram the geometry of the music...

typical window

special windows move up and down like musical notes

5 lines descending ascending

REST BEAT public lounge

REST BEAT public lounge

BEAT TIME

public retail store

■ BUILDING DIAGRAM...

if you connect the front door of the NEW GRANADA to the front door of the CRAWFORD GRILL, it goes right through the front door of LOU MASON

front door of CRAWFORD GRILL

front door of LOU MASON

front door of NEW GRANADA

3. apply the diagram to sensibly tie the elevation on WYLIE

our building connects the great jazz legacy of the Hill District ⊃⊃

3.30.05

4TH FLOOR
3RD
2ND
1ST

REST BEAT public stair porch

descending

ascending

TYP 24' bay

PER UPA GUIDELINES rooftscape cornice

office windows (less open windows) to open Community space offices

smaller windows

tall, open retail space

42.

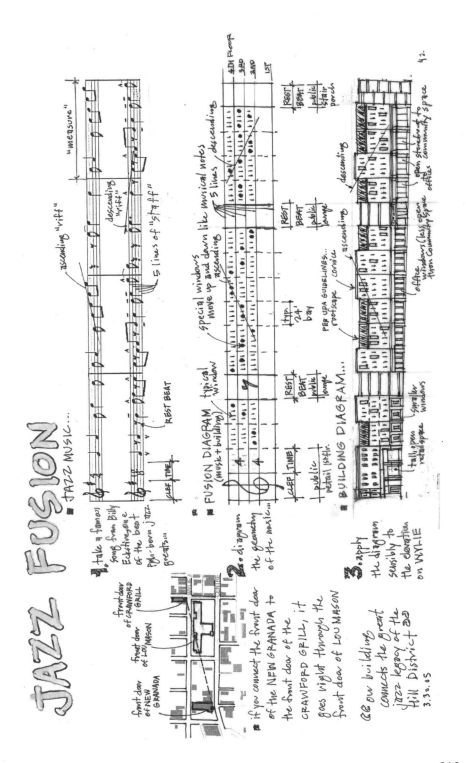

time: honor the truth, avoid harm, and do good. As Dan put it, "There's a difference between being 'not bad' and 'good.'"

The House of Jazz, Terri's project of putting images of jazz artists in the windows of buildings just down the street on Centre Avenue (Figure 5.2), was not the only reminder that jazz was a profound and joyous part of the neighborhood's history. The New Granada Theater and the Crawford Grill, both bordering The Legacy, were two of the most important jazz clubs in the neighborhood.

But what did jazz have to do with affordable housing for seniors? The Design Sketchbook for The Legacy carefully examined the powerful site forces working at that location, including its position on two major avenues, the needs for future development on the site, and an amazing history of jazz venues on either side of the block. Slowly, the pages start to explore what jazz might mean as a site force for the building, playing with idea after idea, until, on March 30, 2005, they make the "Jazz Connection": a line is drawn across the plan and on it is written, "If you connect the front door of the New Granada with the front door of the Crawford Grill, it goes right through the entry door of Lou Mason!" (Rothschild Doyno Collaborative 2005, 39).

After a couple of pages that look at the stories of the great jazz musicians of the Hill, a page called "Jazz Fusion" repeats the startling observation about the doors and goes on to say, "Our building connects the great jazz legacy of the Hill District" (Rothschild Doyno Collaborative 2005, 42).

"Jazz Fusion" involved three steps (Figure 8.8): The first was taking a famous song by Billy Eckstine, one of the jazz greats from Pittsburgh. The second was to diagram the geometry of the music. And the third was to apply the geometry sensibly to the elevation on Wylie. With Eckstinian geometry in the driver's seat, the design process homed in rapidly on the concept of changing the steady beat of facade to a syncopated one.

This was a great breakthrough and in the days that followed, the design process flourished. Correctly placed, The Legacy and its jazz panels would have a great effect on the recovery of the Wylie-Centre corridor. In retrospect, it seems obvious that the jazz history of the site was as real as gravity, but the reality is that most designs might stop with only a marker or some historic quotation. For RDCollab, it changed the entire expression of the building from the walls to the details. The joy of the building comes directly from the location. Its connection with people of the area and dialog with its surroundings are key signals of respect, essential to community restoration.

This was such a rich design inspiration that it triggered many other strong and playful concepts. Eventually, the building had carefully located awnings that helped to create the system of visual rhythm. The architects pulled the bricks in one section to make the song, "Just the two of us."

The secret and obvious playfulness of the building was combined with four other features important to its success in meeting complex goals. The first was the ribbon band of names of jazz greats. The ribbon band echoed the marquee of the New Granada just down the street on Centre Avenue. It was in the spirit of the carved names of scientists and philosophers that ring the Carnegie Museum in the nearby Oakland neighborhood. Motivated by this idea, the Housing Authority of the City of Pittsburgh created a ballot with the names of thirty jazz greats. People voted for their favorites, and the top twelve vote getters had their names inscribed in massive stone panels. This had profound meaning for the neighborhood, and, by extension, for all neighborhoods at the juncture of reinvestment. Many other neighborhoods have lost their historic names as African Americans have been pushed out. The assertion of the identity of the African American neighborhood—in a building named "The Legacy"—retains the heritage as the neighborhood moves into the future.

The second act—related to the Hill as a place of "all races"—was to create a visual link to the neighborhood's first synagogue, a modest building around the corner on Erin Street. Rothschild Doyno Collaborative (2008, 8) noted in their publication, *The Legacy of Jazz*, that the "red and gold brick patterning on the neighborhood's first synagogue is repeated in red and gold stripes on the building's three corners to link history with the present."

This tribute to the older history of the Hill has profound significance. The Hill was the entry neighborhood for generations of immigrants to Pittsburgh. It is dotted with the buildings of many peoples, buildings inherited by the African Americans when they became the predominant ethnic group. This multicultural heritage is part of the Hill. In fact, historian Laurence Glasco once told me that he thought it was a real weakness in the plays of August Wilson that he didn't tackle that complexity of the

Hill.[1] The Legacy is not just a legacy of jazz, but also a legacy of multiculturalism that should be treasured, discussed, and, most importantly, *continued*. In its acknowledgment and continuation lie the defeat of sorting and all its attendant horrors.

The third act was that the Urban Redevelopment Authority worked with McCormick Baron Salazar, the developers, to put retail stores on the ground floor of The Legacy. One of the great failings of American public housing was that it was only residential. This kind of monoculture—especially in the large public housing projects—stultified and distorted the diversity fundamental to vibrant urban life, as well as perverting people's ability to have plans of their own. Multiuse buildings are key to using public housing dollars to greatest effect.

The fourth act was that McCormick Baron Salazar worked with Hill House to integrate a remarkable collection of art into the building. They advertised for local artists to submit jazz-inspired artwork to be exhibited at a public art showing that Terri Baltimore organized at Hill House. At the end of the show, McCormick Baron Salazar purchased all of the works for the building. The artwork inspired Dan to create a central element in the lobby, a set of embedded trumpets that support a glass mantle above the fireplace. The set of trumpets and the magnificent fireplace lifted The Legacy from fine to meaningful, making it a showplace for the neighborhood and its residents. One of the people who moved into the building said, "It's the first time in my life I feel respected by the place I live."

At the time RDCollab finished The Legacy in 2007, they wrote, "Since the building has been completed, the announcement of a new library and new YMCA on adjoining blocks has given credence to the catalytic nature of the project. Hope has also returned for the renovation of the adjacent jazz venues: Crawford Grill and the New Grenada Theater" (Rothschild Doyno Collaborative 2005, 16).

Well, the library was completed in 2008. In other neighborhood developments, the Kaufman Auditorium, redesigned as a conference center and concert hall, was completed in 2011, the first phase of infill housing on Dinwiddie Street was completed in 2011, and the construction of the Thelma Lovette YMCA was completed in 2012. The renovation of the historic Miller School and the building of a new grocery store are to be completed in 2013. RDCollab has also been awarded the contract to design The Legacy II.

Yet, it has been a constant and complex effort to extend RDCollab's holistic urbanism to new projects so that they all contribute to creating the welcoming city. Driving down Centre Avenue with Ken, he pointed to the Y, which was under construction, and asked, "Where should the door of that building be?"

I had an intense flashback to medical school, hearing the chief surgeon bark at me, "*Name that artery!*"

I batted the memory away and applied the rule of align and connect. "Opposite The Legacy's door."

He didn't say anything, but the stony silence reminded me of walking with Cantal through Square Bir Hakeim. He was complaining about the extent to which cars were encroaching on the park and muttered, "It's a constant battle."

On another occasion, Ken told me, "To get the great city to emerge, every opportunity needs to realize its full potential. This is design efficiency. It is essential for urban restoration. To put it another way, there are right relations among people and there are right relations in space. We should always strive to be in right relation to the world."

CHAPTER NINE

Element 7: Strengthen the Region

The lake was silent for some time. Finally it said:

"I weep for Narcissus, but I never noticed he was beautiful. I weep because, each time he knelt by my banks, I could see, in the depths of his eyes, my own beauty, reflected."

What a lovely story, the alchemist thought.

—Paul Coelho, *The Alchemist*

The French call the hour between daylight and full dark *entre chien et loup*, between the dog and the wolf, which one translator suggested might be called "the gloaming" in English. It is a magical and dangerous time: we are outside without the protection of sunlight. It was at that time, driving through the city of Bordeaux, that Cantal drove past a *dalle*, the elevated platform on which a tall tower had been built. The *dalle* was deserted, and it cast a pall on the street level.

Then, we turned the corner and entered a section of the old city. A square with a park at its center—sunk just a bit below the street grade to create a serene space in the middle of traffic—was buzzing with light, activity, and people. The thrill of the working city passed through me like a jolt of electricity.

"When they could have this, why do people do that to the city—build structures like that *dalle*?" I asked.

"There are many ways to make war," he muttered.

As I have traveled through regions sundered by sorting, I have often reflected on that comment. How do we come to see one another as friends, how can we learn to accept our inherent interdependence, and how do we step into the reality that we live in the interwoven metropolitan regions?

The seventh element of urban restoration, strengthen the region, involves:

- Recognizing that every part of the region has a right to be loveable;
- Making the vast regional conversation; and
- Building the city on the city.

Recognizing the right to be loveable

Banlieues 89

Banlieues 89 was Cantal's first major regional project in France. This project addressed the failure of French urbanism to connect massive new construction to the existing cities. This phenomenon could be seen in cities, when construction was placed at an edge or in a cul-de-sac, and in the nation's suburbs, *les banlieues*. As the buildings were often meant to house working people and immigrants from the colonies, the obvious classism, racism, and colonialism were not lost on anyone. Cantal viewed this as execrable from the standpoint of common decency and human rights and as dangerous from the standpoint of maintaining civil society.

Cantal had learned in Tunisia that it is helpful to be able to go to the top. While working in southern Tunisia, he was asked to present his ideas to the president of the nation. His presentation, which was scheduled for twenty minutes, went on for two hours. The work of his team gained attention and respect because the president endorsed it.

In *Merci La Ville!*, Cantal (1994) recounted that, in France, a connection to national policymaking in urbanism was opened in 1976 at the 37th Congrès de l'Union des Habitations à Loyer Modéré, the Congress of the Union of Moderate Income Housing (the HLM, which is French for housing projects). That group had just issued a white paper, commending efforts at construction and criticizing problems of *l'insertion urbaine*, urban insertion, that is, the ways in which the projects were set into the urban system. The Clodion project in Perpignan, described in Chapter 6, is an example of the kind of problem they were identifying. Clodion, set in a cul-de-sac formed by a highway, a field, and a stadium, was typical of the egregious errors of urbanism that affected housing projects all over the nation (see Figure 6.4, Before).

It was because of that challenge that Jean-Michel Bloch-Lainé, the inspector of finance and the new director of construction, began to consider the question of urban insertion and convened a group of urbanists for a "National Consultation on Habitat." Cantal worked with Antoine Grumbach, Roland Castro, and Antoine Stinco to visit seventeen cities and debate the issues with mayors, *maitres d'ouvrage,* the construction managers, and local associations. The effort resulted in a report called "Un espace pour la vie" and the book, *La Ville à Livre Ouvert* (Castro, Cantal, and Stinco 1980).

When I asked Cantal, "Does it cost more to make a beautiful building?" he sent me to get a copy of *La Ville à Livre Ouvert*. As we traveled around France, he began to show me some of the laudatory housing projects it documented. One of the first we visited together was a project by Le Corbusier just outside of Bordeaux. The squat houses were meant to be perfect "machines for living," but people had altered them in various ways to suit themselves. This is the fate of all buildings, according to Stewart Brand's (1994) investigation of how buildings change over time. The point was not that Le Corbusier's buildings changed, but rather that they remained attractive and functional housing more than fifty years after they had been built. Several fundamental ideas emerged in that study that challenged the "poor-tall-and-ugly" thinking that dominated French building in the 1950s and 1960s.

The report opened a conversation that continued at various levels of French society. Cantal and his colleagues looked for ways to continue the work, finally proposing Banlieues 89, a five-year project that would end in 1989 at the time of the bicentennial of the French Revolution and an exposition to be held in Paris. In July 1983, President Mitterand agreed to go on an architectural tour, specifically to see the works of Ricardo Bofill. The team seized the opportunity to organize a most unusual visit in the suburbs of Paris, following a line of obsolete forts that encircled the Greater Paris area.

The trip was made by helicopter, by car, and by foot. The helicopters served to show the overview of the new cities and those works of Bofill that merited being seen from the sky. They took the president by foot to see the housing projects so that he would have a first-hand sense of the problems. Cantal (1994, 128–29) wrote, "We put in place an impeccable pedagogy: that which worked and that which didn't, showing him the margins and between spaces, those *non-lieux* which constitute the city frontiers where highways, railroads, public housing and immigrant housing are concentrated."

The highlight of the trip was the comparison between the Butte Rouge at Chatenay-Malabry and the Quatre Mille at La Courneuve. The first project—whose beauty and functionality had been highlighted in *La Ville à Livre Ouvert*—had stately, well-proportioned buildings set in a serene landscape. Although constructed in 1934 and lacking some modern amenities, the Butte Rouge housing project was loved and fully occupied. The second project, Quatre Mille, built in 1963, was already worn out.

The president, who had understood what he had just seen, gave his support to a project to beautify the *banlieues* and improve their relationship to the center. Without money, but with Mitterand's endorsement, Cantal and Castro launched their project, using the old fortifications around Paris as the organizing theme. *Forts et Fêtes*—Forts and Festivities—became one of the slogans. They recruited architects willing to help and asked mayors of the cities in the *banlieues*, "How would you propose to repair, free up, link, modify, identify, invent intercity projects, find the geography, recreate the landscape, reconcile the street and the city, or nourish the site?"

By February 1984, seventy-four mayors, each accompanied by an architect, presented to the president a project that would not only beautify their city but also contribute to the betterment of the region. The whole checkerboard of French politics was involved, from the right to the center to the left. There was a debate about which projects to support. Some argued to support only the best, but others wanted to use the opportunity to curry political favor and picked projects favored by certain influential politicians. Cantal and Castro argued for funding all of the projects, and that carried the day. Six months later, an additional 152 projects, from all over the nation, were funded. Cantal's relationship with Mayor Jean-Paul

Alduy, which was to be so important for them and for the city of Perpignan, dates to this period.

As the projects were getting started, Banlieues 89 created a massive dialogue about what they called "Grand Paris," focusing on projects that would transform the urban structure of Paris and its surrounding suburbs. At that time, this was not a widely held or very popular idea. Cantal and Castro began by making a grid to overlay the circular form of the Paris region (Figure 9.1). This grid, Cantal explained to me, shifted the emphasis from the Champs Elysées to the many delights in the periphery of the capital. A massive investigation was undertaken. It included visits to every square of the quadrillage, as well as a major geographic investigation of the distribution of roads, housing projects, cafés, and many other assets.

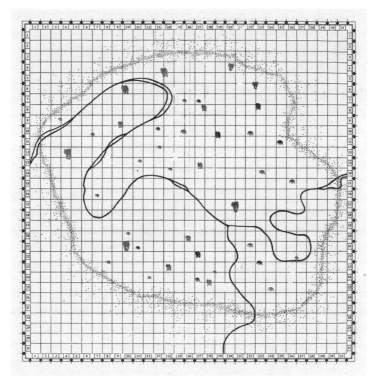

Figure 9.1: Grid of Banlieues 89. A grid divided the Greater Paris region, and Cantal and his colleagues searched for the outstanding elements of urbanism in each section. They argued that every square has a right to be loveable. They placed elephants in many squares of the grid, creating an entirely new way of seeing the Greater Paris region. Each "dot" on this map is an elephant.

Courtesy of Michel Cantal-Dupart.

This investigation both arose from and led to a new way of thinking about the region, which was characterized by five concepts (Castro 1986). The first concept was to think in terms of voyages, because wherever one was, one always wanted to have to opportunity to go someplace else. The second concept was to think in terms of the uncertain, the complex and the multiple, since no project could be guided by simplified ideologies. The third concept was to think in terms of the place more than the object, and to think of the object as containing public spaces and linkages to the city. The fourth concept was to think in terms of the quadrillage, searching for magical places (*lieux magiques*) in every square. The fifth and final concept was to think in terms of finding other relationships (*rapports*) between the universal and the particular. Castro (1986, 6) emphasized, "All the work of Grand Paris is a kind of democratic machine that affirms that every place has the right to exist and the right to make itself loveable."

In December of 1985, people engaged with Banlieues 89 met in Enghien-les-Bains, a beautiful city by a lake just on the outskirts of Paris (see the photo in Figure 9.5). The two-and-a-half day *Assises* (conference) offered Castro and Cantal a chance to explain their thinking to the mayors, architects, and other partners in the effort to beautify the suburbs. A transcript of the meeting, published by *Murs Murs*, allows us to glimpse the vast extent and excitement of the project (Banlieues 89 1986). Cantal and Castro were not only traveling far and wide in France, peering into every corner and dissecting every problem and its possible solutions, but also being invited to go to other countries to understand the similarities and the differences.

In the press of invention, Cantal and Castro articulated a whole style of urbanism. Three features of the style were: gain time with time (*gagner du temps sur le temps*), employ pointillism, and build the city on the city. "It's a nerve-wracking problem," Cantal told the audience, "that urbanism takes a long time and people can become impatient. Therefore, we have to gain time. We all know that ephemeral events—like a fair—can take over a city. Therefore, we can use the ephemeral to create excitement and build momentum while we are waiting for construction to go forward. The parties we are holding in the forts are part of this strategy, and we can think of ways to improve and deepen these crucial events" (Banlieues 89 1986, 19).

Pointillism was perhaps more controversial. How, challenged some, did working on a point help a city? Cantal countered that urbanism was always working at a point. The key for Banlieues 89 was to understand that there were many, many points being activated at once, in a net of solidarity. There were, after all, 226 projects that had been launched. "In the crystallization of salt," he argued by analogy, "we know that a point will start the process. We don't know which point, and we can't predict exactly how it will proceed. But we know that it will proceed from small beginnings to the final crystal and we can say with certainty what that crystal will be like" (Banlieues 89 1986, 85).

The concept of building the city on the city has been one of the most important to emerge from Banlieues 89. At that time, the cities in France were rapidly expanding outward into the countryside. But Cantal and Castro argued that, instead, the cities themselves should be evolving and mutating, looking to wasted space at the margins and abandoned industrial sites and at places that might be densified and made more complex. In this way, the city could be pushed forward without swallowing up farmland and losing the advantages of concentration.

At the end of the *Assises*, President François Mitterand addressed the group. He made it clear that Banlieues 89 held hope for the nation if it could solve the problems of all. He saw in the creative energy and diverse projects a new tool for creating a vast tissue of democracy. "You are the avant-garde, building a form of civilization… I tell you that," he concluded, "this 7th of December, 1985, and in ten years, twenty years, thirty years…. Therefore, make something so solid that, in spite of all the changes in humor and in fashion, others will see it and want to use it" (Banlieues 89 1986, 180).

All kinds of projects were carried out. In Saint-Priest, a suburb of Lyon, the city hall was in the center of town, but facing it were the kitchens and bathrooms of a nearby building. The project consisted of putting in a parking deck, library, and movie theater. Cantal (1994, 131–32) observed, "There was nothing unusual in this idea, but they had the idea to put in a propylaeum—like the columned entrance of the Parthenon—which people really liked. It became an active plaza, where the weekly market was held, the heart of the city."

In La Rochelle, a housing project was falling apart. Its only asset was that it faced the sea. The idea emerged to turn it into vacation housing. A number of agencies were approached, but none were interested in the project. Finally, it was the city that did the necessary renovations. The newly organized vacation housing was an instant hit. "I defy you to find a vacant apartment there," Cantal (1994, 133) challenged the reader of *Merci La Ville!*.

The successes of Banlieues 89 were evident, but the ideas were quite avant-garde. They were not carried forward or universally adopted in the broad way that was clearly called for by the widespread problem of *non-lieux*, the dysfunctional places. The problems of the *banlieues* erupted in riots in 2005 and 2006. That served to emphasize the degree to which these urban centers had remained isolated from the mainstream of urban life in France.

In the meantime, Castro and Cantal took the repertoire of repair into their own urbanism, as did many other progressive urbanists. Among the ideas that Cantal articulated at the *Assises*, and which have characterized his later work, were the need to create spaces to bring citizens, planners, and politicians together to discuss the future of the city, as, for example, in L'Atelier, which Mayor Alduy established in Perpignan; the importance of bringing the edges of the city into relationship with the city's center, as in Rion des Landes; and the crucial role of many points of light, many scattered projects, in illuminating a large area, as with the many projects in Pau.

Perhaps, the most profound intervention Cantal and Castro made was the layering of the grid over the map of the Paris region. I first began to understand the grid, and what that had to do with Banlieues 89, in 2003, when Cantal and his colleagues from the project celebrated the thirtieth anniversary of its beginning with a party at Fort de Champigny in Chenn-evières-sur-Marne. At the party, posters and maps detailed the process and the projects that had been carried out. Several publications revisited what had happened. It was an opportunity for me to dig deeper into what he'd meant.

At the same time, Rod Wallace and I launched our first regional study, an examination of the ways in which urban renewal in the urban core of Newark, New Jersey, had triggered displacement and housing destruction through the whole of Essex County. Out of that work, in 2008, I launched Main Street New Jersey, a study of the role of main streets in people's mental health. That study was designed to look at what was on a main street and how it was used. This was inherently a study of living in the solution, and my first foray into a methodology like Cantal's grid.

Cantal, commenting on the grid, has emphasized that the grid has no inherent place of preference. The grid gives value to everything. This is for us, in the United States, perhaps the most fundamental assertion of the project, as the grid of Banlieues 89 is the antithesis of the redlining map (see Figure 2.3).

The task of the grid is to examine each of the squares in order to find what is useful and what is magical in the entire system of urban structures. The long-term goal is to use those trump cards to make each of the squares an exemplary place to live. "Planners can get in trouble when they start to prescribe exactly what should happen where, especially in a big region. Wherever things start to happen, it's good they are happening. We can support what people like by making it more comfortable, more functional," he elaborated to me.

Making the vast regional conversation

In February 2010, Rothschild Doyno Collaborative (RDCollab) undertook the development of a vision for the 178-acre LTV Steel Hazelwood site, a river plateau that was formerly occupied by a major steel plant, now largely demolished. It is the last large steelmaking site left to be redeveloped in the city of Pittsburgh. In 2002, four southwestern Pennsylvania foundations, sure that its redevelopment had the potential to drive the future of the region, formed a limited partnership called Almono to buy the land. Key to the foundations' thinking was that the redevelopment should focus on all dimensions of the long-term sustainability of the site.

The site was a long gourd-shaped slice of land along the Monongahela River, east of downtown, abutting Hazelwood, a poor and largely African American community that had shrunk from its heyday when the steel mill was there (Figure 9.2). Railroad tracks passed through, running west to downtown. Water passed through, following the runs down to the river. A few historic buildings remained from the site's steelmaking past.

ALMONO PARTNERSHIP MASTER PLAN

Almono Vision, Partnership Meeting 1, February 11, 2010

ECONOMIC:
- Provide site amenities that are supported by **generating tax revenues**
- Do **not overly subsidize** to achieve success
- **Attract developers** to invest and pursue projects
- Incorporate for **profit and non-profit** entities into the planning and use of the site
- Participate in changes in the **energy economy**
- Generate **reinvestment** in the area surrounding the site

SOCIAL:
- Be **welcomed** by the surrounding community
- **Build synergies** among different users
- Attract a **range of interests** that can participate in change making
- Provide **access to the river**
- **Attract new people**, don't just pull from the surrounding neighborhoods

PHYSICAL:
- Learn from visionary precedents
- Plan transportation as both a local and regional asset
- Use best-practices in **sustainable site and building design**
- Advance **alternative energy systems** over time
- Propose **imaginative reuse of existing buildings**
- Provide a **mixture of uses** appropriate to distinct locations
- Create a unified vision

ECONOMIC
SOCIAL
PHYSICAL

2

03-11-10 Partnership Meeting

Figure 9.2: Almono ESP. The aerial photograph on the left shows the setting of the project and the gourd-shaped project site, outlined in white. The key economic, social, and physical goals are listed to the right. This page became the foundation for all subsequent work.

Credit: Design Sketchbook Page courtesy of Rothschild Doyno Collaborative.

What is to be done with a site that is both vacant and active?

As with their placemaking at The Legacy, RDCollab started with a reverence for the site: the railroad, the water, the history, and the remaining industrial buildings. It is from these elements that their plan grew.

The Almono site was rebuilding in an even larger context than The Legacy. The Legacy was located on Centre Avenue, the emerging main street of the Hill. Almono is located on the Monongahela River, one of the natural main streets of the region. Nothing about Pittsburgh can be understood outside of the context of the Three Rivers—the Allegheny, Monongahela, and Ohio. They are, literally, the source. Just as The Legacy needed to animate Centre Avenue, the Almono site needed to animate the Monongahela and the region it serves. Indeed, the name Almono is composed of the initials for the Allegheny, Monongahela, and Ohio Rivers, which implies that the site is seen as central to the reanimation of the whole region.

RDCollab worked programmatically, and the process was constantly taken back to the economic, social, and physical outcomes endorsed by the Almono partners, what they were FOR (Figure 9.2).

I visited RDCollab's office in October 2010 while this process was in full swing. The movable walls in their Strip District office were covered with sketchbook pages looking at every aspect of the site. There might have been a hundred pages on display at that time. The wealth of information was breathtaking, as was the care with which it was presented. When I had the opportunity to study the reports to the partners, a set of ten Design Sketchbooks, what impressed me was how much attention had been paid to making the information on the pages accessible. I am not an entirely naïve reader, but I have not paid that much attention to railroad right-of-way or combined sewer outflow problems. Yet, I felt that I could understand a great deal about these issues from careful perusal of the pages, as they colorfully and playfully mixed words with pictures.

The genius of the Design Sketchbook is that the pages keep active the many threads of a complex process. RDCollab was examining twelve domains, divided equally among the economic, the social, and the physical, as the process evolved from questions to design solutions. In addition to keeping all the threads active, the sketchbook keeps the many participants looking at the same body of information. The participants, a group numbering easily in the hundreds, included the partnership of owners, key stakeholders including from many city agencies, and four advisory communities.

By examining Design Sketchbook pages with maps, tables, diagrams, and photographs, that complex group of people could master the issues that had to influence the decisions. Massive site forces, for example, were impinging on the site, including railroad tracks, highway right-of-way, and an outdated sewer system. These were realities that would have to be managed in the redevelopment plan. And they weren't the only ones. All of those who engaged deeply in the project, as the leading representatives of the partners did, could juggle the same information RDCollab was juggling. This meant that a massive group of people was moving together towards crucial decisions, acknowledging the complexity of competing interests.

In Rothschild Doyno Collaborative's (2011) *Almono Vision*, a page, entitled "What We've Heard," offered a brief overview of what the stakeholders had said during the process. It hints at the range of issues that the Almono project had to tackle. Here are a few sample comments that Rothschild Doyno Collaborative (2011, D17) collected:

> "The level of service along Irvine St./Second Avenue is awful for the traffic and for the business district. Getting trucks through Hazelwood has been an issue for decades."—Pat Hassett, City of Pittsburgh.

> "The Run and Saline Streets only have one way in and out and we are concerned that this is dangerous but any connection to Neville needs to be slow and safe."—Bill Smith, Greenfield Organization.

> "I'm concerned for the businesses and residents that will be threatened by change no matter what. Some may not want to be more connected but would rather be left alone."—Rev. Leslie Boone, Hazelwood Presbyterian Church.

> "We're going to protect South Oakland as a high quality residential neighborhood. For us that means less traffic cutting through to Swinburn Street and better connection to the park."—Wanda Wilson, Oakland Planning and Development.

A crucial piece of such a process is that it takes time. People have to study the data, get to know one another, think through philosophical and ethical issues, and consider options. There is no way to rush such an exchange. A substantial investment was made in meetings, which are the heart of consideration, building trust, and negotiation. Ken always emphasizes his process goal of "align and connect," and this was certainly a core activity of the Almono vision process.

In terms of the sorted-out city, I would argue that there were three key issues on the table. The first issue was the possible negative effects of the Almono project on the fragile Hazelwood community to the south, that is, the threat of gentrification. One of the economic summaries noted, "The location of this site between the **economic centers** of Downtown, the rivers and hillsides and the historic neighborhoods of Appalachia requires a configuration that reflects and connects the inherent **value of community** with the economic purpose and drive embodied in technology and knowledge industries" (Rothschild Doyno Collaborative 2010, 7; emphasis in the original).

This was taken very seriously by the planners, who noted, "The economic difference between the proposed site use and the existing community is both an opportunity and a threat to the existing social fabric in communities in the Hazelwood Peninsula" (Rothschild Doyno Collaborative 2010, 9).

They concluded that this serious threat required what they called a "mediatory framework," which had been begun with the development of the project's advisory communities. They also examined the ways in which the guidelines for development could nudge investment in paths that would be inclusive and not uprooting. They asked the partners, "What should be regulated?" and included on the list of possible regulations such issues as job generation for a range of skill levels and interaction with the community.

The "Social Vision Diagram" by Rothschild Doyno Collaborative (2011, D14) in *Almono Vision* pulled together the solutions with a focus on the proposed Hazelwood Flats, the section of the new development that would abut the existing Hazelwood neighborhood (Figure 9.3). Hazelwood Flats would differ from the older community by having larger, multifamily dwellings, which would also be newer and likely

Development Guidelines

SOCIAL VISION DIAGRAM

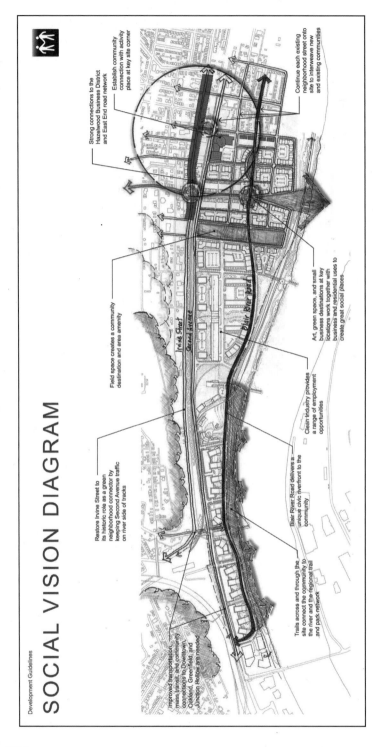

Restore Irvine Street to
its historic role as a green
neighborhood connector by
keeping Second Avenue traffic
on river side of tracks

Field space creates a community
destination and area amenity

Strong connections to the
Hazelwood Business District
and East End road network

Establish community
connection with activity
place at key site corner

Continue each existing
neighborhood street onto
site to interweave new
and existing communities

Art, green space, and small
business destinations at key
locations work together with
business and residential uses to
create great social places

Clean industry provides
a range of employment
opportunities

Blair River Road delivers a
unique civic riverfront to the
community

Trails across and through the
site connect the community to
the river and the regional trail
and park network

Improved transportation,
mass transit, and community
connections to Downtown,
Oakland, Greenfield, and
Junction Hollow are needed

Irvine Street

Second Avenue

Blair River Road

Figure 9.3: Fourth corner. The Almono Project proposed to redevelop a Brownfield site next to a poor neighborhood. Ensuring that the existing neighborhood would not be harmed by this was the focus of a good deal of the planning effort. In this diagram, the physical integration is examined. The solution was to posit that the Almono would not be a gated, disconnected new community, but rather the "fourth corner" of a major intersection in Hazelwood, a part of the neighborhood and connected via important roadways and paths.

Credit: Design Sketchbook Page courtesy of Rothschild Doyno Collaborative.

more expensive than the existing houses in Hazelwood. The differences are bridged by continuing the neighborhood streets onto the site, and by placing linking buildings and open space at three key locations, two at the edge and one in the interior. These buildings and activities invite people to move through each other's communities, sharing resources and getting to know one another. A major perspective to the river would offer an irresistible invitation to visit and increase the movement to and fro. This created the possibility that the new investment would support the older housing, rather than destroy it.

As Reverend Leslie Boone of Hazelwood Presbyterian Church had commented, it is frightening to see new development come into a marginalized poor community. In the past, this has meant only one thing—the destruction of the community. But Dan's story of the panels going up on The Legacy and creating a new hope of inclusion is useful to remember. With a new thesis of how we put our communities together, we can make redevelopment work successfully. Dan pointed out, and I reiterate here, "There's a difference between being 'not bad' and 'good.'" In making Hazelwood Flats the "fourth corner" of the existing neighborhood, RDCollab did good.

The second sorted-out-city issue on the table for Almono was that, in the redlining paradigm, investment gets concentrated in one site, to the detriment of other sites. Rapid investment in a project as big and beautiful as Almono would be cataclysmic for other parts of the region. Many Design Sketchbook pages helped to place the regional problem of unequal investment in the conversation.

I found two of the solutions that emerged to be particularly powerful in this regard. The first was the simple decision, made at the outset, not to overly subsidize the development. The foundations that are partners in Almono have substantial endowments and could conceivably make massive investment to jumpstart the redevelopment. Quick investment by powerful players would likely draw similar investment by other major players. This, however, would trigger a rush of capital to the site that might potentially have the most draining effect on the larger area, not to mention the most destabilizing effect on the surrounding neighborhoods.

Second, the vision plan called for an organic process of using the site to create interest and demand. The early uses RDCollab suggested were quite

DEVELOPMENT VISION
ROLLING LIKE A RIVER

Riverview Campus

Four Mile Run Falls

Riverview Campus

Roundhouse

Washworld Research and Bioremdiation

Strawberry Fields

Forever Over Geothermal Robotic Farm

Green Fuels Off-barging facilities

Mill 19 Pond

A Place to Play

Hazelwood Pond

Meeting the Neighbors

09-21-10 Partnership Meeting

Figure 9.4: Blair River Road. Blair River Road was designed to roll through the Almono site, connecting all the places inside and outside the development.

Credit: Design Sketchbook Page courtesy of Rothschild Doyno Collaborative.

modest and put the site at the service of those most local. This included extending a bicycle trail that connected to an existing trail that leads downtown. I was in Pittsburgh on June 15, 2012, and attended the party for the opening of the trail. The party featured the local organizations and residents and provided free bicycles so anyone could try out the trail. Standing around the site, listening to music created by local youth bands, I had the opportunity to appreciate the bowl of green that embraces the plateau. We were standing at its broadest point, and the counterpoint of flat open space and a ring of tree-covered hills behind me and across the river created just that longing to *go there* that will sell the space to astute developers. This kind of organic development-by-living has the potential to create a process of people investing because they've gotten to know the existing scene—the edge of Appalachia—and want to connect to what's there, extending the living Hazelwood all the way across the 178-acre site.

The final sorted-out city issue had to do with the site itself—abandoned, desolate, and in desperate need. As Roland Castro put it in Banlieues 89, it had a right to be loveable. Dan's advice that we can heal the city by doing *meaningful* placemaking rang in my ears as I was studying the Almono sketchbooks. I had learned, looking at The Legacy sketchbook, that there would be a moment when the design clicked. As the sketchbooks I was studying were the summaries for the partners, I didn't get to see the actual "ah ha!" moment.

But I could certainly see the before and after. July's sketchy plan called for a "signature avenue." By September, there was a glorious realization of Blair River Road, understood as a street-as-river curving and winding its way through the entire site, making both the old and new parts of the neighborhood a riverside neighborhood, a reconnected tributary of the Three Rivers (Figure 9.4).

"How did that happen?" I texted to Ken.

He wrote back, "It was an in-house design session, with Dan, Kate, José, and me. Dan was the brilliant man with the colored pencils as the four of us raised the idea from the page and the site forces. It was truly a magical moment when the sketch went on the wall and we stepped back and saw the whole city connected at all of those scales."

Elephants everywhere!

Figure 9.5: Wonderful sights were discovered everywhere in Greater Paris. Clockwise from top left: Baby Buddha by the side of the road; Lakeside café in Enghien-les-Bains; Plain of France; Women shopping in the market at Gennevilliers; an abandoned industrial building decorated with graffiti; tourist boat on the Canal St. Martin.

Photo credits: Mindy Fullilove, except Baby Buddha, by Léa Znaty, used with permission.

Building the city on the city

Grand Pari(s)

In 2008, the opportunity to intervene at the national level, this time with President Nicholas Sarkozy's blessing, arose again in the form of Grand Pari(s), a project that asked ten international teams of architects and urbanists to propose ideas for the future of the Greater Paris region (Nouvel, Duthilleul, and Cantal-Dupart 2009). The title is a play on words. Paris is, of course, the name of the city, while *pari* is a bet. So Grand Pari(s) indicates both the city and a bet on the future. Both the term, Grand Paris, and the *jeu-de-mot*, Grand Pari, it should be noted, were used in Banlieues 89.

Cantal worked with Jean Nouvel and Jean-Marie Duthilleul; I was a part of Cantal's team. Cantal augmented his encyclopedic knowledge of the Paris region with a rigorous regime of site visits, traveling by train, car, bicycle, and foot. When I arrived in July, he had a long list of places that he wanted me to visit and photograph (Figure 9.5).

The first trip, on July 4th, Bozena Kluba led us to Gennevilliers, Epinay-sur-Seine, and Enghien-les-Bains. Gennevilliers was an old industrial city on the Seine. We visited the traditional center, where we saw a lively market frequented by a diverse group of people. After a bit of searching, we found our way to the Seine, where there were abandoned factories and a deserted waterfront. In Epinay-sur-Seine, we met a young woman who worked for the rehabilitation office. She explained that vast renovations were going on, affecting 60 percent of the people in the city. She shared that 40 percent of the people in the housing projects were unemployed.

We visited Orgemont, a housing project that was being rehabilitated. Already, a gorgeous new playground for children was in use. We asked two passersby how they liked what was happening. They put down the heavy bags they were carrying from the supermarket at the far end of the complex. "People from the suburbs are coming to see what's happening here and that's never happened before," they told us with warm smiles. We made a detour to see a soon-to-be demolished historic train station with a view of the Eiffel Tower.

After a drive of one and a half miles from Epinay-sur-Seine, we arrived at Enghien-les-Bains, where the Banlieues 89 *Assises* had been held in 1985. Enghien is a resort town and filled with the sights and sounds of a lakeside resort in midsummer. Signs announced the Enghien Jazz Festival. We stopped for drinks at a lakeside café and were entertained by music coming from a performance in an adjacent park.

On the second day, Cantal led the trip, pushing hard to cover a lot of territory as he tried to fill out a section of the map that was incomplete. We visited Versailles. Outside the city, we passed by a man mounted on a beautiful horse, out for a ride in the countryside. Then, we mounted the plateau of Saclay. This is a remarkable place—envisioned as the Silicon Valley of France. This plateau has, among other remarkable features, a system of water collection built in the 1600s that fed the fountains of Versailles through a series of ponds, canals, and rills that collected water on the plateau and funneled it down to the great garden. We passed by a number of the institutions that were slated to be the foundation for the proposed technology center. We passed through a number of towns as well, among them Palaiseau, which straddles the edge of the plateau. Cantal's pace was furious and there was little time for questions or photographs, though he seemed quite content with the day's work by the time we returned to Paris.

For the third trip, on July 6th, Léa Znaty took us to Pantin, Bourget, Gonesse, Goussainville, and Louvres. In Pantin, we saw a worn-out housing project. In Bourget, we stopped to see the old airport, transformed into an air and space museum. Like many early airports, it has an intimate relationship with the city. The line of stores and restaurants facing the airport reminded me of many French seaside towns where the main street fronts the ocean—Collioure and Capbreton came immediately to mind. I joked to Cantal that we could call it the "*front de l'aeroport*" (airport front), a play on oceanfront, which, in French, is "*front de la mer.*"

Near Bourget, we stopped to see the garden apartments of Blanc Mesnil, another notable housing complex discussed in *La Ville à Livre Ouvert*. It is decorated with elegant tile and sculpture, and its solid design has endured since the 1930s. Gonesse was famous as the site of the crash of the Concorde in 2000. Goussainville, also close to Charles De Gaulle International Airport, was a small village that had been closed because it was in the flight path. But Goussainville didn't seem closed to me. On the afternoon of our visit, we found an old car show going on and the Big Barbecue—a party organized by La Force des Iles, people from the islands and Africa—in full swing. On the road back to Paris, we passed by a water tower, a giant baby Buddha statue, a highly decorated abandoned factory, and a dock where tourists were clambering onto a canal boat.

On day four, Bozena and I traveled to Euro Disney (Disneyland Paris), the center of an explosion of urbanization. We visited a new town called Serris, which has a traditional Haussmannian look, but had just been built. We noticed that control was tight all over this new city: we had to get permission to visit a garden by city hall, we were forbidden to film in a "street" that we learned was a mall, and we noticed that the public square was surrounded by high iron gates. We got back in the car to drive to Euro Disney, and we were greeted by a water tower with a Mouseketeer hat.

The last stop of the journey was Ivry-sur-Seine, a working-class city on the edge of Paris. We parked by a place called L'Atelier, the Workshop, which was so interesting that we stopped for a tour. It was a site for artists to work, and it honored the history of industry and working people in the city. At the time of our visit, the site was celebrating the seventieth anniversary of the victory of the Popular Front, a progressive movement that succeeded in establishing vacations for working people, among other great accomplishments. After that, Bozena took me to see a remarkable housing project that juts out in all directions, creating many varied shapes for living. Designed by French architect Jean Renaudie, it was covered with trees, on balconies and roofs, so that it seemed like a forested hillside. In the center of the city was a skateboard park, covered with young boys who were part of a special school that traveled the Paris region to enjoy the skate parks. In the plaza in front of city hall, we saw the end of the market and people relaxing in the city. As we traveled around Ivry-sur-Seine, there were posters everywhere, and it reminded me that I hadn't seen any posters in Serris.

I produced a report and a photo-essay, *Grand Paris: Quatre Jours, Une Americane* (Grand Paris: Four Days, One American Woman) (Fullilove 2008). The complexity of the Parisian terrain raised the problem that Rod had posed for me, that of creating effective collective consciousness. How was the well-to-do chevalier outside of Versailles to be engaged in conversation with the Arab women in the market in Gennevilliers? What did the plain of Saclay have to do with the dense urbanization of Ivry-sur-Seine?

What did any of those places, with their real and gritty history, have to do with the newly invented and tightly controlled Serris?

Would you have to be blind?

Bozena kept me informed about the feverish work to complete a final report by the end of the six-month time frame of the project. The team identified six spaces that demanded particular interventions: *les lisières* (the borders between city and nature); *voies, pistes,* and *chemins* (the pathways); *reseaux, connexion,* and *maillage* (networks and interconnections); *transformation, tissage,* and *métissage* (transforming, weaving, and crossbreeding); *quartiers, cités,* and *grand ensembles* (neighborhoods, the center of the city, and housing projects); and *haut lieux* (high places). These ideas were then applied to the four valleys of Grand Paris and to Central Paris. The team also proposed an idea for using art at the scale of the city.

In the project's remarkable book, *Naissances et Renaissance de Mille et Un Bonheurs Parisiens*, Jean Nouvel, Jean-Marie Duthilleul, and Cantal -Dupart (2009) expounded their vision for Grand Paris, to which they gave the new name "Paris aime" (Paris love) or Paris[m]. It was a vision for a well-integrated metropolitan area on its way to more complexity, more connection, and more sustainability.

To writer, filmmaker, artist, and photographer Alain Fleischer was confided the task of articulating the group's vision. Social, economic, and demographic history, he wrote, determined the development of cities. But cities were forced to evolve to meet changing times. Fleischer (2009a, 45) noted,

> An organism that is mutating obeys an obligation to adapt, to perform. Something is lost, and something is gained, and we have to think of the mutation as a loss of the worst with the gain of the best. In mutation, the forms that are deleted to make way for new forms should be less regretful of what's lost and more grateful for what appears. All degeneration is an occasion for renaissance.

How was this evolution to be guided? The team contended that it must be built on the existing city, the same concept of "build the city on the city" that was so powerful in Banlieues 89. Jean Nouvel (2009, 45) asked what was to be done with the ill-conceived constructions of the past eighty years and his answer was firm: "We must transform them, supercharge them, graft them, superimpose on them… We must phagocytose them."

Nowhere was this program for change more succinctly encapsulated for me than in the discussion of *hauts lieux*, the tall places. The center of Paris has largely been guarded at the level of the nineteenth-century buildings. The exceptions can be shocking, like the much-maligned Tour Montparnasse, a building that rises fifty-nine stories above Paris in the fifteenth *arrondissement*. I count myself among its detractors. Alain Fleischer (2009a) argued that the tall buildings of Paris should be thought of as giants who seemed peculiar because they stood out in the landscape and perhaps were not beautiful. But, he pointed out, even the Tour Montparnasse would be seen differently if it were in a group of three or four towers, if it were better integrated into the neighborhood, or if it didn't conclude in such a banal manner.

To prove the last point, the team took sketches from Frank Gehry, made a flamboyant Gehry-esque hat, and showed how it altered the dour Tour Montparnasse. The change was extraordinary, and I completely shifted my view of the whole situation. My point here is that the project team argued throughout for taking the city as it was and reimagining what it could be.

The team—our team, may I say—was the only one of the Grand Pari(s) teams to confront the challenges raised by Banlieues 89, the serious problems of exclusion in French cities. Two sections dealt with spaces of urban fracture, the one we had identified as transforming, weaving, and crossbreeding, and the one we had identified as neighborhoods, the center of the city, and housing projects. Perhaps my favorite line in *Naissances et Renaissance de Mille et Un Bonheurs Parisiens*—although there's a lot of competition for that top ranking—is this, "*La politique mise en oeuvre est incompatible avec l'idée de demolition, d'éradication*" (Nouvel, Duthilleul, and Cantal-Dupart 2009, 298). It translates as, "The policy proposed here is incompatible with demolition, with eradication."

Alain Fleischer (2009b, 300) wrote,

Let us part with the idea that any object—a building, for example – can be irremediably condemned because of its ugliness (or its poverty or its sadness). The ugliness of a building stirs in us a dream of what it might be, what might be its beauty. And nothing is closer to despair than hope. One could then imagine, not destruction of what is accused of being ugly, but rather its transformation, its mutation, its meta-morphosis, by adding or grafting, more than demolishing or suppressing, in the manner of plants that are capable of marrying, conquering, embellishing all disgraceful objects.

This had profound implications for the marginalized housing projects, as it addressed their dignity, their beauty, and the society's obligation to bring them into right relation with the larger region. Adding complexity and connectivity were key to the changes being proposed. It reminded me of Jean-Pierre Dupont, a participant at the *Assises* of Banlieues 89, who complimented Castro and Cantal because their work had led to the suppression of the rule against having bistros in housing projects. "In getting rid of that legislation, it is likely—even certain—that they made the urban" (Banlieues 89 1986, 64).

Jean Nouvel (2009, 42) addressed the challenge that the team's set of ecological strategies presented to French society, saying,

> What changes in Paris[m] enable a different set [of] energy policies—and, as a result, new industries—or a better social structure—one that is, as a result, more just—or a better competitive edge—and, as a result, makes Paris[m] more attractive—or offers the imagination a greater measure of pleasure that allows us to envision a future Paris, one that is illuminated by the hopes and dreams of generations to come?
>
> But look carefully at today's reality: is Paris[m] an open, welcoming city?
>
> What would it take to answer 'yes'? Would you have to be blind? A masochist? A cynic?

A major exhibit of the proposals put forward by the ten teams was held at Palais de Chaillot in the Cité de l'Architecture et du Patrimoine in Paris on April 29, 2009. President Nicolas Sarkozy (2009), in his remarks at the opening of the exhibit, said,

> Breaking with the habits of thought and behavior that for decades placed architecture and urbanism in the background in the major

urban development schemes, I hope that the thinking of architects and planners is the starting point of the development of the project so symbolic of Greater Paris.

This is not a fixed plan, locking hard the future instead of opening it. It is a process of transformation, the exploitation of all possibilities, all the potentialities, it is to continue a history that began long before us and which we want to give a new course, a new direction.

I got to see that exhibit in November 2009. I was thrilled to see my own name printed on a panel. I enjoyed the wild models and over-the-top pronouncements about our urban future. A common theme—build the city on the city—emerged from all of the projects. The teams were searching for ways to bring the parts together and make them stronger, more sustainable, and more interesting, thus creating the foundation for a vibrant future. Cantal emphasized to me that, while Grand Paris might have been considered a crazy idea when he and Castro were first putting it forward in 1983, by 2008, it had become a necessity, essential for the development of the region and the nation. President Sarkozy played a key role in its emergence, forcing destiny by calling the international teams together to explore new directions.

Palaiseau and the *front de campagne*

In the aftermath of Grand Pari(s), Cantal was asked to help the small town of Palaiseau, on the plateau of Saclay, with an extension of the town on the top of plateau. He used this opportunity to implement the ideas of Grand Paris. His former student, urbanist Isabelle Trider-Andorin, took the lead on the project. She took me to the site and also gave me a tutorial on the ways in which Grand Paris was infused in the project.

"I took *Naissance and Renaissances de Mille et Un Bonheurs Parisiens* and examined how the six key ideas might guide our thinking," she explained to me. "One of the most important for us was the idea of *les lisières*, the shorelines, so speak. Palaiseau is at the edge of the farmland of the plateau. The idea is to create a living, vibrant space that demarcates the transition from urban to farmland. There are many ways to accomplish this. We want to use the idea of *front de campagne* (country front)—like *front de mer* (oceanfront)—to indicate looking out over the great expanse of open country. We have proposed that the buildings at the edge of the city look out, just as buildings facing the ocean would look out across the water. This honors the edge, and links city and country. It uses the great tool of perspective to help people see and appreciate the world of nature that is at their doorstep.

"This new development will be organized around a central square. It will be in walking distance of schools and other urban infrastructure. It will be linked by bus to the rest of Palaiseau and to the nearby train station. The idea is that people who work in the nearby research centers and universities will be able to use a bus system to get around the area. If they can shop, get to recreation, and get to work without cars, some will choose not to have automobiles, and this helps to create a sustainable future.

"Remember," she asked, "about the system of collecting water for the fountains of Versailles? There are rills that are part of that system that run through Palaiseau. We will make sure they are rehabilitated and we will install signage so that people understand the massive historic water system that laces through their city. This project is exciting because we are the first to take the ideas of Grand Paris onto the ground. I feel like we are inventing the future based on the ideas that the president generated."

The elephant is in the house

For my Main Street NJ project, I found it useful to spend time in Orange, New Jersey, and HANDS, Patrick Morrissy's community development organization, served as my base of operation. I slowly sketched out the county's dense web of main streets, which replaced the tic-tac-toe board of highways as my way of traveling the area. The more I looked, the more elephants I discovered: museums, libraries, rail lines, schools, historic churches and cemeteries, great eats and fine dining, statues, and smokestacks.

While it might seem ludicrous to compare Essex County, where Orange is located, with Greater Paris, in the essence of what an urban region is, they are quite similar. The great psychiatrist and anthropologist Arthur Kleinman taught me that essentializing can be quite dangerous for a scientist, and I acknowledge that proviso in making this comparison. What I am trying to highlight is that we can identify in each case a complex regional entity that contains a great diversity of people, a variety of land forms and uses, an energetic economy, great evidence of history, and potential for a meaningful future.

Planners concerned about eliminating inequity in our landscape have turned to regional interventions to find solutions. This is a powerful tool, and one that has rarely been used to its full potential. It is the elephants that are the key, I think, to making regional plans work. Cantal, at his retirement party in 2010, showed a slide of a giant mechanical elephant that strides a dockside plaza in Nantes (Figure 9.6). His grandchildren, who live near the elephant, were wide-eyed with wonder and asked their parents, "Did *Grandpère* invent the elephant?" The parents—not wanting to disappoint their children—said that he did.

"I don't want my children to lie to their children—I don't think that's right," he told me a few days later. "But, in a way, I did. In Banlieues 89, we put elephants wherever we found something wonderful. We made elephants a symbol of revitalization. The elephant in Nantes was designed

Figure 9.6: The elephant of Nantes. This massive mechanical elephant strides an old port area in Nantes.

Photo credit: Mindy Fullilove.

to reanimate an empty waterfront, so it is an elephant and it is an elephant in the sense of a symbol of coming back. So it is possible that my elephants made a small contribution to the elephant of Nantes, and in that sense, the parents did not lie."

As they say in the clubs, "The elephant is in the *HHHHHOUSE!*"

PART IV

Connect

CHAPTER TEN

Element 8:
Show Solidarity with All Life

Behold a certain lawyer stood up and tested him, saying, "Teacher, what shall I do to inherit eternal life?"

He said to him, "What is written in the law?"

He answered, "You shall love the Lord your God with all your heart... and your neighbor as yourself."

He said to him, "You have answered correctly."

But he, desiring to justify himself, asked Jesus, "Who is my neighbor?"

—"The Good Samaritan,"
the Gospel according to Luke 10:25–29

My first lesson in the psychology of place had to do with coffee grounds in the sink. The third floor of 513 W. 166th Street in New York City was occupied by a number of different groups that reported to different employers and did different activities. We were all organized into strong teams, but the teams had no connections to each other. The space, however, did not echo our fundamental disconnection. It was weirdly open and people walked through the space of other groups all the time. There was also a no-team's-land that included the hallways, bathrooms, conference rooms, and kitchen. These were messy because they belonged to everyone and to no one. To use Mark Granovetter's (1973) language, the strong ties of teams existed, but there were no weak ties to link the teams to one another. It was the weak ties that would have helped us keep the common spaces clean. The nasty messes that grew in the kitchen sink really sickened me, but I had no idea what to do to get them to stay clean.

A high school student, Maureen Turner, showed up, interested in competing in the Westinghouse Science Competition. I said, "Well, we have a problem with the kitchen sink." She observed what was going on and documented what we felt: the good spirit of the individual teams and their lack of control over the common space. She came up with a plan that teams each "adopt" one of the common spaces. One of the great organizers in our group got everyone to participate in this "Adopt-a-Space" program. On a certain day, we were to have our spaces "ready" and we would have a party. All kinds of decorating and cleaning went on—the spaces were transformed with paint, wall hangings, dishtowels, and flowers. When Maureen did a follow-up inspection, the spaces were remarkably different. This experiment was so successful that she was selected a semifinalist in the competition, a great honor for a young scientist.

What we found interesting was that not only did teams succeed in taking ownership but also people got to know each other. The cooperation among teams, so easily organized, led to much better interpersonal working relationships across teams and throughout the floor. This was the model that we then used to organize NYC RECOVERS and CLIMB.

A settlement house tackles the same problem—lack of weak ties—and solves it the same way: by creating common space within which individuals from disconnected groups can connect in new and interesting ways. In the context of those new openings for exchange, new capacity is created for problem identification and solution. Trust grows. People begin to extend their connections outside of their immediate networks of family, church, and ethnic group. As the weak ties accumulate, the capacity to function is restored. Eventually, people go to the library and get a card, and this will always be true whatever a library is and whatever a card becomes.

This takes us to the eighth element of urban restoration: show solidarity with all life. This involves:

- Organizing by listening;
- Reassembling the fragments; and

- Weaving society with solidarity.

Organizing by listening

The expressions "top down" and "bottom up" describe two kinds of processes, one in which the authorities—whoever they might be—impose, and the other in which there is a rising up from the bottom and the people assert their desires. These options oversimplify the complex process in which many groups organize to contribute to the process. I want to foreground the role of organizers.

In this regard, Cantal likes to tell a story about Bob. We were walking on the grounds of a housing project in Bègles, a city on the edge of Bordeaux, when we saw some people having a barbecue and playing some music. A man started over towards us, not sure who we were or what we intended. Bob, sensing his unease, immediately started a conversation about the music, which he recognized. He segued into being from New York, and in no time, he and the man were great friends, and we had met all the people at the barbecue.

Organizers are essential in situations of oppression because the oppressed need direction in order to take on the force majeure that is holding them down. It is not simple to win in these situations. My dad, Ernie, thought the people could win if they had superior organization and attention to detail. This requires superb leadership. Ernie's theories arose from his decades of experience, successfully organizing unions and political power. He knew how to win against the odds, but he'd also seen lots of people lose and he'd lost some battles himself.

The key, he told me, when I made my first tentative organizing effort, was to get some people. As I was morbidly shy and thus thoroughly inept at the getting of people, my little project went nowhere. By contrast, for my college honors thesis I was able to produce an oral history of his organization, the National Negro Labor Council (Thompson 1978). After watching that, he had a second piece of advice for me. "You have a great talent for finding information. Organizers always need information and they will look to you for guidance. You can be a people's researcher." And that is how I came to found the Community Research Group in 1992. Our slogan was, "Facts people need, publications they can use."

In my role as a student of social process, I have met hundreds of organizers and I've studied the work of a good number of them. The organizers in this book—Terri Baltimore, Lourdes Hernández-Cordero, Molly Rose Kaufman, Bonnie Young Laing, Mike Malbrough, Pat Morrissy, and Carl Redwood—are among the best I know. All of them lead by listening. They have vivid visions of the direction—toward a more just society—but they are constantly integrating daily life into the actual steps to be taken to get closer to that vision.

Pat Morrissy, for example, went into a community meeting to present a plan for the development of some new housing. A woman at the meeting told him, "That's nice, but can't you do something about the vacant houses that are so disruptive?"

He hadn't thought about that problem, but became convinced that it was the key to stabilizing neighborhoods. HANDS stopped building new housing and focused on a "vacant and problem properties" campaign, which eventually succeeded in lowering the number of such properties from 392 to 49. When the foreclosure crisis hit, the number bounced back up. Pat immediately began to organize to halt the abandonment of properties and to protect the hard-won stability.

We gather at the invitation of the organizers because they know us, care about us, and have provided sound advice in the past. Organizers communicate their solidarity in myriad ways, but one that strikes me is the ability to just talk about whatever seems important to talk about: the garbage in the street, the sweet smile on the grandchild's face, the problems of changing tires, the great collard greens at the new restaurant, the early spring, the late winter, and the need to plant bulbs in the fall. In these innumerable conversations about "ships and sails and sealing wax and cabbages and kings," they build bonds of commonality. If they ask us to do something, it's because they know that it matters to us.

A second thing about the organizers who do work in the era of Simms III, the time of unexpectancy, is that they must be able to connect to the many, many fragmented groups, making common ground in haunted space. Lourdes's walking meetings traveled through Highbridge and other abandoned spaces as a way of exorcising the ghosts there. She led the CLIMB consensus group by inviting everyone to walk together and was constantly creating a larger and larger set of people who knew each other.

Under the tent of a common search for a better city, organizers are ready to participate in the conversations with planners that will teach them how to repair the city.

Reassembling the fragments

Planning with Simms III in mind

In 1998, Cantal took me to Argenteuil, a housing project on the outskirts of Paris. It was one of those built after World War II, when there was a massive housing shortage and a great influx of immigrants from the former colonies. This de facto segregation was reinforced by the physical marginalization of many of the projects. Some were far, some were located away from transportation lines, and some were set back in cul-de-sacs that created the feeling of isolation even though the city was around the corner. As I have mentioned before, Clodion in Perpignan is typical of that problem (see figure 6.4, Before).

The project we were visiting was typical of that era, a set of tall buildings built up on a *dalle*. It was an awkward distance from Paris, which contributed to a feeling of geographic isolation. I was there to speak in one of the common rooms. About ten people were present, mostly young men of North African descent. They were angry, and I was an object of their anger. "You live in the United States," they pointed out. "So why haven't you stopped imperialism? What do you have to say about that?"

I hadn't stopped imperialism, something I kick myself for every day, but I hadn't precisely seen its continuation as *my* fault. What could I tell them about my efforts? I thought of the word *militante*, which seemed to me to mean "activist." I tried to say I was a civil rights activist. "What!" they shouted. "You're a communist? And you drink Coca-Cola?"

I do love Diet Coke, so I just sat there, guilty as charged.

As we were leaving at the end of the evening, Cantal smiled broadly. "That was great, wasn't it? You got to see the real issues we're facing here in France."

This reminded me of earlier training in family therapy, when I was a psychiatric resident. "Your first job," my supervisor Hector Goa told me, "is to connect to every member of the family. You can only help if they all trust you."

One day, a family came in, every member on edge and each easily provoked into screaming at the others. I was in the treatment room with the family, while Hector and the rest of the team were watching behind the one-way mirror. We were connected by a telephone. Within seconds of the family's arrival, the phone rang and Hector called me to the observation room. "You have only a few seconds before it explodes. I want you to send the children out. Then, go in the garbage and pull out a paper. Say that the family gets treated like garbage, but is really a wonderful tender marshmallow. Then, ask the children to come back in. Let's see how it goes and I'll tell you what to do next."

I walked through this complicated process, the metaphors lowering the tension, and the phone breaking it up as it started to rise. The constant shifting of the groupings in the room helped to break up the habitual patterns of antagonism. Suddenly, I discovered that the family had a sense of humor and we all started to laugh. It was the beginning of some healing.

Cantal has such a science for entering cities. He is an elegant man, which attracts attention when he enters a room. He uses that moment to connect to people and to show them respect. He has taken me to meetings at the French Senate and housing projects on the outskirts of Paris. I've seen him with top politicians, world-famous architects, hippies, homeless people, and Americans of all shapes and sizes—he was always at his ease and always interested. I asked him how he managed that. "I think I got that from my father," he reflected. "He was an architect and music critic, but he also loved horse racing. His acquaintanceships spanned a very wide range of people. He was always gracious with everyone, no matter what their social standing was. I try to be like him."

This welcoming stance was, I believe, fortified by the seven years he spent working in Tunisia at the start of his career. As opposed to many French people, who have lingered in the colonial era, Cantal got born into the future while working in a postcolonial setting.

In Pittsburgh, he learned about a funicular—in Pittsburghese, it is called an incline—that connected the Hill to the Strip District. He wanted to find the site where it had been. He studied the map in advance of a group bus trip to the Hill, thinking that would be a perfect opportunity to go look for the site. When the bus stopped, he quickly descended and began to run, not waiting for anyone to go with him for protection or guidance. The Hill, like Harlem and many other inner-city neighborhoods, was considered a "no fly" zone for white people. The sight of a white man running *into* the ghetto was extraordinary for all the Americans, white and black, who were involved. His credibility was greatly enhanced simply by doing that. But, better yet, he beelined right to the old pillars of the incline, located alongside coach Leroy Dillard's house (you can see the site he found in Figure 10.2).

"Yeah, that was our incline," the old-timers said, acknowledging he'd hit the nail on the head.

As daring as he had seemed to the onlookers, Cantal told me that he's not reckless in his travels. He knows perfectly well when he's in a dangerous neighborhood. "I go in the morning," he said, "because the *malfaiteurs*—the bad guys—don't get up very early. Still, going is often seen as foolhardy. It's part of the horrible racism. For my part, I go everywhere. It is how I show respect. It is the beginning of the work of repair."

I was telling this story to Rod one day, and he joked, "Cantal is a one-man weak tie, holding France together."

Find the Rivers!

When Cantal came to Pittsburgh in 1998, he gave us long lists of things to do for placemaking. When I asked him for his final advice, as we were putting together Hillscapes, he sent a series of maps (one of which is shown in Figure 10.2). Those maps highlighted the problem of disconnection. "Reconnecting the Hill to the flow of the city is the fundamental problem that must be resolved in order for the neighborhood to work. It's nice to repaint the New Grenada, but it's not enough. You have to work on the connections," he said in summary.

Terri and Denys took up this challenge. At the point they started the organization, Find the Rivers!, much groundwork had already been covered in terms of small conversations about people's stories and finding elders who thought it was a good idea. Mr. Dwayne Cooper, Ms. Edna Council, and Ms. Lauretta Comans bought the idea of finding the paths to the rivers. George Moses, one of the colleagues from the Coalition for a Healthy Urban Habitat, also understood the search for connections and the link to housing. They became constant supporters of Find the Rivers!. Once the Consensus Group had endorsed the idea, Terri and Denys launched their first project, creating plans for a linear park along the length of Kirkpatrick Street.

Find the Rivers! obtained a grant to hire a landscape architect. All of the elders—who were always addressed by their title and last name as a sign of respect—helped interview firms. Dina Klavon won the contract with her clear presentation and strong interest in working with community people. With her leadership, Terri and Denys launched the next phase of the work: exploring the terrain. Terri described, "From the planning process on, Mr. Dwayne Cooper, his wife Mrs. Myrtle Cooper, and Mrs. Comans were the people who were really in it. They did the boat rides, meetings, walks, and mapping. They would come to community meetings and talk about the process. It was really interesting—on the boat rides, there was a changing cast of characters, but they were constants. On one of the last boat rides we did, there was a whole group of twentysomethings and eight elders."

The constancy of these elders helped Terri and Denys think through what should happen in the many spaces they visited. They remained engaged, thinking through what could be and what they remembered. "On one of the coolest trips, we rented a van and the Coopers, Denys, and I went to visit a program in Baltimore, Maryland. It was a project that took kids sailing. It was a rainy, cold day, and we were sailing and there were the Coopers with their rain gear and disposable cameras."

These were people who had seen things come and things go. They were thoughtful, considerate people who were well respected in the neighborhood. "When they stood by you, it made a difference," Terri said. "People would joke, 'Have you found the rivers yet? Ha-ha.' Mr. Cooper would say, 'We're still looking—making those connections.' They wouldn't let us get discouraged, they wanted to know what was happening and how our trips—like the trip to France—went."

Early on in their organizational efforts, Terri and Denys traveled to France to get advice from Cantal. In an undated report, Denys documented the activities they engaged in and the lessons they learned (Candy, n.d.). He noted, "Michel Cantal-Dupart walked down a spillway at the edge of the Seine and rolled up his sleeves. 'It is vital,' he said, 'for people to touch the water. We must be able to put our hands in the water. There are eight million people in Paris. How many of them actually touch the water?'" (Candy, n.d., 3).

In visits to the Seine in Paris and the Loire in Nantes, Cantal demonstrated the need for the development of the relationship to water in three domains: on the water, on the banks of the rivers, and on the streets that access the rivers (Figure 10.1). On the water, there should be houseboats, tourist boats, and transit boats, all offering opportunities to experience the river as fish and birds might, as well as in all the ways people can. On the banks, there should be places for walking, sunning, fishing, and visiting. On the streets that have access to the river, there should be places to look over the river, enjoying the ever-changing scenery.

Denys, after describing the careful dialogue that Cantal advocated for linking bridges, stairs, and vistas, noted that a parallel dialogue needed to occur among the citizens of Pittsburgh. He argued:

Planning for the rivers and creating increased access to them must, by definition, be a process that builds new bridges among the diverse people of Pittsburgh. A bridge to the future depends on remembering

Figure 10.1: Find the Rivers! in Nantes. Terri Baltimore, Carol Tileston, Xavier Cantal-Dupart, Michel Cantal-Dupart, Christelle Nori, Denys Candy, and Joëlle Perron during the tour of the Loire River in Nantes.

Photo credit: Pierre Perron.

community history and honoring the multiple perspectives and stories of that history. It's easy to say. The question for us in Pittsburgh is, are we ready to do so? (Candy, n.d., 5)

The explorations took people out on the vacant hillsides overlooking the river, searching for clues about the lost access points. One day, I got to search with them, bushwhacking my way through urban forest, up a little-used trail that led to a hilltop clearing with spectacular views of the river and the new HOPE VI development that had replaced Allequippa Terrace. Part of the way, the old stairs were functional. A hat and child's toy gave the impression that people passed that way from time to time. On one of the stairways down towards the river, at a point that overlooked a tangle of highways and a bridge, someone had written in silver marker, "Dear Mom, it's been five years since I wept. Love, Jesse."

Having searched the hillside, we went out for a boat ride. We got on the boat downtown. We went up the Monongahela for a while, then turned and went back. We looked at the Ohio, but our route took us up the Allegheny for a bit, to see the Hill District, enjoying coach Leroy Dillard's house from another perspective. It was a good size boat with strong engines. The point where the three rivers meet is broad, and the blue-brown waters flow quickly. There were not too many other boats out that day, so the broad expanses were ours. It was not exactly quiet, with the churning motor and the chatter of our group, but there were none of the usual sounds of sirens, trucks, and car radios. The absence of our everyday offered a kind of peace to do the work of looking around and looking up from the water to the hills we had just walked.

In addition to the support offered by the Coopers and Mrs. Comans, Carl Redwood, head of the Consensus Group, always stood by Find the Rivers! He made sure they had time on the agenda of the Consensus Group. He recognized that this was a different angle from the focus on Centre Avenue, which was the preoccupation of most people. Find the Rivers! was demonstrating that there was much to see and think about in other parts of the neighborhood. "Denys always said, 'We don't have a dog in that Centre Avenue fight,'" Terri remembered.

The solidarity of the elders allowed the organization to get off the ground. As it began its work, Terri and Denys began to connect with others

Searching for the connections

How do we get from here to there?

Foundation of old incline.

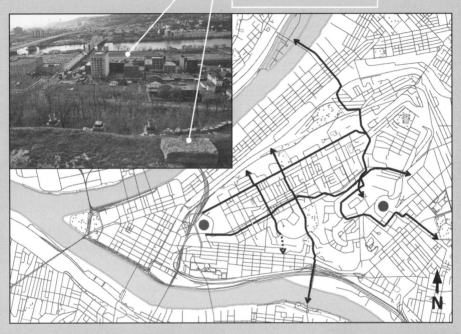

Figure 10.2: Find the Rivers! has led the search for connections between the Hill District and the Three Rivers of Pittsburgh. The photos depict the activities of looking on land and on water. The arrows of connection were first suggested by Cantal in the sketches for *Hillscapes* (Robins et al. 1999).

Photo credits: Mindy Fullilove, except bottom left, by Denys Candy.

interested in green space. The Herron Avenue Corridor Coalition was one of the groups they connected to. It had started at John Wesley AME Zion Church, which was suffering due to old mines that sat beneath the property, referred to as "undermining." They wanted to get the mine water out of their basement. They talked to many kinds of people and ended up with a geothermal heating and cooling system for the church and capacity for a second building they hoped to develop in the future. They started thinking about taking that idea and making the area a geothermal corridor. With help from Luis Rico-Gutierrez, a professor of urban planning at Carnegie Mellon University, and the Urban Land Institute, they got a plan of their own.

Find the Rivers! also connected with Landslide Farm, a group that was farming in the Hill, because they were taking people to look at the Mon (as Pittsburghers call the Monongahela River). That farming group connected with the Martin Luther King Jr. Reading and Cultural Center to create a greenhouse. While each group had its own projects and interests, they could call upon one another for help. This was real evidence of a deepening solidarity among the many splintered groups on the Hill.

Pittsburgh's Riverlife (formerly Riverlife Task Force) has led much of the work of making the rivers a worthy destination. Terri and Denys connected to them in the beginning of their work with Find the Rivers! and argued that there was a great need for the Hill, as a landlocked neighborhood, to be part of the conversation about the city and its rivers. Lisa Schroeder, head of Riverlife, would later support Find the Rivers! when it undertook a major ecological planning process, the creation of the Greenprint (Hood Design Studio and ARUP Spatial Practice 2009).

In the interim, through Lisa, Terri and Denys met Peter Fink, a British lighting architect who was looking at the park along the rivers. He agreed to come to the Hill. Terri wanted to make his coworkers and him feel comfortable during their visit. She called the William Penn Hotel, which served high tea in the afternoons. "Do you have scones to go?" she inquired.

It turned out that it was possible to get clotted cream and scones to be served at Hill House. Terri brought in a sterling silver tea service. Her colleagues said, "*What* are you doing?" The day of the visit was rainy and dreary, but the British guests were heartened by the high tea and went out to see the Hill in great spirits. "In the teeming rain on Arcena Street," Terri related to me, "Peter stretched his arms out and said, 'There should be *lights* here—people should be able to see the city from *here*! This neighborhood is so cool and you just need a beacon of light.'"

Having completed a series of plans, Terri and Denys knew that they had to actually build something. They had no idea how to do that. Denys recruited Meg Cheever to meet with them. As head of the highly successful Pittsburgh Parks Conservancy (PPC), Meg had raised millions to restore the city's great parks, which had fallen into disrepair and disuse. Her organization was focused on the four large city parks of Pittsburgh. Denys and Terri took her to the same spot on Arcena Street that had thrilled Peter Fink. She took in the vista and said, "I can feel mission creep."

"We were all uncertain at the beginning. They knew how to build parks. We knew how to build community consensus. It turned out to be a good match," summarized Terri.

The first project the partnership undertook was the Greenprint. "It has been a challenging relationship at times," Terri related to me. "Denys feared that we would get swallowed up and pushed out of the way by their big organization. We've had to push back to make a good relationship. But with work, we've started to rub off on each other. I've learned their strategic planning for space, and they've learned community process. Prior to working with us, they worked in the Great Parks where they had a good deal of say: the parks didn't belong to any particular community. Rather, those parks belonged to a complex network of users, institutions, special events, neighbors, and civic-minded supporters, a network that had to be developed and made real for actual progress to be funded and peacefully pursued.

"Working in the Hill is completely different. Susan Rademacher, one of their team members, became a real part of the neighborhood. PPC, by 2012, was so much a part of the neighborhood that they became one of nine organizations in a neighborhood partnership thinking about merging the social and the ecological. All of this work has opened their organization and shifted its mission to be more inclusive of the neighborhood parks."

Cliffside Park emerged as the first building project. While raising the funds, it was important to create the sense that something was happening. Park cleaning seemed to be the right intervention. Cleaning days were

Clean-up at Cliffside Park

Figure 10.3: A series of clean-up days were organized at Cliffside Park. Weeds were whacked and refrigerators and tires were removed in preparation for the park's restoration.

Photo credits clockwise from top left: Rich Brown; Terri Baltimore; Terri Baltimore; Rich Brown; Terri Baltimore. Used with permission.

organized by the PPC, by the Cliff Street neighbors, and by Terri and Hill House. The engagement of building companies and the maintenance staff of the University of Pittsburgh meant that equipment was available: weed whackers, a water buffalo truck, and the equipment to haul air conditioners and other large waste off the hillside. At the same time, the team decided to include a lot across from the park in the project. The owner gave permission. Donated shrubs, grasses, and flowers were planted. Reused bricks were brought in from other sites and used to create pathways. One group of volunteers included construction workers from Massaro, a local building company. After planting trees, ornamental grasses, and flowers, some volunteers started carefully placing large stones around some shrubs. They paid homage to Stonehenge, a loving tribute to such a special space. "People that have worked planting or clearing debris return again and again, interested in checking how their work is holding up or caring for the tender plants. Many are not from this community, but they feel the same kind of ownership that the neighbors who work there feel. I *love* that spot!" Terri concluded.

Weaving society with solidarity

In the summer of 2000, Cantal and I went to the French city of Agen to see a school for prison guards (Fullilove 2001). We stopped for lunch in a small restaurant on a winding mountain road. Cantal asked if I remembered about his lesson on perspective at Vaux-le-Vicomte. "Yes," I replied, "and I read Erik Orsenna's (2000) book that you lent me, *Portrait d'un Homme Heureux*, about André Le Nôtre."

"Good," he responded, "because we are going to see perspective today. This is a school for prison guards, recently built. There was a competition to design the grounds. The school authorities had proposed a design of a school surrounded by a wall."

He pulled his ever-present black felt tip marker from his pocket and drew the proposed layout on the placemat. "There was to be a cafeteria shared with another school and that was to be placed just inside the wall. Then, the school building would be all the way at the back of the walled area. I said, 'This is too much like a prison. If we put the guards in prison, how will they be able to help the prisoners return to society?

Perspective on liberty

Figure 10.4: The School for Prison Guards in Agen, France, was built in a park modeled on the classic French château, Vaux-le-Vicomte (see Figure 6.3). Its central feature is a canal that leads the eye to a nearby church spire.

The reintegration of prisoners is the goal of national policy. The guards can't achieve that goal unless they themselves feel free and integrated into French society. What is required is an open campus.'

"The old school was set up against a prison on two sides, so it was very closed in. The students had planted many rare trees, as nature is one way to counter a prison. The other is perspective, and that is what I will use here.

"I am using Vaux-le-Vicomte as the model. I plan to use a canal to create a dynamic center. The canal will guide the eye to a church spire in the distance—my Hercules (see Figure 6.3). This links the campus to the town just beyond its borders. The school will be placed at the entrance, as it should be. The shared restaurant will be at the end, and the students from the other school will cross the grounds of the school for prison guards."

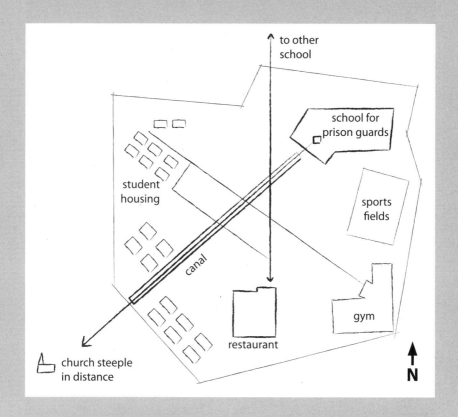

Photos courtesy of Michel Cantal-Dupart.

Map redrawn by Sarah Schell from the original plan by Michel Cantal-Dupart.

He put down his pen and picked up his glass of wine, a contented and even triumphant smile hovering on his lips. After lunch, we finished our drive to the school. We parked near the main school building and strolled the park, which was bisected by a canal that ran from the school toward a church spire off in the distance. It was filled with reeds, and frogs were hopping about, croaking greetings to each other. They splashed into the canal to hide from us. I flashed back to Vaux-le-Vicomte and its formal stone canal. I had encountered this in Cantal's design work in Rion des Landes, another place where he had used the lessons of Vaux-le-Vicomte. There he'd used a curving path, where André Le Nôtre would have used a straight one. Here, he was using grass and wildlife to riff on the formal stone canal of Vaux-le-Vicomte.

We went back to the school a few years after it opened and we met with the director. He gave us copies of a beautiful book of watercolors of the ceremonies to close the old school and open the new one (Herrenschmidt 2001). He then told story after story of the adventures they'd had, ranging from the frogs keeping everyone up at night during mating season to the judo team opening up the school's athletic space to the local area. "Some local people complained that we have an armory here. They wanted guards posted to safeguard the guns. I said that a guard wouldn't do any good. Furthermore, this is a school of guardians; everyone here is a guard. All of us are responsible, not just some of us. That argument carried the day and so far it's working."

In 2011, local people who'd come to love the school argued that its park needed to be protected as part of the area's cultural patrimony. "Otherwise, they'll build on it," was the local wisdom. Cantal was pleased that the park had won fans who were not even part of the school. "That is proof that we built a bridge we could only dream about before. You know, right after the school opened, France established a new ministry for prisons. The minister thought the school was not enough like a prison and wanted to close it. The directors of the school and the unions of the prison guards were united in saying, 'No! We live our lives in prison. We return to the school often during our careers and on those occasions, we don't need more prison, we need perspective.'"

"Really?" I asked. "They said, 'perspective'?"

"Of course," Cantal said. "It's a common word."

"Indeed, it is," I replied, "but not many Americans—and this included me before I started to study with you—are aware of this need for open sight lines in our daily lives."

He looked at me in thoughtful consideration of my point. "Perspective is the warp of the city," he said. "And its woof is solidarity. That's what makes this school so important to people: here, we have the two together."

Layers and levels

I would say that every bit of Cantal's work flows from a devotion to creating solidarity. He jokes that he is a "Bricoleur des Villes," a Mr. Fix-it of Cities, because he is always mending, patching, repairing, and putting back together. His life's work is to enlarge the frame by which any of us views any of the rest of us. There are a million examples of this that I could cite[1], but here's just one.

Bob got really sick at one point and had to have open-heart surgery. I called Cantal to tell him. There was a brief period—about four days—before the surgery. Cantal called me every day, chatted briefly about the weather and promised to call the next day. When Bob pulled through the surgery in great shape, I got Cantal on the phone and he celebrated with me.

A few years later, we were at dinner with friends and I mentioned that he had done this and what a comfort it had been to me at the time. He nodded. "I had a friend, Bob Guerin. He was a contrabassist and a jazz musician. He was going to come to my fortieth birthday party in 1980, and I had gotten a piano for the occasion. He committed suicide. I had neglected to call him. Since then I've thought that if I can make a phone call to help, I will. I know what it's like to go through a period waiting for surgery. I knew I could help you get through it, and then you could help Bob, so I called."

That is, for me, the heart of solidarity.

CHAPTER ELEVEN

Element 9:
Celebrate Your Accomplishments

"But while he was still a long way off, his father saw him and was filled with compassion for him; he ran to his son, threw his arms around him and kissed him.

"The son said to him, 'Father, I have sinned against heaven and against you. I am no longer worthy to be called your son.'

"But the father said to his servants, 'Quick! Bring the best robe and put it on him. Put a ring on his finger and sandals on his feet. Bring the fattened calf and kill it. Let's have a feast and celebrate. For this son of mine was dead and is alive again; he was lost and is found.' So they began to celebrate."

—"The Prodigal Son,"
the Gospel according to Luke 15:11–32

One evening, after dinner, a few of us were gabbing around the table in the *salle à manger*—the small dining room—at Cantal's house in Saugnac. The subject of his fiftieth birthday party came up and one of his children said, "We have a video."

"Let's watch!" everyone said.

Cantal's fiftieth birthday party was held in Gabarret, the village where he was born. The guests arrived on Friday to a big feast. On Saturday, there was a rugby game, that being Cantal's favorite sport. Saturday night, there was a big party with singing and dancing. And Sunday, there were more

La fête à la mode Cantalienne

Figure 11.1: These are photos from Cantal's parties. Clockwise from top left: Mindy and Bob in the crowd when Cantal was awarded the Legion of Honor; In costume for Cantal and Marie-Dominique's "Come as Your Favorite Movie Star" wedding dinner are Molly, left, as the Elven maiden Arwen Undomiel from *Lord of the Rings*, and Lily, right, as a cheerleader from *Bring It On*; The brass bands playing at the conclusion of Cantal's last lecture; Guests shucking oysters in the garden at Saugnac for Cantal and Marie-Dominique's wedding breakfast.

Photo credits: Mindy Fullilove except top left, Pierre Perron, used with permission.

festivities until everyone hit the road to go home. I was astonished: I'd been to lots of birthday parties, but they'd lasted three hours, not three days.

When I told my daughter Molly about Cantal's party, she was inspired and used it as the model for the celebrations around her graduation from college. My son Bobby flew in from California, and son Kenny, his wife, and daughter came up from Atlanta. My mother, daughter Dina, and her daughter Lily, as well as Molly's father, stepmother, and sisters, Sadie and Gahlia, came, too. We drove to Amherst, Massachusetts, for a series of festive events. Friday night, we had dinner at Amherst Chinese Restaurant with several other families. A May snowstorm on Saturday challenged all of us, and we struggled to stay warm. I had a great time giving the commencement speech, inquiring why someone would ring a bell until his hands bled. Sunday, we had a wonderful family brunch at the Lord Jeffrey Inn in Amherst. It was a glorious weekend and it helped our family begin to appreciate and accept its complexities and quirks.

Cantal's seventieth birthday, in November 2010, coincided with mandatory retirement from his position as professor and chair of the department of urbanism and the environment at CNAM—the National Conservatory of Arts and Trades—in Paris. He decided to celebrate with a *leçon de cloture*, a last lecture, and a party on a restaurant boat on the Seine, which was docked next to the houseboat where he and his wife lived. Molly and I decided to go. We arrived in Paris on Monday morning and had two days to get over our jet lag before the party. Molly's friend Kate McNamara, who was a visiting curator in Antwerp, joined us in Paris. Cantal said he would meet us for dinner and would be there in a few minutes. We strolled over to the appointed spot, and Cantal rode up on the bicycle that had become his favorite method of transportation around Paris. We had a great dinner as he explained all that he was looking forward to at the lecture and the party. "I want to show them something they've never seen before!" he announced with delight.

CNAM consists of a set of buildings organized around a courtyard accessed through a gate on Rue St. Martin, in the third *arrondissement*. On entering, one faces a broad flight of steps leading up a church. Several fanfares had installed themselves on the steps and were playing sprightly marching music in honor of Cantal. All of the musicians were decked out in black, with black hats of various lineages and the red scarves of bullfighting fans—these reading "*Banda Cantal*" (Cantal's Band)—around their necks.

Cantal's friends streamed into the courtyard and down the stairs to the brightly lit underground amphitheater where the lecture was to take place. Cantal entered with a fanfare, literally, and took his place at the podium wearing an elegant academic red robe, trimmed with black, with a white cravat tied at his neck. He looked like he had stepped out of an etching of a nineteenth-century professor or lawyer.

He lectured about himself, reflecting in a quite personal manner on his life, a style of talking that is not as common in France as it is in the US. He explored the challenges he'd faced and the ideas he'd had. He talked about a style of living. He illustrated his style with a costume change—from his academic robe to *torero landais*, the costume he'd worn for his wedding—and with intermissions for the fanfare to play. In the corner, a group of friends spent much of the time getting into a bull costume and they joyfully butted Cantal at the end.

Afterwards, everyone—people of all ages and from a vast range of stations in life, from ministers in the French government to people far from that—made their way by car or metro to the restaurant boat, where the party went on until four o'clock in the morning. Cantal had promised to be at the office at ten the next day to work with me, but that didn't happen. He showed up late, happy, and chomping at the bit to get on to the next project.

The ninth element of urban restoration is celebrating your accomplishments. This has two parts:

- Giving parties to make the city; and
- Seeing the change in ourselves.

Giving parties to make the city

Why urbanists give parties

In 2012, Lourdes and I were teaching a seminar on emerging issues in urbanism when the topic of parties came up. "Why do urbanists give parties?" was the question of the day. Lourdes said, "Parties are one of the basic structures of the city. If you think about going to church once a week, that's a weekly party that gives order to everything in the city. When we urbanists give parties, we are building on our collective understanding that a city is made by its parties.

"We give parties to affirm, make connections that build over time, establish a sense of community, create solidarity, and understand people who are different from us in a different context.

"Here's another point about urbanists' parties: ownership is shared. In 2011, a week before Hike the Heights, I got a call from a community partner. She said, 'We have fifteen giraffes for Hike the Heights—where do you want them?'

"It turns out that the workers at the home visiting program she ran had learned how to make giraffes, and then they had helped mothers and their children make them during home visits. The fifteen giraffes were proudly displayed at the entrance to the party and everyone admired them. I had nothing to do with getting that organized—it happened because everyone pitched in and shared what they have.

"And that's how cities work, too. So we give parties to build the city and learn how to be better caretakers of our metropolis."

For her part, Molly, reflecting on why she gives parties, said, "I love parties. Parties allow us to step outside of our normal lives. We work, we take care of other people, and we take care of ourselves so that we can work and take of care others. When we have a party, it is something else. We get to experience ourselves in a fuller way. So a party can be any size—my mother, my niece, and I having cupcakes—but it makes my life richer and happier."

The six parts of the party

The urbanist's party has six parts: arriving, engaging, détente, reengaging, going home, and recap. Détente and reengagement can be repeated as often as you like as the party goes on over more days, the idea being that people are gathered in different configurations over the period of time.

Arriving

Cantal likes to have people travel to a party. "It gives them something to talk about when they get there. Invariably, a car broke down, a train was late, or someone missed their flight. It gets the excitement going. It gets people out of their daily routine. And I think it's really great if people have to prepare something for the party, like a costume. Then, they're really in the mood when they arrive."

One of the great challenges of the urbanist's party is picking the right spaces. The space must be the right size. If it is too large, the party will be lost, but if too small, the party won't be able to gain speed. The spaces need light and warmth and the sparkle that comes from proper care. Bedraggled spaces call attention to themselves in a doleful manner, and this could ruin the mood of the party. It goes without saying that the space should be well designed and built with substantial materials. Architects like Cantal have a horror of the fake. They might have to use it for some projects, but they don't party with it.

Engaging

Although we often think of a party as getting together for eating and drinking, the urbanist's party has content that is related to city making. The content might be a ceremony, a visit to a show, a trip to a museum or exhibition, or a dinner in a special location. All of the ways in which we reflect on the city can be ways to celebrate the city during a party.

The great challenge is that the presentation of the content cannot be too didactic. Cantal's last lecture, for example, was full of light moments to get the crowd laughing and enjoying themselves. On the other hand, it must not be too thin either. But what makes it playful and joyous *and* meaningful?

Détente

The urbanist's party has at least arriving, engaging, going home, and recap. If it is to be a more complicated party, then there is a period of détente. During the Cold War, there was a period of easing in the tension that came to be called détente, from the French word meaning a loosening or a relaxation. This period of the party provides a transition between two parts. It has modest definition, but the guests are largely on their own: this gives them time to interact. The détente is a time when people encounter each other in a relaxed fashion. Conversations on the wing can plant seeds of relatedness that will blossom days or years later.

The great challenge of détente, I think, is that people want to give it more form and content than it needs to have. Helping people relax, hang out, and enjoy each other is the shared work of the hosts and the guests in this transition phase.

Reengaging

The reengagement, in Cantal's hands, is designed to be in a different place with different activities. If the first part was serious, the second will be playful. If there had been talk, it will be followed by food. During a symposium on urbanism and governance in 2007, Cantal organized an outing to the Louise Catherine, a *peniche*, a French barge, with a special history, what he called the "five patrimonies." First, it was one of the first peniches to be built of concrete, so it represented an invention. Second, it was purchased by the Armé de Salut, the Salvation Army, to shelter homeless people, an important act of solidarity. Third, the sponsor of the homeless shelter was Madame Singer Polignac, of the sewing machine family, so it represented the history of philanthropy. Fourth, the interior for the shelter was designed by Le Corbusier, so it was important in the history of architecture. And fifth, it was being renovated by l'Ambasade de la Seine, so it represented urbanism in action. He gave us a tour and, in particular, explained Le Corbusier's thinking about the organization of space.

After the tour was over, we relaxed with food and wine on the roof of the boat. After that was over, our group was invited to dinner on the boat of the project leaders, just next door. The leisurely dinner outside and the soft rocking of the Seine were a great counterpoint to the more serious discussion of how to rehabilitate a boat and honor a great architect.

The organization of the reengagement poses the same kinds of issues of space that the original engagement raised. How will the group change? How will the activity change? What complements the experiences that have already transpired? Cantal's wedding was a masterpiece of complements, enhancing our experience of the city as we were slowly wending our way from the joy of the ceremony to the happy chaos of the wee hours of the morning and then on to a day-after wedding breakfast in Cantal's garden in Saugnac.

Going home

At the end of *Ferris Bueller's Day Off*, a great film of a daylong party, Ferris looks into the camera—that is, at the audience—and says, "You still here? Go home." We laugh and leave, but the pertness is a tiny sting: we have been faithful watchers up to that point and wonder why we are suddenly the objects of irritation. In general, I'd say that dismissing the audience is not the usual way urbanists end their parties. They are trying, after all, to build solidarity and welcome in the city. Shooing people away is not *comme il faut*, how it's done. Nor does Cantal shower people with presents: gift bags are definitely not his thing. The experience was the offering from Cantal to his friends. How, then, is the parting managed?

Cantal largely counts on the natural orders of life to handle the endings. At the luncheon after he was awarded the Medal of the Legion of Honor, the dessert served as the finale. People began to circulate in the room, did some singing, and started to drift away. I think there is always the feeling with Cantal that one is shortly to be invited back. He'll have something to show and talk about, some great new event that you'll be dying to go to, a new party to enjoy. The parting is temporary: after all, we are making the city together. I have left the many Cantal parties I've been to with the great satisfaction of the experience and a thirst for more.

Recap

If one is an urbanist, one often has work to do during a party. And if one happens to be shy, as I am, one finds parties stressful. In either case, I really love the last part of the urbanist's party, which is recap. It's the time when the Monday-morning quarterbacks get to do their thing, looking at the tape, raising the tough questions, and generally trying to understand what worked and what didn't. It is the time when long lists of do's and don'ts are created, and these guide future parties, making the efforts stronger with each passing year. At least, that's the ideal. Mostly, we tend to sit around with silly grins on our faces, saying, "I had such a good time!"

We are making and remaking the city

We don't always think of celebrations as including the times we gather in our grief. But in times of mourning, it is necessary to gather. When we share our loss, we affirm our future. I learned about this from Hirofumi

Minami, an environmental psychologist on the faculty at the Kyushu University in Japan. I met him while he was on sabbatical and in New York for eight months. He arrived in January 2002, just as the city was trembling from the anthrax attacks that rocked us after the attack on the World Trade Center. It was exhausting and tense. I had organized NYC RECOVERS and we were trying to think about Cantal's science of cities as a source of ideas for the badly shocked metropolitan region. Hiro joined us in that effort. What was remarkable was that he brought with him a deep knowledge of the story of Hiroshima. It was fifty-six years since the United States had dropped an atomic bomb on Hiroshima, causing massive destruction in the city and 160,000 deaths that unfolded over more than a decade. Paradoxically, it was not the tragedy, but the recovery that Hiro helped us to understand, creating a long perspective that New York would heal.

In 2006, he arranged for me to visit Japan (Figure 11.2). I spoke at a conference he had organized and then traveled to Hiroshima for the observances on August 6th, the anniversary of the bombing. We had to leave early in the morning, as the ceremony unfolds around ringing a bell at 8:15 a.m., when the bomb exploded over the city. Standing in the immense ceremonial square as the bell sounded, surrounded by so many people, I gained a deep new perspective on my own decades of peace and antinuclear activism. Later that day, Bob and I strolled around the city and went to the museum that detailed what happened in the bombing.

We then traveled from Hiroshima to Kyoto, a city where temples occupy a hilly district in the northwest part of the city. Hiro and a group of colleagues joined us, and we spent a day strolling the temple district, sharing insights. It was with the utmost joy that I approached Ryoan-ji, a temple graced by a garden created in about 1450. I had actually made a three-dimensional model of that garden in my History and Theory of Landscape Design class, a model that caused me much emotional turmoil, but which was well received by my teacher, Marta McDowell. By a happy accident, I had corrugated cardboard at home and that is exactly how the roof looks at Ryoan-ji. She didn't mind that I placed just three stones. I didn't know then that there were really fifteen stones in five groups.

A set of wooden stairs ran along one wall and offered people a place to sit and contemplate the groups of stones set in sand. When I entered, I was

Meditation in Japan

Figure 11.2: Photos clockwise from top left: on Hiroshima Day, a memorial in that city was one of many draped in chains of paper cranes, a symbol of the quest for peace; a garden in the Kyoto Temple District; Hirofumi Minami explaining Zen Buddhism to me while sitting in the Temple Garden at Ryoan-ji.

Photo credits: Hiroshima Memorial and Kyoto Garden, Mindy Fullilove. Mindy and Hiro in the garden at Ryoan-ji, Mami Kano, used with permission.

still quite shaken by the feelings of Hiroshima Day. I sat on the worn and friendly stairs and tried to take in the contents of the garden.

How does one comprehend fifteen stones set in sand?

I could not, and I had to surrender to that truth.

At that moment of letting go, I was suffused with the spirit of the place, a warmth and a happiness that I can only compare to an old turtle I saw a little bit later, sunning herself on a rock in the temple's lake. Unlike the regal Vaux-le-Vicomte, the exuberant North Hills, or the diffuse 488, Ryoan-ji is a garden of surrender.

Hiro came over after a bit and sat next to me, explaining Zen Buddhism and sharing his thoughts about the place. We were both attuned to the spirit of Ryoan-ji, and I could feel the perfect nature of friendship.

When we left, we continued our walk around the temple district, seeing various temples and deciphering the history of the dense neighborhood that was in the process of evolution, having lost some of the small stores that had once served the local people.

We were all eagerly anticipating a visit from Hiro in 2011 when the Tōhoku earthquake and tsunami devastated the northern part of Japan. He came as planned, but the occasion was a time to reflect again on grief and mourning. He addressed a colloquium Lourdes and I organized at Mailman School of Public Health. "When I came to New York in 2002," he related to us, "I wanted to do a psychoanalysis. I'd wanted to do this for a long time, but there aren't many psychoanalysts in Japan and they are busy with people who really need the help. My trip to New York offered a wonderful opportunity, and I undertook a twice-a-week psychoanalysis during the eight months I was here.

"I hadn't expected that I would find it so disorienting. I would come out of the sessions and have to walk around the city until I could go back to my normal routine. It turned out that the unspoken tragedy of Hiroshima, where I grew up, became the central story I explored. The story of my city was interwoven with my story, and I started to do a psychoanalysis of cities, weaving together my personal story with the story of my city. I used family photographs and random walks the way a person might use dreams—to free the process of association and open up the hidden stories and meanings that were eluding me.

"The nuclear attack has been memorialized in the massive Peace Park on the site of our ground zero, and it is solemnly commemorated every year. But it was only when I had a son that my father began to speak of his experience, arriving in the city two days after the attack and being part of the effort to get the city started again. More recently, people who lived near the center, which was destroyed—the people of the place and the place are gone. But, the people who lived nearby have memories of that place and its daily life. They are now opening those memories so that we can learn how the people lived.

"I think back to NYC RECOVERS, and the idea that we worked with then—the idea of parties everywhere—and I think that is the right idea. Just before I left Japan for this trip, it was the time of graduation. The schools that had survived the tsunami were now serving as shelters. But for that day, the shelters were transformed into places of celebration. It gave people hope. Many of the people who live in the north are elderly, and seeing the young graduate is a source of comfort and pride. It lifted the spirits of the nation to see the graduations.

"I am not sure how we will think about those places that are wiped out and the people who are gone. Who will remember them? How will we think about them? It is in that context that the celebration of life has a new meaning."

Seeing the change in ourselves

One June

The NYC RECOVERS "Year of Recovery" was launched on September 15, 2001, in the immediate aftermath of the 9/11 terrorist attacks and lasted until December 2002. It is in that spirit that my 2012 June community-building party season started in April and ended in July.

The first party was Placemaking IV: The People's Poetry, the signature urbanism event of the University of Orange. This annual event had started out with Cantal's first visit in 2009, and originally was a time of serious speeches and workshops. It had evolved. Molly developed our "Jan Term" and Summer Urbanism sessions for teaching and began to use placemaking for the experience of being in the city.

In 2012, it was the Guerilla Haiku Movement that took us to many parts of the city to write poetry with passersby and chalk our poems onto sidewalks, streets, rooftops, bridges, stairs, benches, and light poles. Invented by artist and actress Calley Vickerman, Guerilla Haiku was an opportunity to write poetry in the city, celebrating the city. We all started out a little tongue-tied, but quickly learned that if somebody throws out an idea and everybody counts on their fingers, it is pretty easy to come up with three lines of poetry, with five, seven, and five syllables, in that order. By the end of the day, we were thanking each other with haiku notes and howling with laughter at watching everyone's fingers count out the beats. When I went to the train station on Monday morning, I enjoyed the colorful poetry that had been left there for me and for all of us.

The first weekend in May 2012 was devoted to a Jane Jacobs Walk, organized by the urbanism students at Columbia University's Mailman School of Public Health. They had located sights and tastes of Inwood, and the walk turned out to be a time for a reunion of urbanism students. We arrived at Inwood Hill Park by way of the farmers market. We were loaded down with wonderful things to eat, and we picnicked in the grass.

June 2nd was our annual Hike the Heights, our biggest and best ever. We hosted about fifteen-hundred people in the Sunken Playground of Highbridge Park. An adventure that had begun with Lourdes and Anthony climbing the rocks along the trail took on new stature as REI, the outdoor store, hosted real rock-climbing at the site. Maudene presided over a truly sumptuous and healthy feast. Arelis made sure that everything worked. But there were new partners who had designed and made the T-shirts, new partners who had organized the entertainment, and many new partners who had helped to set-up and break down the event.

As we were getting ready for the day, Lourdes said she thought we'd have a big crowd, maybe even fifteen-hundred people. I replied, "Do you think we can fit that many people in the Sunken Playground site?"

She organized the next planning meeting as a site visit. She divided people up into groups of "first-timers" and "old-timers," depending on how many Hike the Heights people had attended. They were each assigned a set of questions about the event and asked to explore the terrain to find the best answers.

The **space** is the thing

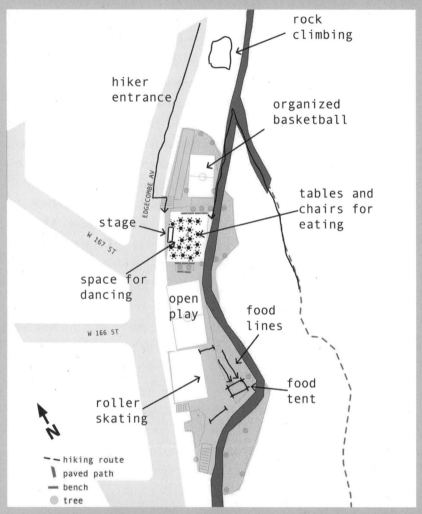

Figure 11.3: Cantal (1994), in *Merci La Ville!*, said that every successful party organizer knows that the key is to fill the space. Here's how the Hike the Heights 8 team laid out the Sunken Playground area so that it could welcome 1,500 hikers.

Sketch by: Sarah Schell.

After careful consideration, everyone present at the site visit agreed—indeed, they were adamant—that the Sunken Playground was the spot for our event. They did propose a reorganization of the space, managing to make it substantially larger and more integrated. At one end was the food table and at the other, the rock climbing—anchors of the event and its process in more ways than one.

On June 9th, I was back in Orange for the Valley Arts, Music and Poetry Festival (VAMP), which Molly and Mike Mal were organizing for ValleyArts. This event had had some spectacular years, but had been anemic of late, not helped by the wretched redesign of Triangle Park (see Figure 8.4). Molly and Mike had decided to relocate the festival to Ironworks and build off the energy they'd created there at the Big Top. The crew of emerging artists pitched in to come up with an exciting live program.

I didn't have too many duties at VAMP, so I just laughed and took photographs and enjoyed the huge crowds—about eight hundred people attended—that floated through all day.

One more thing: I tried to finish my poem for the 8 p.m. Poetry Lounge. I had one idea, but I trashed that and started to work on a new poem. Little did I know that most of the evening's poets were scribbling as frantically as I was. Just as the Poetry Lounge was about to start, I got a call that I had to pick Lily up. I was tense about missing my performance, but it all worked out. Things started late, as they often do, and went long, which also happens. Lily came with me. As we walked in, one man was reciting a poem about life on the mean streets of Newark. Lily wondered how my poem about a white carpet and blue paint was going to work.

But the crowd loved poetry and loved words, and loved mine as well as they loved everyone else's. I felt tenderly welcomed and supported. They laughed at the silly parts of my poem and sighed at the sad ones. After it was over, I got hugs and compliments from many of my younger peers. I went home feeling great.

And the party season was only beginning.

Ken, as the new president of the Community Design Center of Pittsburgh, which they had just renamed the Design Center, had asked if I would give a talk for them. I told him that to advance the shared vision—to align and connect—we needed to have a penumbra of parties. He is, quiet as it's kept, a master host, and the list of parties quickly grew into a

"Welcome City Weekend." It got so interesting that Molly and Lourdes decided to come, which added new layers of connection and meaning.

The Design Center and its new leadership needed to prove themselves. They went all out advertising my lecture entitled, "The Meaning of Things: Pittsburgh's 21st Century Triumph over 20th Century Urban Renewal." I was startled to find my face plastered all over town. But I wasn't surprised when four hundred people showed up at the August Wilson Center in downtown Pittsburgh: It was June 2012, and I was realizing that people were longing to be together in finding solutions to our common problems.

And they wanted to know about this triumph I was talking about, as they were not entirely sure that they'd seen it! Some left as skeptical as

Party on, Wayne!

when they came. But others bought my argument that the brutal, top-down imposition of urban renewal-type planning seen in 1997 was different from the revitalization flowing from neighborhood visions seen in 2012.

The next weekend, I, for one, rested up, because there was another weekend of community-building parties in my future. I'd been invited to Little Rock, Arkansas, by the We Shall Not Be Moved Coalition, which was fighting the threatened displacement of an inner-city neighborhood for a proposed technology park. They'd arranged for me to speak at the University of Arkansas Clinton School of Public Service and then go to a series of events and celebratory meals with various groupings of the coalition. I entitled my talk, "Neighbor Like You Mean It," and took as my

Figure 11.4: Images from the 2012 June Community Building party season. Clockwise from left: Eva-Marie Simms and Terri Baltimore enjoying the Patio Party at Ken Doyno's house; Mailman School of Public Health Jane Walk; Hike the Heights 8 climbing the 155th Street stairs (see Figure 6.1); Battle of Brooklyn, Little Rock; Guerilla Haiku, Orange, New Jersey.

Photo credits:

Simms and Baltimore, Beatrice Spolidoro, used with permission.

Jane Walk, Mindy Fullilove.

Guerilla Haiku, Courtesy of the CRG Collection.

Battle for Brooklyn in Little Rock, Demetria Edwards, used with permission.

Climbing 155th, Mindy Fullilove.

theme the story of the Good Samaritan in the Gospel according to Luke. It was a happy choice for a weekend in the Bible Belt.

Two of my hosts, Reverend Dr. Anika Whitfield and Reverend Demetria Edwards, Esq., had, at my suggestion, come to the Welcome City Weekend in Pittsburgh. You might say they honored Ken and the Design Center by making every effort to outdo them during my visit to Little Rock. At any rate, we tried to use the time effectively to deepen the understanding of coalition, to strengthen connections among people, and to argue for the preservation of neighborhoods.

Threaded through this work was time to appreciate the gentle beauty of Little Rock and the kindness of the people who live there. While driving from one place to another, we stopped by the state capitol building and explored the extraordinary classical garden that surrounds it. The designer had opened the perspective in all four directions and had judiciously placed magnificent trees in a combination of well-ordered allées and specimen plantings in slightly surprising locations that punctuated the order to make it more exciting. It is such visits that delight our senses, deepen our understanding of the city, and make a party weekend an *urbanist's* party weekend.

As if all those events weren't enough, on July 4th, I got to go to a community barbecue at Barrow Mansion in Jersey City, around the corner from where I used to live. It was a chance to see old friends, catch up on news, listen to stirring speeches, and eat wonderful food.

I got home from the Fourth of July celebration, the last event of my June community-building party season, grateful for time with so many good people, all so deeply committed to making a better future in our cities. It was easiest for me to see how a great series of events had built relationships in Orange. From Placemaking IV to VAMP, I'd written haiku, gone to arts shows, shared pizza, listened to music, and recited poetry in my neighborhood with family, friends, and neighbors. I knew more names and had more associations with people than I'd had before. In addition to those connections, there'd also been plenty of time to complain to each other, to consider the problems of the city, and to reflect on next steps. All of that was crucial to my growth as an urbanist and community member.

The June community-building party season was so full and so fabulous that it reminded me of the Saturday Night Live skits about Wayne's

World. One of the great exchanges was Wayne saying to his friend Garth, "Party on, Garth!"

And Garth would reply, "Party on, Wayne!" (Figure 11.4).

The change is in ourselves

After the celebration of Cantal's seventieth birthday in 2010, he announced that he had to go to Perpignan. The timing of his trip couldn't have been worse from my point of view, as I'd hoped to review some questions so that I could finish this book. But it couldn't be helped. He had to speak at the annual colloquium of the citizens' urbanism atelier. He couldn't stay in Paris, but it turned out that I could travel to Perpignan.

I enjoyed the colloquium and got to tell the story of the apatosaurus machine that ate part of the building in Clodion. I visited some sites with Cantal, including going by Clodion to see the park, which had just been installed. And, finally, on Saturday, the day I was returning to Paris, we had a quiet hour and I posed the questions that had been on my mind.

Towards the end of the hour, he leaned back in his chair and looked out the window of the Park Hotel toward Square Bir Hakeim. "I think," he said, "that you've learned everything you need to learn about me and about my work. I think what's missing is the connection to your own work. You're a scientist, you study cities: why do you find my projects important? That's what needs to be written."

A few minutes later, we set out for the airport and my return flight to Paris. The flight back was a good time to reflect on the party and all that I had learned. I also had time to reflect on the profound question Cantal had posed to me. It would take two years to answer, and would profoundly alter what I had to say.

That is why urbanists give parties.

Conclusion:
Give Me Your Hands

Gentles, do not reprehend:
If you pardon, we will mend:
And, as I am an honest Puck,
If we have unearned luck
Now to 'scape the serpent's tongue,
We will make amends ere long;
Else the Puck a liar call:
So, good night unto you all.
Give me your hands, if we be friends,
And Robin shall restore amends.

—Shakespeare, *Midsummer Night's Dream*

Here's my prescription for the American city: "Take nine elements of urban restoration, and apply liberally to the affected area."

Once we have the city in mind, know what we're for, and make a mark, we will start to see change. From there, the improvements will accumulate, the clarity of unpuzzling, the excitement of unslumming, and the heart's ease of meaningful placemaking will strengthen the city and energize the region. Then we can show solidarity and celebrate our achievements.

This restoration will proceed from many initial points. Cantal talked about this as the process of the crystallization of salt, while Ken viewed it as the effect of many points of light making a whole area bright. They are

The nine elements of urban restoration

Element	In the crazy sorted-out city...	Solution	Key Stories
City-in-mind	People can't see/know the whole.	Get to know the whole city in order to have a proper foundation for the future.	Is this a welcome?
Find out what you're FOR!	Rupture of networks leads to loss of shared sentiments, history, direction.	Community clarifies its vision, finds common ground, begins to work with others for change.	Programmatic Cat and the New Day Platform.
Make a mark	The inability to read the "other" makes us feel excluded.	Explain the obscure so that it has meaning for all.	No more redevelopment!
Unpuzzle	People have difficultly navigating because it is fractured and disconnected.	Straighten out the disconnects so that people have 1) clear vision and 2) safe passage.	Across the speedway.
Unslum	Population is in constant motion. People don't understand where they live or why they live there.	Jane Jacobs: "We need to discern, respect and build upon the forces for regeneration that exist in slums themselves, and that demonstrably work in real cities."	Rice truck brings peace.
Make meaningful places	Deprivation and displacement destroy meaning.	Restore hope and give a gift to the community.	The Princess and the medina.
Strengthen the region	Regions are as splintered as cities are.	The healed city is an engine of problemsolving and can extend its net of concern to include the region.	Every place is lovable.
Show solidarity	People only help their own.	Recognize inherent worth and dignity of every person. Identify, don't compare.	Can we get there from here?
Celebrate	People are isolated and demoralized.	Parties set up a new feedback loop: hard work > collective joy > hard work.	Making and remaking the city.

Figure 12.1

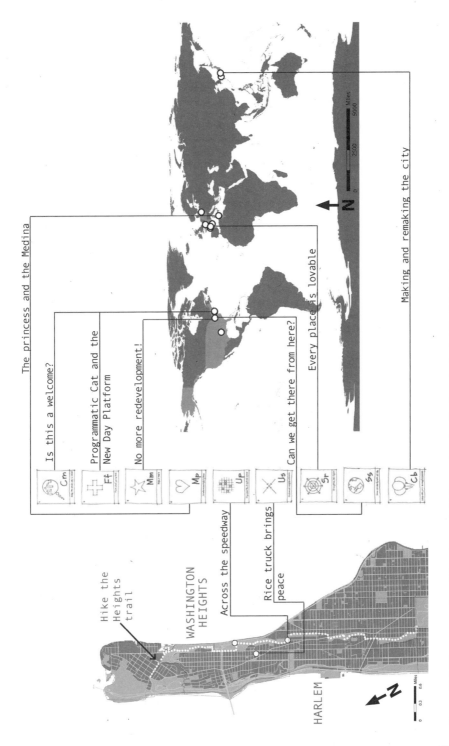

Figure 12.2: The geography of the elements. This map locates the key stories told in this book.

both pointing to the coalescence of the many small efforts into a larger whole, which is the eventual goal of urban restoration. Cantal's story of UNESCO helping the Medina of Tunis, my story of the Rice Truck on 166th Street, and Dan's story of the jazz panels on The Legacy may seem small and disconnected, but they are exactly the kinds of points of light that are accumulating as people work to make their cities places of welcome and hope.

Yet Puck, in *Midsummer Night's Dream*, talks about amends—that is, change—and that is a fundamental topic to address as this book comes to a close. That is because, however effective the nine elements of urban restoration might be, they cannot work in the face of the ongoing sorting of the city. In 1994, I started a research project looking at the work of Harlem Congregations for Community Improvement (HCCI). At that time, the Bradhurst neighborhood was in desperate shape, and HCCI was bringing the first investments into the neighborhood. They were guided by a savvy plan created by Lionel McIntyre, and the congregations had a deep commitment to rebuilding Harlem for the existing African American community.

I was proud and delighted to report what we saw unfold (Fullilove, Green, and Fullilove 1999). I watched with eager anticipation, expecting to see more of the same. Instead, things started to change. The first inkling I had that something was different was when colleagues in AIDS housing services stopped placing people in Harlem. "The prices are just too high," they told me.

What was happening was gentrification, and it took off. I went to a meeting one evening in 2010 and I passed by a well-lit first floor gym in which little white girls were taking a ballet class. I stopped in astonishment. A couple of years later, I got invited to a protest led by Harlem clergy who did not want to be zoned out of Harlem. I was glad to go, but I thought it possible that we were ten years too late. The work is *not* restoration if the marginalized people are ejected in the process of change. If we make things better without stopping the process of sorting, in the end, sorting triumphs.

What can we do? We must, I believe, follow the advice of the comedian, Steve Harvey, who said to women stuck in dead-end relationships, "Don't hate the player, change the game" (Parker 2012).

The current game, according to Elliott Sclar (1990), an esteemed member of the planning faculty at Columbia University, is musical chairs. Each time we sort the city, we take away a chair, that is, we take away housing, historic structures, and social relationships. In doing so, we are destroying the very fabric of the nation.

I am proposing, instead, that we play the game that Cantal plays—and that he has taught his motley crew of friends and family, *Banda Cantal*, as he called us at his retirement party—the "game" of urban alchemy.

South Orange, a city near my home, prides itself on being a liberal place, but deep racial tensions undermine this ideal. Imagine that the city wanted to solve its social problems, where might it start? In the spirit of urban alchemy, it could take a very fine drumming circle that meets in a small park on Sunday evenings. The city could nurture this activity that's working, that's "unslumming" in the best Jane Jacobs's sense of the word. The city could incorporate drumming into the schools, provide instruments in their great park on Sundays, bring ribbons for children and adults who want to spin and twirl, and invite the whole city to drum and dance together. Out of those distinct rhythms would arise a sense of South Orange, energized and united. They would have woven something larger and stronger, something that emerged organically from the fabric that is already in their fingers. That is urban alchemy; it is the magic that is possible, that is all around us, that is the new game we might play.

So what?

So we restore a city, what then? I want to end with that most important question. It is my contention that the city is an engine of our society, a machine for problem solving, a mill to grind issues until they are fine and can be baked into the bread of change. Our machine is broken, and our mill wheels are out of kilter. We must fix them. But this is not just so that they are fixed, it is because we need this machine in good working order to solve the problems of our times.

This machine, to give it a name, is our collective thinking. We can't think collectively if we can't live together, and we can't live together in the sorted-out city. To get the economic, social, and physical connections needed for effective collective thinking, we must restore the urban ecosystem. Then, we can use our collective thinking to answer the hard questions of our times, questions like: What kinds of work will Americans do in the years to come? How will we manage the consequences of global warming? How will we harvest the oil in the sky and replace ancient sunlight? How can we learn to build and expand our nation's wealth together? And how can we learn to live in peace?

I went to an art show by Der Fehler, a young woman from Portugal who had arrived in Newark two months before the show and was astounded by what she saw. In the two rooms of the gallery, she included an installation of tall sawhorses, called *Monument*, some paintings of weird hands and feet on the walls, some photos of the city with texts she had written, and a set of drawings riffing on a nineteenth-century shepherdess. For me, the dominant image was of many hands, joined at the wrist but pointing in an impossible number of ways.

I experienced this disjointed set of objects and images as a representation of our social disconnection. Der Fehler's art represented the same disconnection that Eva-Maria Simms described in Simms III, the era of

Figure 12.3: Hands ready for work. *4th World*, needlepoint by Maggie Thompson. Photo: Mindy Fullilove.

unexpectancy, the same disconnection that I talk about in my model of community collapse, and the same disconnection that is the end result of sorting-out the city.

My mother, Maggie, made a needlepoint of hands, but her image was of four hands locked together. She named it *4th World* (Figure 12.3). I remember that when I was young, she taught me to lock hands in that way for what she called the "Firemen's Carry." "It's a way for two people to work together to carry a person," she explained. "Our hands, locked like this, are firmly united. The person we are carrying is very safe. We can get them out of a burning house."

We practiced by carrying my brother, Josh, around the house, to the great delight of all of us.

To be continued…

Cantal and I talked endlessly during my trip to France in 2012, the last I'd make before finishing this book. We kept opening up new topics, finding that there was so much to do and say. Finally, Cantal said, "You know, we'll never finish the conversations we're having. So when you get to the end of this book, just put *à suivre*, to be continued, and we can start the next book."

à suivre
to be continued

Afterword
by Ken Doyno

Where we find ourselves

As we read this book and connect its teachings to what we do, as we become conscious actors in our city and our community, we become urban alchemists, trying to weave a whole and healthy community into the glorious golden city. In *Urban Alchemy*, Mindy challenges us by illustrating how we have the power to unsort and reshape our cities so that they are welcoming, inclusive, connected, creative, and productive in the future. The motivation to participate in moving towards unsorted communities is driven by the recognition that failure to address mad plagues and unexpectancy is a threat to each and every one of us.

What does it take?

Becoming an urban alchemist begins with seeing the desires that are all around us and developing a faith that these can flow together to shape the spaces we share. Much of the sorting that has encumbered our cities and cultures comes from fear of difference. This closes us off from being open to change and to other people. When we loosen the grip with which we hold onto our own conclusions, we can ask both ourselves and others: What is motivating us? What do we see? Is there something that we can do together? We learn that we can say yes to ourselves and to each other. We learn that we can be open, rather than closed, and come to know each other's stories.

As these stories converge and diverge, we find that it is difficult to contribute alongside others, especially when faced with big decisions and responsibilities; we struggle to comprehend *how* we will make our contribution. Can my personal aspirations interact with others and make an outcome that serves us all? Do I trust myself and others to do their best? When we gain more understanding of each other, we can work to make our city better together. The greater our differences, the more we're challenged to recognize what each of us brings to the table. Can we be patient and find the ways to learn from what others are doing, support our efforts, and allow their goals to influence us?

Consciously or not, we answer these questions every day of our lives. The more we can craft answers that are in accord with our greater intentions, the better we can find the right places for our contributions and interweave with those we walk beside.

See stories everywhere

I'm reassured by the image Mindy describes in which we are made stronger with many hands working together toward a common purpose (see Conclusion, Figure 12.3). As an architect, I have long realized that it takes many hands, hearts, and minds to build a building. As an urbanist, I am constantly learning how these hands come together to form a community in all of its complexity. When this complexity overwhelms me, I seek comfort in watching others working to make change. I am humbled by the knowledge that resides in the hands of a mason who practices every day. Those hands will always know more about placing a brick than mine ever will, and I am dependent upon that knowledge being applied.

When we can expand trusts, align intentions, and connect people and purposes, the action and the materials that we change transcend their moment and become part of the spirit of the places in which we live our lives. What we make with our hands, hearts, and minds becomes the future—the welder who said, "This is how I will live forever," or the painter who said, "This is where I'll bring my grandkids." With each effort, we create memories that live on across our communities. We build our own stories and find joy in each other's, and this joy resonates through the connected city.

The process is hard, but of course it is!

As I work with clients and communities, I am constantly seeking ways that I can help people connect with, influence, and ultimately come to see themselves in the outcomes of our work. This is a path with many twists and turns. When I come up against issues that are unresolved or that I don't understand—some of which are becoming more evident to me through working with Mindy on this book—I have to remind myself of the greater purposes that underlie what I am doing. I know that the magic of the journey will continue on.

Every project I've worked on has moments of hope and excitement where purposes, people, and site forces flow together. New ideas, solutions, accomplishments, and new places seem to emerge, almost of their own accord. Those same projects have moments of anxiety where the people and forces are turbulent, as if the future seems blocked by something that no one can see. Or worse, we discover economic, social, or physical conditions are at cross-purposes that we can't yet name. Like a dam, the unknownness blocks the solutions. Our faith in the possibility of resolution gets shaken.

Nothing to fear

It is precisely at those points where I find it vital to listen actively, sketch what I hear from others, share what I see, reflect what I learn from people, and foster conversations until the ideas illuminate a path. Every time I have gone through these passages, what emerges surprises everyone because the outcomes were not foreseen by any single participant. I have learned to embrace and celebrate these moments, when we are overcome by joy with the passage that we have traversed. In my bravest hours, this feeling drives me to continue to search out and embrace the unknown. My understanding has deepened as much, perhaps even more, from trying to clear the turbulent waters—turning blockades into relationships, transforming conflicts into understandings, and reshaping divergent complexities into a shared clarity.

The path from careful observer to grassroots activist to humble participant in a thriving, verdant, metropolitan ecosystem can seem risky and uncertain. But it is nurtured by building and expanding networks of purpose, difference, and trust. This path starts by recognizing that where and how we live our lives already intersects with a more positive and inclusive future. From those meeting points, we can elevate and increase connections with the situations and people who are different from us.

Align and connect

So go and make your mark.
Have a potluck, have a yard sale,
invite people from different communities.
Help actions and change to emerge
help people to hear each other's stories
and tell your own stories,
to learn how you came to be in the position and places that you
  are in
connect these with other places and people in your community
let stories flow together
learn how you can, from where you find yourself, make a mark
that makes the world a better place
by connecting people and recognizing all of the needs and
  aspirations that flow around us
open up to those needs and aspirations
so they may flow with your own
if this is meant to be
practice saying yes, and find your own yes.
let live and live yourself
most of all, go and do.

Acknowledgments

This book was developed through a process of co-storytelling with urbanists from the United States and France. I have served as a participant-observer, visiting cities with my co-storytellers, collecting notes, photographs, and ephemera, and then writing up what I understood. They have helped me to see what they saw in these many situations. I appreciate the tolerance shown by all of them. Any errors or misunderstandings that remain are entirely my own.

My father, Ernest Thompson, was my earliest mentor. He taught me that it was important to listen. He was a pioneer of the civil rights movement and an outstanding urbanist. Working with him on his book, *Homeboy Came to Orange: A Story of People's Power*, determined my life path.

Dr. Rodrick Wallace has been my mentor in understanding the connections between urban ecosytems and disease. We have coauthored numerous papers and a book. His insistence on respect for urban ecology is, I hope, thoroughly reflected in all my writings.

Michel Cantal-Dupart, a renowned French urbanist who has pioneered strategies of urban restoration in France, Tunisia, Madagascar, Morocco, and the United States, worked closely with me for many years to help me understand cities and their repair. He also consulted with me on projects in three US cities: Pittsburgh, Pennsylvania; Orange, New Jersey; and New York City, New York. His generosity and welcome cannot be overstated: he is the source of this book. His family—his wife, Marie-Dominique, son, Xavier, and daughter, Leïla—have welcomed me into their homes and shared their knowledge and expertise with me on many occasions. The superb team that works with him has also supported me over the years, especially Sibylle Rérolle. I owe all of them a profound debt.

The projects in Pittsburgh, Orange, and New York City have their own leaders. I am very honored that Terri Baltimore, Lourdes Hernández-Cordero, Molly Rose Kaufman, Bonnie Young Laing, Michael Malbrough, Patrick Morrissy, and Carl Redwood agreed to be part of this process. Their generous contributions of time and materials are gratefully acknowledged.

Through my 2004 book, *Root Shock: How Tearing Up City Neighborhoods Hurts America and What We Can Do About It*, I made the acquaintance of architects Ken Doyno and Dan Rothschild. Their generous and spirited collaboration helped me to connect French urbanism to the United States. Other members of the Rothschild Doyno Collaborative, and especially Kate Tunney, Michelle Nermon, Melanie Buzgan Dower, Jennifer Zaffuto, and Beatrice Spolidoro, have also been very generous with their contributions to my work.

I am indebted to many others, whose gracious support helped me carry out the work described here. Robert E. Fullilove, III, a.k.a. Bob, was codirector of the Community Research Group (CRG) of Columbia University and New York State Psychiatric Institute from 1992 to 2012. Bob provided major assistance with negotiating the French language and translated the Foreword by Jean Nouvel. He shared documents from his library, read drafts, verified details of our trips, and provided insight into the culture and politics of France. He provided many suggestions for making this book useful for students.

CRG carried out the two decades of work reported here. I had the honor of working with a very gifted team that included, in addition to Molly and Lourdes who are mentioned above: Lesley Rennis, Jennifer Stevens Dickson, Véronique Héon-Klin, Moriah McSharry McGrath, Mark Boutros, Evelyn Joseph, Howard Joseph, Arelis De La O, Beverly Xaviera Watkins, Caroline Parsons Moore, Sara Booth, Helena Hansen, and David Swerdlick.

Sarah Schell served as the chief illustrator. Pam Shaw, Rich Brown, Dan Rothschild, Ken Doyno, and Beatrice Spoliodoro provided advice and assistance. Dan Rothschild contributed the Periodic Table of the Elements of Urban Restoration. Thomas Hanchett created the 1875 map of Charlotte, North Carolina. Pam Shaw created the cover, which, for me, is the perfect embodiment of urban alchemy.

Writing this book required new skills. I got a certificate in landscape design from the Continuing Education Program at the New York Botanical Garden. I am especially grateful to Bill Einhorn and David Dew Bruner, who understood what I was trying to learn and did everything in their power to help me on my way. I also studied storytelling with Murray Nossel, cofounder of Narativ. He, the Narativ team, and my fellow students in the master classes helped me break out of the rigid habits of speaking and writing I'd developed over so many years of doing science. I am also grateful for the careful reading and fine advice I was given in a fiction writing workshop organized by the Columbia University Narrative Medicine Program and led by Chris Adrian and Nellie Hermann. David Chapin, Roy Crystal, Serena Crystal, Bozena Kluba, Zoë Levitt, and Victor McTeer read drafts and provided helpful advice.

Assistance in acquiring photographs was rendered by Mary Yearwood at the Schomburg Collection of the New York Public Library; David Rosado of the New York Public Library; Gilbert Pietrzak of the Carnegie Library of Pittsburgh; and Laurel Mitchell, the coordinator of rights and reproductions of the Carnegie Museum of Art.

For permission to use their photographs, I am grateful to Terri Baltimore, Rich Brown, the Carnegie Library of Pittsburgh, the Carnegie Museum of Art of Pittsburgh, Demetria Edwards, Robert Fullilove, Mami Kano, Maulin Mehta, the New York Public Library, Pierre Perron, Sarah Schell, Beatrice Spoliodoro, Rodrick Wallace, and Léa Znaty. Of the many photographers who have contributed to the Community Research Group collection, I am honored to include photographs by Lesley Rennis, Howard Heyman, Amelia Krales, Rojelio Rodriguez, and David Swerdlick. For allowing my adaptation of texts they created, I am grateful to Michel Cantal-Dupart, Molly Kratz, and Patrick Morrissy.

New York State Psychiatric Institute has been critically important to the accomplishment of all the tasks represented in this book. Dr. Anke Ehrhardt and Dr. Zena Stein secured my position there and set this work in motion. Dr. Bruce Dohrenwend, chair of the division of social psychiatry, has provided impeccable scholarly leadership and intellectual freedom.

My gratitude to my writing group, Ann Burack-Weiss, Lourdes Hernández-Cordero, Helena Hansen, and Jack Saul, knows no bounds. They read many, many drafts of this book with unwavering enthusiasm for the project. The founders of the Writing Group, Adolph Christ and Grace Christ, were always present in the methods of work that they so ably modeled.

Allan Rosenfield, Phil Hallen, Don Mattison, Richard Jackson, and David Satcher provided critical support to my research, starting long before the study of urban ecosystems had entered the mainstream of public health research. I am eternally grateful for their insight and enthusiasm.

Many urbanists, including teachers, colleagues, and students, have taken time to visit cities with me. In addition to all the cities I have studied in New York, New Jersey, Pennsylvania, France, and Japan, I have been deeply influenced by the work of urbanists in Enschede, the Netherlands; Anniston, Alabama; Atlanta, Georgia; Baltimore, Maryland; Detroit, Michigan; Charlotte and Asheville in North Carolina; Houston, Texas; Madison, Wisconsin; New Orleans, Louisiana; Roanoke, Virginia; St. Louis, Missouri; Memphis and Nashville in Tennessee; San Francisco, California; Seattle, Washington; Syracuse, New York; and Washington, DC. I am grateful to all of them, and many others in cities I have not listed. I look forward to future collaboration.

My family has been steadfast in its support. I am grateful to my brother, Josh Thompson, for the wonderful wordsmithing that led to "Urban Alchemy." My nephew, Avery Thompson, provided sage advice on the epigraphs, and my niece, Jaden Thompson, spent one lovely afternoon in the library with me selecting them. My children and their families—Bobby Fullilove in Japan, Kenny Kaufman in Atlanta, and Dina Kaufman in Hackensack—have been my cheering section, as have all the Hale-Crystals. My granddaughter, Lily Johnson, lived with me through this whole thing. She gave me tons of splendid advice and, when things worked out as she had said they would, never hesitated to remind me, "Grandma, I told you so!"

There are four people to whom I owe very special thanks. Sarah Schell, who undertook the task of making all the illustrations, sat with me through some very hot summer days. Her calm in the face of thousands of photographs, hundreds of maps and charts, and piles of draft illustrations gave me heart. The way she took the messy originals and transformed them felt to me like the realization of my own vision in my own aesthetic. It helped enormously to have what I was seeing in my mind's eye so clearly laid out on paper. She was a remarkable ally, kind, patient, and present at all times.

Ken Doyno, in addition to sharing the work of his firm and placing at my disposal the vast store of his knowledge, took on the role of urbanist Zen master. This took the form of quests and koans, the first nudges about unfinished work and the second ideas that could only be integrated through meditation and reflection. Indeed, I had the feeling that, between February and August 2012, I pulled together twenty years of psychiatry-meets-the-city. This was a trippy process, and Ken's calm in the face of such was absolutely commendable. He inspired me to work hard and laugh a lot, a combination that made it possible to get to the heart of the matter and finish my book.

Molly Rose Kaufman played many roles in this process. She is a gifted urbanist and has worked on many of the research projects that inform this work. She is a leader in Orange and helped me understand how she was using the tools of urban restoration in her work. She is a journalist and writer and offered excellent advice on the writerly aspects of the project. And finally, she remained calm and serene during the months when I was tripping on Ken's koans, providing Lily and me with the emotional, moral, and spiritual support we desperately needed. I couldn't have made it through without every bit of her wisdom and kindness.

My mother, Maggie Thompson, who died in February 2012, reread my other books in her final months. "Now that I'm a writer," she told me, "I have a much better appreciation for what you have accomplished." Though sad she wouldn't get to read this one, she helped choose the title. The last photograph she took was of my brother and me batting around names. She worked her entire life to make the world a better place. May we always remember the Peace of Olcott Street.

Notes

Chapter 1

1. Cantal (1993) elaborates on these points in "La crise des villes," published in *Les Temps Modernes*.

Chapter 2

1. The report *Hillscapes: Envisioning a Healthy Urban Habitat* (Robins et al. 1999) tells the full story of the Falk Fellowship.

2. The Design Sketchbook process is described on Rothschild Doyno Collaborative's website at http://www.rdcollab.com/sketchbook_process.html.

Chapter 6

1. During one visit to Perpignan, Cantal took me to see St. Michel de Ceixas, one of the monasteries from which stones were taken to be used at the Cloisters in New York.

2. Loïc Wacquant (2008, 1–2) argues in *Urban Outcasts*: "This book takes the reader inside these territories of relegation in two advanced countries—namely, the black ghetto of the United States and the working-class banlieue of France—to show that… urban marginality is not everywhere woven of the same cloth, and, all things considered, there is nothing surprising in that. The generic mechanisms that produce it, like the specific forms it assumes, become fully intelligible once one takes caution to embed them in the historical matrix of class, state and space characteristic of each society at a given epoch."

Chapter 8

1. Glasco (2011) describes the diversity in an essay in *August Wilson: Pittsburgh Places in His Life and Plays*, edited by Laurence A. Glasco and Christopher Rawson. Glasco's (1989) writings on black life in Pittsburgh are informative, and I recommend also looking at "Double Burden: The Black Experience in Pittsburgh," published in *City at the Point*, edited by Samuel P. Hays.

Chapter 10

1. Cantal played a major role in liberating his friend, Jean-Paul Kaufmann, who was seized in Lebanon in 1985 and held hostage for several years. Cantal's efforts in that important campaign are described in my book, *Root Shock* (Fullilove 2004).

Selected Publications
by Rodrick Wallace
and the Community Research Group

Boutros, Mark. 2006. "Is There Space for Place? Forced Migration and the Psychology of Place." Dissertation, Teachers College, Columbia University.

Fullilove, Mindy Thompson. 1993. "Perceptions and Misperceptions of Race and Drug Use." *Journal of the American Medical Association* 269: 1034.

———. 1996. "Psychiatric Implications of Displacement: Contributions from the Psychology of Place." *The American Journal of Psychiatry* 153: 1516–23.

———. 1998. "Comment: Abandoning 'Race' as a Variable in Public Health Research—An Idea Whose Time Has Come." *American Journal of Public Health* 88: 1297–98.

———. 1998. "Promoting Social Cohesion to Improve Health." *Journal of the American Medical Women's Association* 53: 72–76.

———. 2001. "Root Shock: The Consequences of African American Dispossession." *Journal of Urban Health* 78: 72–80.

Fullilove, Mindy Thompson, Gina Arias, Moises Nunez, Erika Phillips, Peter McFarlane, Rodrick Wallace, and Robert E. Fullilove III. 2003. "What Did Ian Tell God? School Violence in East New York." In *Deadly Lessons: Understanding Lethal School Violence*, edited by Mark H. Moore, Carol V. Petrie, Anthony A. Braga, and Brenda L. McLaughlin, 198–246. Washington, DC: National Academies Press.

Fullilove, Mindy Thompson, and Robert E. Fullilove. 1999. "Stigma as an Obstacle to AIDS Action: The Case of the African American Community." *American Behavioral Scientist* 42: 1117–29.

———. 2000. "What's Housing Got to Do with It?" *American Journal of Public Health* 90: 183–84.

Fullilove, Mindy Thompson, Robert E. Fullilove, Michael Smith, Karen Winkler, Calvin Michael, Paula G. Panzer, and Rodrick Wallace. 1993. "Violence, Trauma, and Post-Traumatic Stress Disorder among Women Drug Users." *Journal of Traumatic Stress* 6: 533–43.

Fullilove, Mindy Thompson, Lesley Green, and Robert E. Fullilove. 1999. "Building Momentum: An Ethnographic Study of Inner-City Community Development." *American Journal of Public Health* 89: 840–44.

Fullilove, Mindy Thompson, Lesley L. Green, Lourdes J. Hernández-Cordero, and Robert E. Fullilove. 2006. "Obvious and Not-So-Obvious Strategies to Disseminate Research." *Health Promotion Practice* 7: 306–11.

Fullilove, Mindy Thompson, Veronique Héon, Waquiria Jimenez, Carolyn Parsons, Lesley L. Green, and Robert E. Fullilove. 1998. "Injury and Anomie: Effects of Violence on an Inner-City Community." *American Journal of Public Health* 88: 924–27.

Fullilove, Mindy Thompson, Lourdes Hernández-Cordero, Jennifer Stevens Madoff, and Robert E. Fullilove III. 2004. "Promoting Collective Recovery through Organizational Mobilization: The Post 9/11 Disaster Relief Work of New York City Recovers." *Journal of Biosocial Science* 36: 479–89.

Fullilove, Mindy Thompson, and Rodrick Wallace. 2011. "Serial Forced Displacement in American Cities, 1916–2010." *Journal of Urban Health* 88: 381–89.

Fullilove, Robert E., Lesley Green, and Mindy Thompson Fullilove. 2000. "The Family to Family Program: A Structural Intervention with Implications for the Prevention of HIV/AIDS and Other Community Epidemics." *AIDS* 14 (s): S63–S67.

Gasch, Helen, Michael D. Poulson, Robert E. Fullilove, and Mindy Thompson Fullilove. 1991. "Shaping AIDS Education and Prevention Programs for African Americans Amidst Community Decline." *Journal of Negro Education* 60: 85–96.

Green, Lesley L. 2002. "Archetypes of Spiritual Awakening: The 12-Step Journey of Redemption." Dissertation, Teachers College, Columbia University.

Green, Lesley L., Mindy T. Fullilove, and Robert E. Fullilove. 1998. "Stories of Spiritual Awakening: The Nature of Spirituality in Recovery." *Journal of Substance Abuse Treatment* 15: 325–31.

Green, Lesley L., Mindy Thompson Fullilove, and Robert E. Fullilove. 2005. "Remembering the Lizard: Reconstructing Sexuality in the Rooms of Narcotics Anonymous." *Journal of Sex Research* 42: 28–34.

Hernández-Cordero, Lourdes. 2003. "Fostering Collective Recovery." Dissertation, Mailman School of Public Health, Columbia University.

Héon-Klin, Véronique, Erika Seiber, Julia Huebner, and Mindy Thompson Fullilove. 2001 "The Influence of Geopolitical Change on the Well-Being of a Population: The Berlin Wall." *American Journal of Public Health* 91: 369–74.

Madoff, Jennifer Stevens. 2002. "Islands of Success in the Midst of Inequality: The Situation of AIDS Care for Women of Color." Dissertation, Mailman School of Public Health, Columbia University.

McGrath, Moriah McSharry, Robert E. Fullilove, Molly Rose Kaufman, Rodrick Wallace, and Mindy Thompson Fullilove. 2009. "The Limits of Collaboration: A Qualitative Study of Community Ethical Review of Environmental Health Research." *American Journal of Public Health* 99: 1510–44.

Wallace, Deborah. 2011. "Discriminatory Mass De-Housing and Low-Weight Births: Scales of Geography, Time and Level." *Journal of Urban Health* 88: 454–68.

Wallace, Deborah, and Rodrick Wallace. 1998. *A Plague on Your Houses: How New York Was Burned Down and National Public Health Crumbled.* New York: Verso Press.

———. 2000. "Life and Death in Upper Manhattan and the Bronx: Toward an Evolutionary Perspective on Catastrophic Social Change." *Environment and Planning A* 32: 1245–66.

———. 2002. "The Recent Tuberculosis Epidemic in New York City: Warning from the De-Developing World." In *The Return of the White Plague: Global Poverty and the "New" Tuberculosis,* edited by Matthew Gandy and Alimuddin Zumla, 125–46. New York: Verso Press.

———. 2003. "Chronic Community Stress and Individual Demoralization within a Cohort of Prenatal Clinic Mothers: Evidence for Social Signal Transduction and Implications for Community Stability." *Social Science and Medicine* 56: 2467–78.

———. 2008. "Urban Systems during Disasters: Factors for Resilience." *Ecology and Society* 13: 18.

———. 2011. "Consequences of Massive Housing Destruction: The New York City Fire Epidemic." *Building Research and Information* 39: 395–411.

Wallace, Rodrick. 2007. "Plague and Power Relations." *Geografiska Annaler B* 89: 319–39.

———. 2011. "Forced Displacement of African Americans in New York City and the International Diffusion of Multiple-Drug-Resistant HIV." In *Megacities and Public Health,* edited by Omar A. Khan and Gregory Pappas, 155–72. Washington, DC: APHA Press.

Wallace, Rodrick, and Mindy T. Fullilove. 2008. *Collective Consciousness and Its Discontents: Institutional Distributed Cognition, Racial Policy, and Public Health in the United States.* New York: Springer.

Wallace, Rodrick, Mindy Thompson Fullilove, and Alan J. Fisher. 1996. "AIDS, Violence and Behavioral Coding: Information Theory, Risk Behavior and

Dynamic Process on Core-Group Sociogeographic Networks." *Social Science and Medicine* 43: 339–52.

Wallace, Rodrick, Mindy Thompson Fullilove, Robert E. Fullilove, Peter Gould, and Deborah Wallace. 1998. "Will AIDS Be Contained within US Minority Urban Populations?" *Social Science and Medicine* 39: 1051–62.

Wallace, Rodrick, and Kristin McCarthy. 2007. "The Unstable Public Health Ecology of the New York Metropolitan Region: Implications for Accelerated National Spread of Emerging Infection." *Environment and Planning A* 39: 1181–92.

Wallace, Rodrick, and Deborah Wallace. 2005. "Structured Psychosocial Stress and the US Obesity Epidemic." *Journal of Biological Systems* 13: 363–84.

———. 2010. *Gene Expression and Its Discontents: The Social Production of Chronic Disease*. New York: Springer.

Wallace, Rodrick, Deborah Wallace, Jennifer Ahern, and Sandro Galea. 2007. "A Failure of Resilience: Estimating Response of New York City's Public Health Ecosystem to Sudden Disaster." *Health and Place* 13: 545–50.

Wallace, Rodrick, Deborah Wallace, and Robert G. Wallace. 2004. "Biological Limits to Reduction in Rates of Coronary Heart Disease: A Punctuated Equilibrium Approach to Immune Cognition, Chronic Inflammation, and Pathogenic Social Hierarchy." *Journal of the National Medical Association* 69: 609–19.

———. 2009. *Farming Human Pathogens: Ecological Resilience and Evolutionary Process*. New York: Springer.

References

Acker, Caroline Jean. 2009. "How Crack Found a Niche in the American Ghetto: The Historical Epidemiology of Drug-Related Harm." *BioSocieties* 5: 70–88. doi: 10.1057/biosoc.2009.1.

Bacon, Edmund. 1974. *Design of Cities*. New York: Penguin Books.

Banks, James, Michael Marmot, Zoe Oldfield, and James P. Smith. 2006. "Disease and Disadvantage in the United States and England." *Journal of the American Medical Association* 295 (17): 2037–45.

Banlieues 89. 1986. *De la démocratie urbaine: Première Assises d'Enghien, 5, 6, 7 Décembre 1985*. Paris: Murs Murs.

Bishop, Mary, and S. D. Harrington. 1997. "The Invisible Inner City: Poverty, Crime and Decay in Roanoke's Oldest Neighborhoods." *The Roanoke Times and World News*, June 1–22.

Bolin, Doub, and Christopher Moore. 1991. *Wylie Avenue Days*. DVD. Pittsburgh, PA: WQED Multimedia.

Brand, Stewart. 1994. *How Buildings Learn: What Happens After They're Built*. New York: Viking.

Brix, Michel. 2004. *André Le Nôtre: Magicien de l'Espace*. Versailles: Artlys.

Bruner, Jon. 2012. "Ten American Comeback Cities." *Forbes*, March 5.

Candy, Denys. n.d. *Connecting Pittsburgh's Neighborhoods to Our Rivers: Lessons from France*. Pittsburgh, PA: Find the Rivers!.

Cantal-Dupart, Michel. 1993. "La crise des villes." *Les Temps Modernes* 49 (567): 261–63.

———. 1994. *Merci la Ville!* Bordeaux: Investigations Le Castor Astral.

Castro, Roland. 1986. "Une nouvelle manière de penser." *Murs Murs*, April 5-7.

Castro, Roland, Michel Cantal-Dupart, and Antoine Stinco. 1980. *La Ville à Livre Ouvert*. Paris: La Documentation Francaise.

Covey, Stephen R. 2012. "The 7 Habits of Highly Effective People: Habit 2: Begin with the End in Mind." FranklinCovey. Accessed November 28. www.stephencovey.com/7habits/7habits-habit2.php.

Devine-Wright, Patrick. 2009. "Rethinking NIMBYism: The Role of Place Attachment and Place Identity in Explaining Place-Protective Action." *Journal of Community & Applied Social Psychology* 19 (6): 426-41.

Diderot, Denis, and Jean le Rond d'Alembert. 1751–72. *Encyclopédie, ou diction-naire raisonné des sciences, des arts et des métiers*. Paris: André le Breton, Michel-Antoine David, Laurent Durand, and Antoine-Claude Briasson.

Eck, Joe. 2005. *Elements of Garden Design*. New York: North Point Press.

Epting, Chris. 2009. "The Last of the Polo Grounds: New York City Will Repair a Forgotten Staircase." *Preservation*, March 6. www.preservationnation.org/magazine/story-of-the-week/2009/the-last-of-the-polo-grounds.html.

Fleischer, Alain. 2009a. "Mutations, Quand La Règle Est De Changer." In Nouvel, Duthilleul, and Cantal-Dupart 2009, 256–57.

———. 2009b. "Les Quartiers." In Nouvel, Duthilleul, and Cantal-Dupart 2009, 300–01.

Freud, Sigmund. 1961. *Civilization and Its Discontents*. Translated by James Strachey. New York: Norton.

Fullilove, Mindy Thompson. 1993. "Minority Women: Ecological Setting and Intercultural Dialogue." In *Psychological Aspects of Women's Health Care*, edited by Nada Stotland and Donna Stewart, 519–39. Washington, DC: American Psychiatric Association Press.

———. 1996. "Psychiatric Implications of Displacement: Contributions from the Psychology of Place." *American Journal of Psychiatry* 153 (12): 1516–23.

———. 2001. "Links Between the Social and Physical Environments." *Children's Environmental Health* 48 (5): 1253–126.

———. 2004. *Root Shock: How Tearing Up City Neighborhoods Hurts America and What We Can Do About It*. New York: Ballantine/One World.

———. 2008. *Grand Paris: Quatre Jours, Une Americane* [Grand Paris: Four Days, One American Woman]. Paris: Atelier Cantal-Dupart.

———. Forthcoming. "'The Frayed Knot:' What Happens to Place Attachment in the Context of Serial Forced Displacement?" In *Place Attachment: Advances in Theory, Methods and Research*, edited by Lynne Manzo and Patrick Devine-Wright. London: Routledge.

Fullilove, Mindy Thompson, and Terri Baltimore. 2012. "Freedom Corner: Reflections on a Public Space for Dissent in a Fractured City." In *Beyond Zuccotti Park: Freedom of Assembly and the Occupation of Public Space*, edited by Ron Shiffman, Rick Bell, Lance Jay Brown, and Lynne Elizabeth, 99–111. Oakland, CA: New Village Press.

Fullilove, Mindy T., Lesley L. Green, and Robert E. Fullilove. 1999. "Building Momentum: An Ethnographic Study of Inner-City Redevelopment." *American Journal of Public Health* 89: 840–44.

Fullilove, Mindy Thompson, Véronique Héon, Walkiria Jimenez, Caroline Parsons, Lesley L. Green, and Robert E. Fullilove. 1998. "Injury and Anomie: Effects of Violence on an Inner-City Community." *American Journal of Public Health* 88: 924–27.

Fullilove, Mindy Thompson, and Rodrick Wallace. 2011. "Serial Forced Displacement in American Cities, 1916–2010." *Journal of Urban Health* 88 (3): 381–89.

Garcia-Soto, Maribel, Katherine Haynes-Sanstad, Robert E. Fullilove, and Mindy Thompson Fullilove. 1998. "The Peculiar Epidemic, Part I: Social Response to AIDS in Alameda County." *Environment and Planning A* 30: 731–46.

Gilman, Sander L. 1996. *Smart Jews: The Construction of the Image of Jewish Superior Intelligence*. Lincoln, NE: University of Nebraska Press.

Glasco, Laurence. 1989. "Double Burden: The Black Experience in Pittsburgh." In *City at the Point*, edited by Samuel P. Hays, 69–110. Pittsburgh: University of Pittsburgh Press.

———. 2011. "The Hill and the African American Experience." In *August Wilson: Pittsburgh Places in His Life and Plays*, edited by Laurence A. Glasco and Christopher Rawson, 29–53. Pittsburgh: Pittsburgh History and Landmarks Foundation.

Granovetter, Mark S. 1973. "The Strength of Weak Ties." *American Journal of Sociology* 78: 1360–80.

Hall, Edward T. 1966. *The Hidden Dimension*. Garden City, NY: Doubleday and Co.

Haller, William. 2005. "Industrial Restructuring and Urban Change in the Pittsburgh Region: Developmental, Ecological, and Socioeconomic Trade-offs." *Ecology and Society* 10 (1): 13.

Hanchett, Thomas W. 1998. *Sorting Out the New South City: Race, Class, and Urban Development in Charlotte, 1875–1975*. Chapel Hill: University of North Carolina Press.

Hartmann, Thom. 2000. *The Last Hours of Ancient Sunlight: Waking Up to Personal and Global Transformation*. New York: Three Rivers Press.

Harvey, David. 2003. *The New Imperialsim*. Oxford: Oxford University Press.

Héon-Klin, Véronique, Erika Sieber, Julia Huebner, and Mindy Thompson Fullilove. 2001. "The Influence of Geopolitical Change on the Well-Being of a Population: The Berlin Wall." *American Journal of Public Health* 91: 369–74.

Herrenschmidt, Noëlle. 2001. *École Nationale d'Administration Pénitentiarie de Fleury—Mérogis à Agen*. Agen, France: ÉNAP.

Hood Design Studio and ARUP Spatial Practice. 2009. *The Hill: A Village in the Woods*. Pittsburgh, PA: Find the Rivers!.

Houser, Mark. 2008. "Hill Coalition OKs Pact for Development Near Arena." *Tribune–Review/Pittsburgh Tribune–Review*, May 11.

Humphrey, Nancy P. 2005. "Does the Built Environment Influence Physical Activity?" *TR NEWS* 237: 31–33.

Jacobs, Jane. 1991. *The Death and Life of Great American Cities*. New York: Vintage Books.

Karno, Marvin, Joseph Brunon, and Patricia Waldron. 1977. "Therapeutic Use of Generative Graphics: I." *Art Psychotherapy* 4 (2): 79–88. doi: 10.1016/0090-9092(77)90004-7.

Kaufman, Molly Rose. 2007a. *Raccommodage: Mending Our Destiny*. DVD. New York: Community Research Group.

———. 2007b. *Road to Recovery*. DVD. New York: Community Research Group.

King, Martin Luther, Jr. 1963. *Letter from a Birmingham Jail*. Accessed August 12, 2012. http://www.africa.upenn.edu/Articles_Gen/Letter_Birmingham.html.

Laing, Bonnie Young. n.d. *Blueprint for a Livable Hill Proposal*. Pittsburgh, PA: One Hill Coalition.

———. 2009. "Organizing Community and Labor Coalitions for Community Benefits Agreements in African American Communities: Ensuring Successful Partnerships." *Journal of Community Practice* 17 (1–2): 120–139. doi: 10.1080/10705420902862124.

Leighton, Alexander H. 1959. *My Name Is Legion: Foundations for a Theory of Man in Relation to Culture. Vol. I, The Stirling County Study of Psychiatric Disorder & Sociocultural Environment*. New York: Basic Books, Inc.

Lieblich, Amia. 1995. *Seasons of Captivity: The Inner World of POWs*. New York: New York University Press.

Madoff, Jennifer Stevens. 2002. "Islands of Success in the Midst of Inequality: The Situation of AIDS Care for Women of Color." Dissertation, Mailman School of Public Health, Columbia University.

Nouvel, Jean. 2009. "Naissances et Renaissances de Mille et Un Bonheurs Parisiens." In Nouvel, Duthilleul, and Cantal-Dupart 2009, 37–53.

Nouvel, Jean, Jean-Marie Duthilleul, and Michel Cantal-Dupart. 2009. *Naissances et Renaissances de Mille et Un Bonheurs Parisiends*. Paris: Éditions de Mont-Boron.

Orsenna, Erik. 2000. *Portrait d'un Homme Heureux*. Paris: Fayard.

Parker, Lonnae O'Neal. 2012. "Steve Harvey Discusses What Men and Women Think about Love." *Washington Post*, April 14. www.washingtonpost.com/entertainment/steve-harvey-discusses-what-men-and-women-think-about-love/2012/04/12/gIQAfEiCFT_story.html.

Pattou, Jean, and Michel Cantal-Dupart. 1991. *Les Ponts de Paris: Voyage Fantastique*. Marseilles: Éditions J. Lafitte.

Piercy, Marge. 1971. "The Seven of Pentacles." *Best Poems Encyclopedia*. www.bestpoems.net/marge_piercy/poem-12709.html.

Redwood, Carl, and Bonnie Young Laing. 2012. *Organizing for Economic Justice: A Model*. Pittsburgh, PA: Hill District Consensus Group.

Robins, Anthony, Mindy Thompson Fullilove, Robert E. Fullilove, Tracy Myers, and Terri Baltimore. 1999. *Hillscapes: Envisioning a Healthy Urban Habitat*. Pittsburgh, PA: University of Pittsburgh Graduate School of Public Health.

Rothschild Doyno Architects and Brean Associates. 2004. *Development Guidelines for the Center of East Liberty*. Pittsburgh, PA: Rothschild Doyno Architects and Brean Associates.

Rothschild Doyno Collaborative. 2005. *Lou Mason, Jr. Design Sketchbook*. Pittsburgh, PA: Rothschild Doyno Collaborative.

———. 2008. *The Legacy of Jazz*. Pittsburgh, PA: Rothschild Doyno Collaborative.

———. 2010. *Almono Vision: Executive Summary*. Pittsburgh, PA: Rothschild Doyno Collaborative.

———. 2011. *Almono Vision*. Pittsburgh, PA: Rothschild Doyno Collaborative.

Sarkozy, Nicolas. 2009. "Discours prononcé le 29 Avril 2009 à la Cité de l'Architecture et du Patrimoine." Speech at the opening of the Grand Pari(s) proposals exhibit, Palais de Chaillot in the Cité de l'Architecture et du Patrimoine, Paris, April 29.

Sclar, Elliott D. 1990. "Homelessness and Housing Policy: A Game of Musical Chairs." *Americal Journal of Public Health* 80: 1049–52.

Simms, Eva-Maria. 2008. "Children's Lived Spaces in the Inner City: Historical and Political Aspects of the Psychology of Place." *The Humanistic Psychologist* 36 (1): 72–89.

Simon, R. 1986. "Across the Great Divide. A Mental Health Center Opens Doors in the South Bronx." *Family Therapy Networker* 10 (1): 20–30.

Stillwell, Paul. 1993. *The Golden Thirteen: Recollections of the First Black Naval Officers*. Annapolis: Naval Institute Press.

Strunk, William, Jr., and E. B. White. 2007. *The Elements of Style (Illustrated)*. New York: Penguin Books.

Swerdlick, David. 1990. *Mazeway Disintegration*. New York: Community Research Group.

Task Force on Community Preventive Services. 2002. "Recommendations to Increase Physical Activity in Communities." *American Journal of Preventive Medicine* 22 (4S): 67–72.

Thompson, Ernest, and Mindy Thompson. 1976. *Homeboy Came to Orange: A Story of People's Power*. New Jersey: Bridgebuilder Press.

Thompson, Maggie. 2011. *From One to Ninety-One: A Life*. Orange, NJ: University of Orange Press.

Thompson, Mindy. 1978. *National Negro Labor Council, 1951-1956: A History*. New York: AIMS.

Thompson, Mindy, and Maudene Nelson. 1976. *Summer of the Guerilla: Community Nutrition in Newark*. Newark, NJ: Tri-City Citizens Union for Progress.

Vergara, Jose Camilo. 1995. *The New American Ghetto*. New Brunswick, NJ: Rutgers University Press.

Wacquant, Loïc J. D. 2008. *Urban Outcasts: A Comparative Sociology of Advanced Marginality*. Cambridge, United Kingdom: Cambridge Polity.

Wallace, Anthony. 1957. "Mazeway Disintegration: The Individual's Perception of Socio-Cultural Disorganization." *Human Organization* 16: 23–27.

Wallace, Rodrick. 1988. "A Synergism of Plagues: 'Planned Shrinkage,' Contagious Housing Destruction, and AIDS in the Bronx." *Environmental Research* 47: 1–33.

Wallace, Rodrick, and Mindy T. Fullilove. 2008. *Collective Consciousness and Its Discontents: Institutional Distributed Cognition, Racial Policy, and Public Health in the United States*. New York: Springer.

Wallace, Rodrick, Mindy Thompson Fullilove, and Alan J. Flisher. 1996. "AIDS, Violence and Behavioral Coding: Information Theory, Risk Behavior and Dynamic Process on Core-Group Sociogeographic Networks." *Social Science and Medicine* 43: 339–52.

White, E. B. 2000. *Here Is New York*. New York: Little Bookroom.

Wilkinson, Richard G., and Kate Pickett. 2010. *The Spirit Level: Why Greater Equality Makes Societies Stronger*. New York: Bloomsbury Press.

Wolfe, Tom. 1987. *The Bonfire of the Vanities*. New York: Farrar, Straus and Giroux.

Index

Page references followed by *fig* indicate an illustrated figure or photograph.

Community Research Group (CRG): CLIMB, 141–47, 256, 258; Community Burn Index tool developed by, 58–59, 66*fig*–67*fig*; Croton Aqueduct Trail restoration by, 182*fig*; going upstream to find solutions to problems, 34–40; Highbridge Park work by, 173–77; origins of the, 33, 257; selected publications by Rodrick Wallace and the, 3, 15

The Complete Tales of Winnie-the-Pooh (Milne), 193

complexity: Cantal on the cities and their, 84–86*fig*; of the city of Paris, 245–46; of the Hill District, 221–22

connections: align and connect process of making, 237, 306; Cantal's approach for creating city and neighborhood, 214; community gardens for creating, 6; economic centers that connect inherent value of community, 237; Find the Rivers! used for finding the, 265*fig*; Ken's "align and connect" process goal, 237, 306; public space used to make meaningful, 197; ravine of Hédas plan to create, 200*fig*–201*fig*, 202–03; restoring the center, the edges, and, 202–10; unpuzzling fractured space by opening, 152–60; weak ties, 255–56, 261. *See also* disconnection; fractured space

Consensus Group (Hill District), 109, 111, 114, 126, 264

"contagious housing destruction," 17

Cooper, Dwayne, 261, 262, 264

Cooper, Myrtle, 262, 264

Le Corbusier project (France), 227

Council, Edna, 42, 261

Covey, Stephen, 38

crack addiction, 16, 17

crime. *See* violence and crime

Croton Aqueduct (Highbridge Park), 175, 182*fig*

d'Alembert, Jean le Rond, 85

dalle (elevated platform), 225

danger. *See* violence and crime

Dar Lasram (Tunisia), 194–195

The Death and Life of Great American Cities (Jacobs), 168, 190–91, 199

De La O, Arelis, 33

desegregation, 11–14

desenclavement (emancipation), 154, 155

designing gardens, 134–137

Design of Cities (Bacon), 130

Design Sketchbook: the "ah ha!" moment of using the, 241; Almono project use of, 235–36; description of the, 62–65, 68; Jazz Fusion page in, 218*fig*–219*fig*, 220; Ken's review of Mindy's pages, 197–98; The Legacy, 64*fig*–65, 68, 116, 126*fig*, 214; *Lou Mason, Jr. Design Sketchbook* (RDCollab), 218–20; page by Sarah Schell, 103*fig*, 126*fig*; "Sense of Place" page in, 218; "What We Heard" page, 117

détente during parties, 280–81

Devine-Wright, Patrick, 39, 40

Diaz, Sandra, 189*fig*

Dickson, Jennifer Stevens, 33, 80

Dick Whittington and His Cat (Brown), 73

Diderot, Denis, 85

Dillard, Leroy, 261

disconnection: fractured space and, 28–38; objects and images represented our social, 300–01. *See also* connections

discrimination, 164–165. *See also* segregation

The Door (New York City), 187

Doyno, Ken: "align and connect" process goal of, 237; commitment to restoration work by, 61, 62, 63, 68, 69, 70, 115–16, 117; co-storytelling by, 3; East Liberty project role by, 161–64; gift of absolute attention from, 197–98; helping to celebrate the Hill District, 289–90; on memory used to make a meaningful place, 196–202; on the No Redevelopment Beyond This Point! billboard, 131, 132–133*fig*; reflections on becoming urban alchemists, 303–06; reflections on designing The Legacy, 215–18, 223; on restoration as many points of light, 295, 298

droit de siegneur (the king's privilege), 151

drug use/abuse, 16, 17

Dupont, Jean-Pierre, 248

Duthilleul, Jean-Marie, 243, 246, 247

East Liberty Project (Pittsburg), 160–66

East-West German separation, 75–79

Eck, Joe, 35, 38, 135, 136

ecological resilience, 2–7

economic centers, 237

ecosystems: collectively restoring the urban, 299–300; complexity of city, 84–86*fig*; showing solidarity with all life to protect, 39

Edison, Thomas Alva, 91, 93, 95, 96, 207

Edwards, Rev. Demetria, 292

Elements of Garden Design (Eck), 35, 135

The Elements of Style (Strunk and White), 35, 147

elephant of Nantes, 251*fig*–252

empowered collaboration, 56–57

encyclopedists, 85–86*fig*

engaging during party, 280

entre chien et loup (twilight hour), 225

Epting, Chris, 146

equity: how Penn Circle (Pittsburg) acted as barrier to, 160–61, 162, 165; unpuzzling fractured space by creating, 160–66

eutrophication, 2

Fagles, Robert, 41

Falk Fellowship, 58

fear of danger, 169–72

Fehler, Der, 300

Ferrara, Anj, 188, 190

Ferris Bueller's Day Off (film), 282

Find the Rivers! project, 60, 261–64, 265*fig*

find what we are FOR element: addressing the sorted-out city, 104–15; calling on the art and science of urban restoration, 115–20; defining what we are FOR, 109, 111–15; introduction to the, 3, 4–5, 38, 99–100; New Day platform for including

249–50

Panasci, Stephen, 187

Paris (France): L'Atelier (the Workshop) of, 245; Banlieues 89 project in Greater, 226–32, 233, 248; building the city on the city (Paris Grand Pari(s) project) in, 243–49; CNAM in, 85, 277; complexity of, 245–246; *Grand Paris: Quatre Jours, Une Americane* (Grand Paris: Four Days, One American Woman) [Fullilove], 245–46; grid of Banlieues 89 of Greater, 229*fig*, 233; *hauts lieux* (tall buildings) of, 247–48; helping to build a barbecue by the river in, 83–84; how the Seine River shapes, 82; *Isle de la Cité* (City Island) of, 95; Paris Plage festival of, 83; Tour Montparnasse of, 247; wonderful sights discovered throughout Greater, 242*fig*. *See also* France

Parker, Lonnae O'Neal, 298

parties: as basic structure of the city, 278–79; Cantal's great joy in giving, 275–78, 279–82, 293; making and remaking the city through, 282–83, 285–86, 296*fig*, 297*fig*; six parts of an urbanist's, 279–82

Partnership for Parks, 183

path dependence principle, 179

Pattou, Jean, 22

Pease, Robert, 160

Penn Circle (Pittsburg), 160–61, 162, 165

people of color, AIDS epidemic's disproportionate impact on, 1

periodic table of the elements of urban restoration drawing, 37

Perpignan (France), 153–60, 207–10, 226–27, 259

Perron, Joëlle, 263*fig*

Perron, Pierre, 276

perspective: creating form and, 26*fig*; East Liberty project incorporation of, 164; school for prison guards design using, 269–72; unpuzzling fractured space by opening the, 145–51; of the Vaux-le-Vicomte gardens, 148*fig*–151, 164, 269, 270*fig*–271

Phillips, Matt, 89

Pickett, Kate, 12

Piercy, Marge, 68, 189*fig*

Piercy Principle, 68–69

Pittsburgh: "Allegheny Center" renewal project of, 61–62; Almono project for LTV Steel Hazelwood site development in, 233–41; arrows that became gold in, 6–7; Design Sketchbook approach to urban renewal in, 62–65, 68; East Liberty Project creating equity in, 160–66; Find the Rivers! project in, 261–69; HOPE VI initiative in, 42, 43–44, 60; redlining and sorting-out process in, 46*fig*–49. *See also* Hill District (Pittsburgh)

Pittsburgh Courier, 46, 49, 216

Pittsburgh Parks Conservancy (PPC), 267, 269

Pittsburgh Penguins, 111, 114

Pittsburgh Post-Gazette, 60

Pittsburgh Steelers, 4–5

Pittsburgh Steelers metaphor, 4–5

Pittsburgh Tribune, 114

Pittsburgh United, 113

place: Bedford Dwellings and new awareness of, 68; creating places where we want to stay, 184–91; damange of fractured space on, 28–38; French practice of linking taste to pleasure of, 125; *hauts lieux* (tall places), 247; make meaningful, 3, 4–5, 39, 193–223; psychology of, 179–80, 255–56; sense of belonging through, 43. *See also* communities; neighborhoods; space

placemaking: Cantal's teachings about, 79, 215, 261; including both sociopetal and sociofugal in, 203; The Legacy process of, 235; meaningful, 241, 295; Molly teaching about, 286

Placemaking II (2009), 137–38*fig*

Placemaking IV (2012), 286–87, 292

"place-protective behaviors," 39–40

"planned shrinkage" policy (New York City), 16–17

Poe, Edgar Allan, 175

pointillism, 230–31

Les Ponts de Paris (The Bridges of Paris) [Pattou and Cantal-Dupart], 22

Portrait d'un Homme Heureux (Orsenna), 269

Portuguese, Hilda, 13–14

power/governance: One Hill coalition finding allies among those with, 112–13; sorted-out city power concentration with haves, 108–09

Pride and Prejudice (Austen), 11

Princess and the Medina, 193–96, 296*fig*, 297*fig*, 298

PRIZM system, 107*fig*–108

"The Prodigal Son" (Luke 15:11–32), 275

programmatic approach, 38, 101, 112, 235

Programmatic Cat, 99, 120, 296*fig*, 297*fig*

Programmatic Tree, 99, 100

Proposition 13 (California), 15

"The Psychiatric Implications of Displacement: Contributions from the Psychology of Place" (Fullilove), 43, 56

psychology of place, 179–80, 255–56

public policies: comparing French and US historic influences on, 155–56; "contagious housing destruction" through, 17; desegregation, 11–14; forcing population sorting by race, class, and lifestyle, 28–31*fig*; French *mixité* (mixing), 155–56; HOPE VI program (Pittsburgh), 42, 43–44, 60; *l'insertion urbaine* (urban insertion) white paper by HLM, 226–27; "mad plagues" created by, 15–19, 22; New York City's "planned shrinkage," 16–17; serial displacement of people through, 109; top-down, 116, 133, 257. *See also* governance/power; segregation

public space: comparing Triangle Park with Van Vorst Park, 204*fig*; description of, 197; sociofugal and sociopetal, 203–10. *See also* space

"Puss in Boots" (Lang), 99

Qualters, Robert, 126

Quinn, Sebastian, 134

social class: how policies sort city population by, 28–31*fig*; Residential Security Survey Form used to rate neighborhoods by, 46*fig*–47
social disintegration, 105*fig*, 109
Social Vision Diagram, 238*fig*
sociofugal space: Cantal's work balancing sociopetal and, 206–10; description, 203; transformed into bifunctional spaces, 203
sociopetal space: Cantal's work balancing sociofugal and, 206–10; description of, 203
solidarity. *See* show solidarity with all life element
sorted-out city: Cantal on the dysfunction of the, 33; Charlotte (North Carolina) as, 28–31*fig*; FOR element for addressing the, 104–15; going upstream to find solutions to the, 34–40; need to mesh the, 33–34; Pittsburgh Hill District's redlining creating a, 46*fig*–49; power concentration with the haves in the, 108–09; RDCollab approach to fixing the Hill's state as, 218, 220; rules for restoration of the, 38–39; ways that sorting injures the city, 105*fig*. *See also* cities
Sorting Out the New South City: Race, Class and Urban Development in Charlotte, 1875-1975 (Hanchett), 28
Souleyreau, Alexandra, 156, 157, 160
space: appropriation of, 165; how Pope Sixtus V used four obelisks to organize, 130–31; how site forces impact use of, 131–33; how water shapes city, 82–83, 104, 175; spatial homogeneity of, 105*fig*, 108. *See also* fractured space; place; public space
spatial homogeneity, 105*fig*, 108
Spielberg, Steven, 207
Spolidoro, Beatrice, 199
spray-chalking, 138*fig*
Square Bir Hakeim (Perpignan, France), 207–10
"Stage-State Model of Community Disintegration" (Fullilove and Wallace), 18, 22
Stillwell, Paul, 56
Stinco, Antoine, 227
Stittelman, Martha, 135
"Stop AIDS: Keep the Promise. The Importance of Neighborhoods in the Fight Against AIDS" program (Charlotte, North Carolina), 28
street musicians painting (Johnson), 64*fig*, 212*fig*, 214
strengthen the region element: building the city on the city to, 242*fig*–252; introduction to, 3, 4–5, 39, 225–26; making the vast regional conversation to, 233–41; recognizing the right to be loveable to, 226–32, 233; summary of, 296*fig*
strong ties, 109, 179, 180, 255
Strunk, William, Jr., 35
substance abuse, 16, 17
Sutherland, Jermaine, 189*fig*
Swerdlick, David, 17, 19, 22
Sykes, Ray, 189*fig*
"The Synergism of Plagues: 'Planned Shrinkage' Contagious Housing Destruction, and AIDS in the Bronx" (Wallace), 16
systems therapy, 2

tall buildings (*hauts lieux*), 247–48
taste (*le goût*), 124
"thinking like a city," 79–81*fig*
Thompson, Ernest, 14, 99, 101, 102, 104, 109, 112, 286
Thompson, Josh, 301
Thompson, Maggie, 167–68, 300*fig*, 301
Thompson, Mindy, 13*fig*, 99, 102, 112–13, 181. *See also* Fullilove, Mindy Thompson
Thriller (Michael Jackson), 186
Tileston, Carol, 263*fig*
Tōhoku earthquake and tsunami (2011) [Japan], 285
top-down strategies, 116, 133, 257
Torho, Shirley, 95, 138*fig*
Tour Montparnasse (Paris), 247
"Treasures of the Medina" poster, 194*fig*, 195
Triangle Park (Orange, New Jersey), 204*fig*
Trider-Andorin, Isbelle, 249–50
Turner, Maureen, 256

Udin, Sala, 132
unequal investment, 105*fig*, 106
unexpectancy: acknowledging the pain of, 169–72; dysfunction of, 109; Simms III (1980-2004) as era of, 49, 52–54, 55*fig*, 259, 300–01
University of Orange (U of O): origins and development of, 88, 99, 104; Placemaking II (2009), 137–138*fig*; Placemaking IV (2012), 286–87, 292; Valley Revitalization role of, 186–87. *See also* Orange (New Jersey)
University of Pittsburgh Graduate School of Public Health, 57, 69, 161
unpuzzling fractured space element: CLIMB event for, 141–47, 256, 258; creating equity for, 160–66; introduction to, 3, 4–5, 38; opening connections for, 152–60; opening the perspective for, 145–51; summary of, 296*fig*
unslum all neighborhoods element: acknowledging the pain of unexpectancy, 169–72; creating the places where we want to stay, 184–91; introduction to, 3, 4–5, 38–39, 167–69; reknitting weak ties, 172–84; summary of, 296*fig*
urban alchemy: as going upstream to find solutions, 34–40; identifying the basic rules of, 35–39; illustrated diagram of using, 36*fig*; Ken's reflections on applying, 303–06; playing the game of, 299. *See also* urban restoration
urban disorder: "contagious housing destruction," 17; how shredded networks contribute to, 29–32; "mad plagues" of, 15–19, 22; photographs demonstrating cycle of, 20*fig*–21*fig*; "planned shrinkage" policy leading to, 16–17; ways that sorting injures the city causing, 105*fig*
urbanist's party: Cantal's great joy in giving, 275–78, 279–82; making and remaking the city through, 282–83, 285–86, 286*fig*, 287*fig*; six parts of an, 279–82; why urbanist love to give, 278–79
urban restoration: calling on the art and science